"Louis Markos has done it again! If anything, this book is even more valuable than his earlier *From Plato to Christ*. Plato is generally easier to read, and so Aristotle is more in need of retrieval. Markos shows that, while there are places where Aristotle needs correction, his thought is immensely helpful for Christian reflection on God, human nature, virtue, friendship, politics, and rhetoric. May this book receive the wide audience it deserves, for the benefit of biblically grounded Christian faith and culture."

Matthew Levering, James N. Jr. and Mary D. Perry Chair of Theology at Mundelein Seminary and author of *Proofs of God*

"When one studies the early church mothers and fathers, their debt to Plato is obvious. Unfortunately, few students and scholars continue reading into the high Middle Ages, where Aristotle's thought becomes dominant, especially among the scholastic theologians, giving the impression that Plato's influence is foremost in the history of Christian thought. Louis Markos shows how Aristotle's influence is not just in scholasticism but all over the Christian tradition, reminding us that we owe a great debt to Aristotle too. This accessible book should be read by everyone interested in theology."

Greg Peters, professor of Medieval and spiritual theology in the Torrey Honors College at Biola University

"I have been waiting a long time for a book like this one. We live in a difficult era, caught as we are between two extremes. On the one hand, radicals will tell us that if we listen to Aristotle, we will corrupt Christianity. On the other hand, modernism will tell us that we must dispense with Aristotle for the sake of revisioning classical Christianity. Against the radicals, we would do well to remember that our Protestant scholastic forefathers, many of whom were responsible for our Protestant confessions, critically appropriated Aristotle to further fortify the pillars of theology. Against modernism, Aristotle could not be more relevant, assisting us with the tools required to keep at bay everything from monism to materialism. The beauty of Louis Markos's book is the way he introduces the novice to the wisdom of Aristotle to better equip Christianity with a defense of its foundational commitments. In a secular age prone to skepticism, what student can afford not to read Markos and consider the myriad ways Aristotle can clarify what we believe and why?"

Matthew Barrett, professor of Christian theology at Midwestern Baptist Theological Seminary and author of *The Reformation as Renewal*

FROM ARISTOTLE —TO— CHRIST

How Aristotelian Thought Clarified the Christian Faith

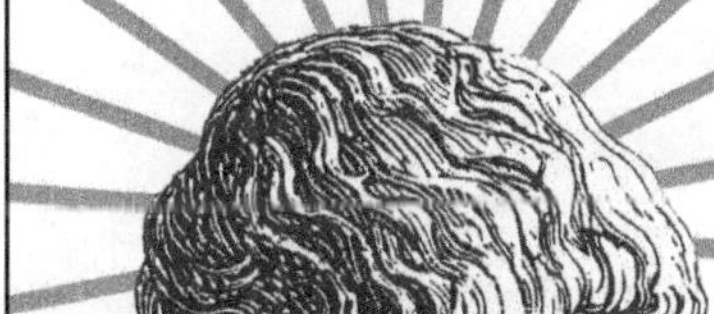

LOUIS MARKOS

Author of
From Plato to Christ

An imprint of InterVarsity Press
Downers Grove, Illinois

InterVarsity Press
P.O. Box 1400 | Downers Grove, IL 60515-1426
ivpress.com | email@ivpress.com

©2025 by Louis A. Markos

All rights reserved. No part of this book may be reproduced in any form without written permission from InterVarsity Press.

InterVarsity Press® is the publishing division of InterVarsity Christian Fellowship/USA®. For more information, visit intervarsity.org.

Scriptures marked KJV are from the King James Version, public domain.

The publisher cannot verify the accuracy or functionality of website URLs used in this book beyond the date of publication.

Cover design: Faceout Studio, Molly von Borstel
Interior design: Jeanna Wiggins
Images: © Grafissimo / DigitalVision Vectors via Getty Images

ISBN 978-1-5140-1132-4 (print) | ISBN 978-1-5140-1133-1 (digital)

Printed in the United States of America ∞

Library of Congress Cataloging-in-Publication Data
Names: Markos, Louis, author.
Title: From Aristotle to Christ : how Aristotelian thought clarified the Christian faith / Louis Markos.
Description: Downers Grove, IL : IVP Academic, [2025] | Includes bibliographical references and index.
Identifiers: LCCN 2025004148 (print) | LCCN 2025004149 (ebook) | ISBN 9781514011324 (paperback) | ISBN 9781514011331 (ebook)
Subjects: LCSH: Christianity–Philosophy–History. | Theology, Doctrinal–History. | Aristotle–Influence.
Classification: LCC BR100 .M2758 2025 (print) | LCC BR100 (ebook) | DDC 230.01–dc23/eng/20250311
LC record available at https://lccn.loc.gov/2025004148
LC ebook record available at https://lccn.loc.gov/2025004149

---

31 30 29 28 27 26 25 | 13 12 11 10 9 8 7 6 5 4 3 2 1

For my good friend, fellow apologist,

and ministry partner

BILL SCOTT

CONTENTS

Preface: A Platonist Learns to Love Aristotle — ix

A Note on Translation — xix

PART 1 — HOW TO THINK LOGICALLY

1. Why It's Impossible to Believe Six Impossible Things Before Breakfast — 3
2. Playing Around in Aristotle's Toolbox — 12
3. Making Arguments That Make Sense — 20
4. Why Things Move and Change — 26
5. Body and Soul in Dialogue — 34

PART 2 — HOW TO READ THE HEAVENS AND THE EARTH

6. Why, Why, Why — 45
7. Where Do I Begin? — 56
8. Wrestling with the Static God of Deism — 66
9. Living in an Ordered Universe — 75
10. Joining the Cosmic Dance — 90

PART 3 — HOW TO BEHAVE

11. Studying the Psyche — 103
12. Virtue as Habit — 113
13. Finding the Golden Mean — 124
14. How to Win Friends and Influence People — 136
15. The Good Life — 146

PART 4 — HOW TO GET ALONG WITH OUR NEIGHBORS

16   The Political Animal   *161*

17   A Critic and a Defender of Aristotle   *175*

18   The Blessings and Dangers of Private Property   *184*

19   The Rule of Law   *199*

PART 5 — HOW TO MAKE BEAUTIFUL THINGS

20   Defending the Art of Rhetoric   *211*

21   Redeeming the Art of Imitation   *224*

22   Purging and Purifying the Emotions   *234*

Conclusion: Aristotle the Prophet   *243*

Glossary   *247*

Bibliographical Essay   *255*

Scripture Index   *261*

Preface

A PLATONIST LEARNS TO LOVE ARISTOTLE

"Every man is born an Aristotelian, or a Platonist. I do not think it possible that any one born an Aristotelian can become a Platonist; and I am sure no born Platonist can ever change into an Aristotelian."

So pronounced from on high the great Romantic poet-critic-philosopher Samuel Taylor Coleridge in his table talk for July 2, 1830. "They are the two classes of men," he goes on to explain, "beside which it is next to impossible to conceive a third. The one [the Aristotelian] considers reason a quality, or attribute; the other [the Platonist] considers it a power. I believe that Aristotle never could get to understand what Plato meant by an idea."[1]

In many ways, Coleridge is correct. Aristotle rejected Plato's central doctrine of the Forms (or Ideas). He could not, as we will see in the chapters below, accept the existence of purely abstract universal forms/ideas that were not connected to something particular and concrete. And yet, Aristotle *did* believe in *real* universal forms that gave shape, function, and purpose to the particulars of our world. Coleridge is right again that Aristotle treated reason as a quality or attribute of the soul rather than a power; yet here too, Aristotle recognized a higher, transcendent, immaterial source for reason.

Like Coleridge, I am a born-and-bred, dyed-in-the-wool Platonist. I published a book a few years back, *From Plato to Christ*, that celebrated Plato's thought and its (mostly positive) influence on Christianity. For several years, I thought, channeling the spirit of Coleridge, that I could not possibly write

---

[1]Samuel Taylor Coleridge, *The Table Talk and Omnia*, ed. T. Ashe (London: George Bell and Sons, 1888), 99.

the necessary sequel to that book, because no true lover of Plato could write an equally celebratory book about Aristotle and the (mostly positive) influence he had on Christianity. That you are holding this book in your hand is proof that I was able to overcome my hesitancy.

That is not to say I have been converted to Aristotelianism. I remain a proud and fervent Platonist. Nevertheless, my yearlong deep dive into Aristotle has convinced me not only of the equally overwhelming genius of Plato's greatest student but of the essential contributions he made to Western and Christian philosophy and theology, ethics and political science, psychology and sociology, cosmology and aesthetics. Aristotle's legacy is a flawed one, and it did not begin to exert direct influence on Christianity until the dawn of the Middle Ages, but it did help to clarify, more for good than for ill, much of what is central to Christendom and to Western civilization.

As with my previous book, I hope that this one will appeal to Christian and non-Christian readers alike. To the latter group, whether you are non-religious, a member of another religion, or a seeker, I ask that you extend me grace as I seek to assess Aristotle's impact on the West, particularly as it was filtered through the church. To the former group, especially those who share my evangelical faith, I ask that you extend grace to the medieval and Renaissance Christians—Catholic *and* Protestant—who were willing to learn at the feet of Aristotle and to be guided in their thoughts and actions by his insights.

Indeed, I think it best at the outset to warn my fellow evangelicals that Aristotle's legacy has been greater among Catholics than Protestants. It was during the Catholic Middle Ages, after all, that Aristotle reigned supreme, exerting a strong influence on Thomas Aquinas and Dante and establishing philosophical methods that undergirded the work of the Scholastics (or Schoolmen).

Sadly, it was precisely Aristotle's connection to Aquinas and the Scholastics that earned him—unfairly—the scorn of both Martin Luther and John Calvin. In the section on the Lord's Supper in his *Babylonian Captivity of the Church*, Luther traces the Catholic doctrine of transubstantiation, with which he disagrees, to a revival of Aristotle and the works of Aquinas. He goes so far as to call Aristotle a beast and accuses the church of showing a blind subservience to Aristotle and the Catholic Scholastics who held him in such a high regard. He even, in a moment of exasperation, exclaims that the "Holy Spirit is greater than Aristotle."[2]

As for Calvin, though he quotes Augustine copiously in his *Institutes of the Christian Religion*, he almost totally ignores Aquinas—as he does the pagan philosopher to whom Aquinas appealed so frequently. In a rare moment, Calvin mentions Plato's greatest pupil only to directly condemn "the frigid doctrine of Aristotle." Later, he extends his condemnation to "the Schoolmen, who have in a manner drawn a veil over Christ . . . besides impairing, and almost annihilating, faith by their obscure definition."[3] With Calvin and Luther sharing such a low view of Aristotle, it is no wonder that early Protestant thinkers in general distanced themselves from Aristotle.

Still, I hope that this sad quirk of history will not prevent evangelical readers from learning from Aristotle. Calvin and Luther, whether they realized it or not, stood firmly in the long tradition of Aristotelian logical, ethical, and political thought. Both Reformers, along with those who followed in their wake, used their hermeneutical skills to understand the Bible in its proper historical context—and that context included the strong and ubiquitous legacy of Aristotle.

According to Galatians 4:4, God the Father sent Christ into the world in the "fulness of time." I believe that fullness includes the law and order Rome brought to the Mediterranean, which allowed the gospel to spread quickly across the empire; I also believe it includes the philosophy of Greece that laid a foundation for the kind of thought needed to articulate fully the revelation of Christ and the Bible. I am convinced that the Bible is the Word of God; I am equally convinced that it is not, nor was it meant to be, a self-contained encyclopedia of all that is good, true, and beautiful.

Just as Moses, who was trained in the pagan wisdom of the Egyptians (Acts 7:22), willingly received management advice from his pagan father-in-law (Ex 18), so Christian apologists from Boethius in the sixth century

---

[2]Martin Luther, *Selections from His Writings*, ed. John Dillenberger (New York: Anchor Books, 1961), 267-70.
[3]John Calvin, *Institutes of the Christian Religion*, trans. Henry Beveridge (Grand Rapids, MI: Eerdmans, 1995), I.5.5, III.2.2 (pp. 53, 470).

to Anselm in the eleventh to C. S. Lewis in the twentieth have effectively used Aristotle's terminology and methodology to defend the faith and work out its full implications. Just as the biblical writers borrowed and transformed literary genres that seem to have their roots in the cultures of the ancient Near East (proverbs, lamentation) and Greece (epistles, biography), so theologians from Augustine to Aquinas, Calvin to Richard Hooker have borrowed—and repurposed—Aristotle's syllogisms, categories, and distinctions to ground their systematic treatises.

In the Catholic Middle Ages, the spiritual vision of man's place in the universe that undergirds Dante's *Comedy* was strongly indebted to Aristotle's cosmology; in the Protestant Reformation and Enlightenment, the social vision of man's place in a well-run state was equally indebted to his political science.[4] When Christians of any age, country, or denomination debate the nature of the good life, the soul, free will, or design, Aristotle lurks behind their logic as well as their rhetoric.

In *From Plato to Christ*, I devoted the first half of the book to Plato's thought and the second to the bearing of that thought on Christianity. Such an approach will not do for the man who invented the system we still use today for breaking down and classifying knowledge into discrete packages— what college students call majors, and their professors call disciplines. One cannot lump together the multifaceted thought of a man who himself distinguished between theoretical thinking, which guides our beliefs; practical thinking, which guides our conduct; and productive thinking, which results in the making of beautiful and useful things.

Accordingly, in this book I will divide Aristotle's thought into five broad categories: logic and science, metaphysics and cosmology, psychology and ethics, social and political science, rhetoric and aesthetics. In each of these sections, I will move back and forth between Aristotle's works and the Christian thinkers he influenced. Though I will critique some aspects of Aristotelianism that I believe led Christianity down some wrong paths, my orientation will be appreciative and joyful, not critical and judgmental.

---

[4] True to the legacy of the classical literature and philosophy that I will be discussing in this book, I will be using traditional English grammar throughout: that is to say, I will use *he* and *his* as the gender-inclusive pronouns, and *man*, *men*, and *mankind* to refer collectively to the human race.

I will not drag Aristotle to the bar and make him apologize for holding beliefs contrary to the zeitgeist of the twenty-first century. To the contrary, I will place myself and my age under his wise tutelage and will endeavor to learn from the thinkers who learned from Aristotle. That modern science has disproven the shape of Dante's universe does not take away from the goodness and truth that continue to flow from the *Comedy*. The cosmology that Dante inherited from Aristotle retains its full beauty and is still capable of provoking awe, wonder, and gratitude in our most jaded of centuries.

Aristotle's *Poetics* and *Nicomachean Ethics* are as true today as they were when they were written; if his *Politics* seems a tad quaint in its refusal to imagine a state much larger than Athens, then at least he erred in the direction of the small, the intimate, and the human. In any case, his treatment of man as a political animal and his analysis of how the good life of the individual should reflect the good life of the citizen has not lost any of its relevance. Our age desperately needs to be reschooled by his clear understanding of how man is both like and unlike the animals in his instincts, passions, and reason.

Much of Aristotle's science has been thrown to the wayside, but not his logic or his clarity of thought. Coleridge complains, in the remainder of his July 2 table talk, that Aristotle, unable to soar as high as Plato, dragged philosophy down to earth, grounding it too much in science and so clipping its wings. Yet, Coleridge cannot help but praise the depth and breadth of his genius: "Aristotle was, and still is, the sovereign lord of the understanding; the faculty judging by the senses. . . . What a mind was Aristotle's—only not the greatest that ever animated the human form!—the parent of science, properly so called, the master of criticism, and the founder or editor of logic!"[5]

* * *

Though my focus in this book will be on Aristotle's works, I would like to pause here to say something of his biography. Ironically, the man who would come to dominate the thought of the Middle Ages and who continues

---

[5]Coleridge, *Table Talk and Omnia*, 100.

to influence how we think about ourselves and our world hailed from the fringes of that cultural and intellectual miracle that historians celebrate as the golden age of Greece.

Unlike Plato (427–348 BC), who grew up in the heyday of the highly civilized, cosmopolitan city of Athens, Aristotle (384–322 BC) was born in Stagira, in the northern frontier region of Chalcis, just east of the growing military power of the hillbilly Macedonians. Whereas Plato was an aristocrat, Aristotle was the provincial son of a working doctor who, for several years during Aristotle's childhood, was court physician to King Amyntas III of Macedon. There is good reason to believe that Aristotle spent some of that time with his father, allowing him to study medicine, including dissection, and to gain a hands-on education in all aspects of health and the human body.

Aristotle's parents died before he reached his teenage years, and he was raised by a relative who had sufficient funds to send the eighteen-year-old prodigy to study at Plato's prestigious Academy in Athens. When the eager lad from the boondocks arrived in Europe's greatest college town, Plato was away in Syracuse, Sicily, attempting, ultimately unsuccessfully, to train the son of a tyrant to become a philosopher-king. But he did return, and he quickly recognized the intellectual prowess of Aristotle, who spent two full decades in Plato's inner circle, learning all he could from the master and his school. Though he would part company with Plato on several of his teachings, Plato would remain the single greatest influence on Aristotle's intellectual life and thought.

After Plato died and was succeeded by his nephew Speusippus, Aristotle decided to seek his fortunes elsewhere, in the Ionian Hellespont of Asia Minor: that strategic strait that connects the Aegean with Istanbul and the Black Sea and that is flanked by ancient Troy on the southern shore and Gallipoli on the northern. Aristotle had been invited there by a fellow student named Hermias who, though a former slave, had risen to be monarch of the region—that is, until he ran afoul of the Persian Empire and was executed. For three full years, Aristotle and a few other Academy expatriates enjoyed Hermias's patronage, setting up their own little school to study not just philosophy but the unique flora and fauna of Ionia and its islands. During this period, Aristotle married Hermias's niece Pythias. He remained happily married to her until her death.

The execution of Hermias closed the door on Aristotle's Ionian idyll, but, as chance would have it, a window was simultaneously and serendipitously thrown open in Macedonia. King Philip II was in search of a tutor for his precocious thirteen-year-old son, and he settled on an Athenian-trained scholar who had grown up in the north and whose father had served one of his predecessors. Thus did Aristotle become the tutor of the young man who would become Alexander the Great and who would conquer and unite a vast empire from Greece to India, Armenia to Egypt. Legend has it that Alexander sent back exotic animals for Aristotle to study, but Aristotle never approved politically of empire, nor of Alexander's idealistic attempt to fuse West and East into a new global culture that, though driven by Hellenic thought, would incorporate "barbarian" ideas.[6]

After Philip was assassinated in 336 and Alexander succeeded him on the throne, Aristotle returned to Athens. As Speusippus had recently died, Aristotle could surely have secured for himself the position of head of the Academy. Instead, he set up his own rival school in a gymnasium attached to the temple of Apollo Lyceus. For the next twelve years, Aristotle led the Lyceum, though he and his students, because of their habit of discussing philosophy while strolling along the portico, also came to be known as the Peripatetics (Greek for "walking around"). The Lyceum did more than discuss and teach every area of human knowledge. It *collected* knowledge as well. Indeed, Aristotle, funded by a generous grant from Alexander, established the first great library in the world, though that library would eventually be dwarfed by the Library of Alexandria, whose foundations Alexander himself would lay.

In addition to books, Aristotle collected maps, artifacts, and all forms of living organisms. These served him well as illustrations for the myriad lectures he prepared on every possible subject. During this rich and fertile period Aristotle wrote nearly all the works that have come down to us and

---

[6] For a wonderful snapshot of Aristotle's influence on Alexander, see Plutarch's *Life of Alexander* 8. According to Plutarch's sources, the young Alexander was once heard to exclaim that whereas his father gave him life, his beloved tutor taught him how to live well.

on which his fame rests. He also wrote dialogues in the mode of Plato, exhortations, and other popular works, but sadly none of those have survived. As head of the Lyceum, he compiled or commissioned the compiling of numerous catalogs of information on various topics. The Lyceum, it appears, possessed a collection of 158 Greek constitutions, and that raw material served Aristotle well when he wrote his *Politics*.

Of the 158, only one survives, *The Constitution of Athens*, but there is strong reason to believe that Aristotle himself wrote it. That is good news for lovers of Aristotle, for it is written in a style that is far more fluid and engaging than his other works. The reason for that is that none of the other books that bear Aristotle's name were prepared by their author for publication. What we read as books are likely his lecture notes, perhaps embellished by his students. I like to think of them as his PowerPoint presentations, for that is very much how they read. Many seem to represent a series of lectures that have been stitched together in the order that seemed best to their editor. Indeed, scholars to this day continue to dispute the proper organization of Aristotle's *Metaphysics* and *Politics*.

When Alexander died in 323, a surge of anti-Macedonian feeling rose up in Athens, which is likely the reason why the conqueror's former tutor felt it prudent that he once more leave Athens. He spent the final year of his life in Chalcis, not the Chalcis of his birth but Chalcis, Euboea, the island city-state that had founded the northern colony many generations earlier. Aristotle had come full circle, dying in the same provincial, outsider state as he was born. Yet, between his beginning and his end, what a marvelous legacy he left behind to those who would build much of that which is best and most lasting, not only in Western civilization but in all those parts of the world that have been influenced by the civilization Aristotle helped to construct.

* * *

In the chapters that follow, I will attempt to unpack Aristotle's thought in the manner and sequence I think he would have preferred, beginning with the true (theoretical thinking that teaches us how to reason logically and how to observe and understand the motions of the heavens and the earth), continuing with the good (practical thinking that teaches us how to behave virtuously and to get along civilly), and climaxing with the beautiful (productive thinking that teaches us how to make things of beauty). Although I think this is the best way to approach the vast Aristotelian corpus, it does have the negative effect of starting out with those parts of Aristotle that are the most obscure, abstract, and difficult to express in layman's terms.

As such, I entreat the reader to be patient as we slog together through the first two sections. I will offer as many explanations and illustrations as I can to elucidate the material, but these portions of Aristotle's writings can be quite abstruse and intractable. Still, the material is essential for fully appreciating and properly assessing Aristotle's influence on the West in general and Christianity in particular. It is also foundational to understanding the more accessible and, I think, more lasting things that Aristotle has to teach us about ethics, politics, and rhetoric. To help sort out Aristotle's difficult, often nonintuitive terminology, I have included at the back a glossary of terms that I would encourage readers to consult frequently as they make their way through each section of the book.

A NOTE ON TRANSLATION

FOR EASE OF REFERENCE and to ensure that all the translations I will be using in this book are in the public domain and easily accessible to readers, I will use the translations of Aristotle's works that are anthologized in *The Basic Works of Aristotle*, edited by Richard McKeon. This book was originally published in 1941 by Random House, and many used copies of this edition are available. It can also be bought new or used in an inexpensive 2001 Modern Library Paperback Edition. Although this fifteen-hundred-page edition is not complete, it has all one needs for a thorough grounding in Aristotle.

All the translations used in McKeon's edition, with one exception, can be read and downloaded for free at the Internet Classics Archive (classics.mit.edu). The one exception is the translation of Aristotle's *Poetics*, which in McKeon's edition is taken from Ingram Bywater but at the Internet Classics Archive is taken from S. H. Butcher. The Bywater translation can be read and downloaded for free at Project Gutenberg (www.gutenberg.org).

As for the referencing of quotes from Aristotle's works, I will *not* be using page numbers from the McKeon edition. Rather, I will include parenthetical references in the text that have two sets of numbers separated by a semicolon: (1) the book and chapter number; and (2) the page, column, and line numbers from the edition of Aristotle's works published in Berlin by Immanuel Bekker in 1831. As most editions of Aristotle's works include the Bekker numbers in the margin or the top of the page, these numbers, together with Aristotle's book and chapter numbers, should allow readers to quickly locate the passage I am quoting, no matter what edition they have. If I quote the first paragraph of book X, chapter 9 of *Physics*, the parenthetical citation will read: (X.9; 217b29-218a3). Which of Aristotle's books I am quoting from will be made clear in the text.

Here is a list of the translations I will be using for each work: *Categories*, E. M. Edghill; *On the Heavens*, J. L. Stocks; *On Generation and Corruption*, Harold H. Joachim; *On Interpretation*, E. M. Edghill; *Metaphysics*, W. D. Ross; *Meteorology*, E. W. Webster; *Nicomachean Ethics*, W. D. Ross; *Physics*, R. P. Hardie and R. K. Gaye; *Poetics*, Ingram Bywater; *Politics*, Benjamin Jowett; *Posterior Analytics*, G. R. G. Mure; *Prior Analytics*, A. J. Jenkinson; *Rhetoric*, W. Rhys Roberts; *On the Soul*, J. A. Smith; *Topics*, W. A. Pickard-Cambridge; *On the Parts of Animals*, William Ogle.

Finally, although all my quotes will be taken from the translations anthologized by McKeon, in my bibliographical essay I will share with the reader a number of more recent translations and editions I have found helpful.

PART 1

HOW TO THINK LOGICALLY

1

WHY IT'S IMPOSSIBLE TO BELIEVE SIX IMPOSSIBLE THINGS BEFORE BREAKFAST

Albert Einstein did not invent the formula, $E = mc^2$; he discovered it. In the same way, Isaac Newton discovered, rather than invented, the laws that govern gravitation. The formula and the laws have been written into creation since the beginning; what Einstein and Newton did was pull the curtain away from nature to reveal the careful fine-tuning that governs life, motion, and change in our ordered universe.

Aristotle is the father of logic, not because he invented it out of whole cloth but because he recognized, clarified, and systematized the rules that govern the proper use of our rational faculties. There is an order without and an order within, and they reflect each other. How did Aristotle happen upon that dual order? By moving past mere thinking to engage in the metacognitive practice of thinking about thinking.

The Egyptian builders who lived and worked before Pythagoras could, it seems, determine whether they had a perfect right angle by aligning a three-inch, four-inch, and five-inch strip of cloth into a triangle. They were thinking. What Pythagoras did is think theoretically about such practical thinking to arrive at his famous theorem that in all right triangles, even ones that are invisible, the sum of the squares of the two sides ($a^2 + b^2$) will always equal the square of the hypotenuse (c^2). Like Einstein and Newton after him, Pythagoras did not fabricate his mathematical formulation to grace a fantasy world; he discerned this pattern of relationship in the very warp and woof of the cosmos.

THE LAW OF NONCONTRADICTION

Some two centuries after Pythagoras propounded his theorem, Aristotle took a close look at the kinds of statements people make about God, nature, and their fellow man. Though he could not always be certain whether a given statement was true, he discovered a way to spot statements that could *not* be true. A statement is necessarily false if it violates the law of noncontradiction: something cannot be itself and its opposite at the same time and in the same way.

We can say someone is a young man and an old man at a different time (twenty-five years old today but sixty-five years old forty years from now) or in a different way (young at heart but old in years), but we cannot say he is a young man and an old man at the same time and in the same way. To make such a statement is to violate the law of noncontradiction and to fall into logical error.

A man may be alive and not alive, or believe and not believe, or start a project and finish it at different times, but he cannot be (or do) both the one and the other simultaneously. A woman can be a primate in the sense that she is viviparous (gives live births) and not a primate in the sense that she has reason; she can be a doctor in the sense that she has a PhD and not a doctor in the sense that she does not practice medicine; but she cannot be both a primate/doctor and not a primate/doctor in the same sense.

Aristotle states this foundational law of logic most clearly in *Metaphysics*: "The same attribute cannot at the same time belong and not belong to the same subject and in the same respect." He then goes on to add:

> It is impossible for any one to believe the same thing to be and not to be.... For what a man says, he does not necessarily believe; and if it is impossible that contrary attributes should belong at the same time to the same subject...., and if an opinion which contradicts another is contrary to it, obviously it is impossible for the same man at the same time to believe the same thing to be and not to be; for if a man were mistaken on this point he would have contrary opinions at the same time. It is for this reason that all who are carrying out a demonstration reduce it to this as an ultimate belief; for this is naturally the starting-point even for all the other axioms. (IV.3; 1005b20-34)

Note that Aristotle does not attempt to "prove" his point. The law of noncontradiction is a foundational principle of logic that is not to be demonstrated but submitted to: one argues *from* it, not *for* it. It is, Aristotle insists, "the starting-point" for all thinking that can properly call itself rational and logical.

The White Queen in chapter five of *Through the Looking-Glass* informs Alice that when she was her age, she was quite capable of believing six impossible things before breakfast. Neither Aristotle nor the sensible Alice will put up with such nonsense. In fact, Aristotle states, boldly and unapologetically, that anyone who thinks that the self-evident law of noncontradiction needs to be demonstrated lacks true philosophical training. To argue against it is to make an argument that, if proved, would make all other arguments impossible. It is to rob the one who denies it of his very status as a rational animal: "If all are alike both wrong and right, one who is in this condition will not be able either to speak or to say anything intelligible; for he says at the same time both 'yes' and 'no'. And if he makes no judgement but 'thinks' and 'does not think', indifferently, what difference will there be between him and a vegetable?" (IV.4; 1008b8-12).

The reserved Aristotle rarely descends to such sarcasm, but he is defending the very possibility of logical thought and rational choice. Using a somewhat snarky reductio ad absurdum—an argument that exposes foundational weaknesses in a claim by showing what happens if that claim is taken to its "logical" conclusion—Aristotle makes it clear that only a fool would refuse to submit, in his daily life, to the law of noncontradiction:

> For why does a man walk to Megara and not stay at home, when he thinks he ought to be walking there? Why does he not walk early some morning into a well or over a precipice, if one happens to be in his way? Why do we observe him guarding against this, evidently because he does not think that falling in is alike good and not good? Evidently, then, he judges one thing to be better and another worse. And if this is so, he must also judge one thing to be a man and another to be not-a-man, one thing to be sweet and another to be not-sweet. . . . Therefore, as it seems, all men make unqualified judgements, if not about all things, still about what is better and worse. (IV.4; 1008b14-27)

Unlike Plato, who put little stock in common opinions held by common people, Aristotle trusted the wisdom of common sense. All of us know quite well that our neighbors, like ourselves, accept without question that two opposing ideas or actions cannot both be true at the same time and in the same way. If we did not do so, our thinking would be random, our judgments haphazard, and our choices indiscriminate.

THE CORRESPONDENCE THEORY OF TRUTH

In Aristotle, we encounter the same firm but jovial common sense of one of the great Christian thinkers of the eighteenth century: British poet, playwright, critic, lexicographer, moralist, and man of letters Samuel Johnson (1709–1784). In his delightful *Life of Samuel Johnson*, James Boswell records an incident from August 1763 in which Dr. Johnson embodied to the full the kind of common-man logical thinking that Aristotle helped usher into the world:

> After we came out of the church, we stood talking for some time together of Bishop Berkeley's ingenious sophistry to prove the non-existence of matter, and that every thing in the universe is merely ideal. I observed, that though we are satisfied his doctrine is not true, it is impossible to refute it. I never shall forget the alacrity with which Johnson answered, striking his foot with mighty force against a large stone, till he rebounded from it, "I refute it *thus*."[1]

Though Christianity is a religion of miracles, it is grounded in the day-to-day realities of history. Indeed, the Christian is only able to recognize miracles because he knows how the laws of nature normally operate and that there is a correspondence between reality and the statements we make about reality. Johnson remains assured that the stone that halts the forward movement of his foot is as concrete, actual, and real as the sharp twinge of pain he no doubt felt when his soft toe connected with the hard rock.

That there is a real, one-to-one correspondence between the things we see around us and the things we say about those things is foundational to Christianity. But it has also been foundational to secular, scientific thought in the West. Neither Baruch Spinoza nor David Hume nor Bertrand Russell nor

---

[1]James Boswell, *Boswell's Life of Johnson* (London: Henry Froude, 1904), 1:315.

Einstein believed in the God revealed in the Bible; all of them were finally materialists, either rejecting God outright or making him equivalent to nature or the universe. Yet, all four of these nontheistic philosopher-scientists accepted the correspondence theory of truth. Had they not, they could not have propounded their theories about the nature of reality.

Here, in a maddeningly tongue-twisting sentence, is how Aristotle defines the correspondent nature of our world: "To say of what is that it is not, or of what is not that it is, is false, while to say of what is that it is, and of what is not that it is not, is true; so that he who says of anything that it is, or that it is not, will say either what is true or what is false" (IV.7; 1011b26-29). Science as we know it, whether theistic or secular, would not have arisen in the West had scientists not agreed with Aristotle that the objects and patterns and motions that make up our cosmos bear a direct relationship to the evidence of our senses, the theorizing of our minds, and the words and symbols we use to express that evidence and theorizing in hypotheses, principles, and laws.[2]

No modern science, then, but also no Christian theology. Apart from Aristotle's correspondent view of truth—a view that is assumed but not expressly stated in Scripture—the doctors of the church, whether Catholic or Protestant, would have been hard pressed to express the work and teachings of Christ in defendable doctrines and disciplines and coherent confessions and creeds.

Combining the law of noncontradiction with the correspondence theory of truth, Aristotle describes what the world would be like if truth and falsehood were interchangeable:

> On the one hand, if all opinions and appearances are true, all statements must be at the same time true and false. For many men hold beliefs in which they conflict with one another, and think those mistaken who have not the same opinions as themselves; so that the same thing must both be and not be. And on the other hand, if this is so, all opinions must be true; for those who are mistaken and those who are right are opposed to one another in their opinions; if, then, reality is such as the view in question supposes, all will be right in their beliefs. (IV.5; 1009a7-14)

---

[2] I discuss the relationship between Christianity and modern science in full in chapter three below.

Only chaos can result when a culture allows contradictory things to be treated as if they were equivalent or cavalierly call something true that does not correspond with reality. Sadly, we are witnessing that very scenario play itself out in North America, Europe, and other countries influenced by modern Western thought.

Increasingly since Samuel Johnson's day, ethical, philosophical, and aesthetic relativism has seized control of academic and popular culture, even making strong inroads into the church. Engaged in a rash, intellectually (and morally) suicidal quest to make all things equally true, we have only succeeded in making all things equally false—erecting in place of Aristotle's search for objective truth a dictatorship of relativism.

The ancient Greeks worshiped a pantheon of arbitrary gods who ruled over a world that was often as arbitrary as they were. Aristotle, like Plato before him, turned the eyes of philosophy toward truths that transcended the petty rivalries and licentious games of Zeus and his divine court. As we will see in part two, the God of Aristotle was ultimately a removed and impersonal one, a fact that unfortunately helped lead Christianity into the dead end of deism during the Enlightenment. Still, by positing an Unmoved Mover who was consistent and coherent, Aristotle brought clarity about the nature of God to the greatest philosopher-theologian of the high Middle Ages.

AQUINAS AND LEWIS ON THE NATURE OF REALITY

Far from an arbitrary deity, the God of the Bible is not only the author of the correspondence theory of truth and the law of noncontradiction; he embodies both in his nature and his being. In question 25, article 3 of his *Summa*, the great Italian Dominican friar, priest, and scholastic Thomas Aquinas (1225-1274) poses an essential question of theology: Is God omnipotent? Although he answers affirmatively, he qualifies his affirmation by referring to Aristotle's law of noncontradiction:

> Now nothing is opposed to the idea of being except non-being. Therefore, that which at the same time implies being and non-being is repugnant to the idea of an absolute possible, which is subject to the divine omnipotence. For such cannot come under the divine omnipotence; not indeed because of any defect in the power of God, but because it has not the nature of a feasible or

possible thing. Therefore, everything that does not imply a contradiction in terms is numbered among those possibles in respect of which God is called omnipotent; whereas whatever implies contradiction does not come within the scope of divine omnipotence, because it cannot have the aspect of possibility. Hence it is more appropriate to say that such things cannot be done, than that God cannot do them. Nor is this contrary to the word of the angel, saying: *No word shall be impossible with God* (*Luke* i. 37). For whatever implies a contradiction cannot be a word, because no intellect can possibly conceive such a thing.[3]

The omnipotent God, Aquinas argues, can do all things that are possible, but even he cannot make being and nonbeing at the same time and in the same way. God cannot do such a thing, not because he is limited in his power but because such a thing is simply impossible, a logical contradiction in terms. The verse he quotes from Luke (Lk 1:37), he argues, does not contradict the law of noncontradiction, for a word that does not correspond with the nature of reality is not a word; it is a meaningless sound, a nothing.

To the modern—or, rather, postmodern—Christian, Aquinas may seem to be guilty of putting God in a box. But that is not his intent. In the tradition of Aristotle, Aquinas seeks to remain faithful to the rational world that God created, a world that reflects his (God's) rationality and that *corresponds* to the rational structures that God inscribed into the minds of his rational creatures— particularly the supremely ordered (and obedient) mind of Aquinas. It is neither improper nor blasphemous to suggest that God, like any just monarch, follows his own rules.

Seven centuries after Aquinas penned his *Summa*, the great British author, academic, and apologist C. S. Lewis (1898–1963) set himself the task of addressing one of the most difficult and perennial questions asked of Christians: Why, if God is all good and all-powerful, does suffering exist in the world? Most Christians over the centuries have accounted for the existence of evil and pain by referring, at least in part, to man's misuse of free will. Few, however, have thought clearly through the implications of God's decision to endow his human creatures with the gift of free will.

---

[3]Anton C. Pegis, ed., *Introduction to Saint Thomas Aquinas* (New York: Modern Library, 1948), I, q. 25, art. 3 (p. 231).

To set the divine parameters for his freewill apologetic, Lewis, in *The Problem of Pain* (1940), makes a direct appeal to Aristotle and Aquinas's law of noncontradiction:

> *Omnipotence* means "power to do all, or everything." And we are told in Scripture that "with God all things are possible." It is common enough in argument with an unbeliever, to be told that God, if He existed and were good, would do this or that; and then, if we point out that the proposed action is impossible, to be met with the retort, "But I thought God was supposed to be able to do anything." This raises the whole question of impossibility.[4]

Lewis clearly alludes here to the passage from Aquinas quoted above, complete with the biblical reference to Gabriel's words to the Virgin Mary about nothing being impossible for God. Yet, Lewis, like Aquinas and Aristotle before him, qualifies the theological tenet of God's omnipotence to refer only to actions that are intrinsically possible.

From here, Lewis offers his own framing of the law of noncontradiction, noting that opposites are impossible unless an "unless" clause is inserted that bridges the contradiction. Thus, to call back an analogy I used earlier, it is impossible for me to be both an old man and a young man, *unless* I am speaking of myself at two different periods of time. Likewise, it is impossible for a human female to be identical to a primate, *unless* you mean she is identical to a primate in the limited sense that she gives birth to live children. In the absence of such an unless, however, the law of noncontradiction applies. That is to say, if something "is self-contradictory it is absolutely impossible. . . . It has no *unless* clause attached to it. It is impossible under all conditions and in all worlds and for all agents."[5]

With that, Lewis springs on his reader the divine implications of a law he learned, via Aquinas, from a pagan philosopher who did not have access to the Scriptures:

> "All agents" here includes God Himself. His Omnipotence means power to do all that is intrinsically possible, not to do the intrinsically impossible. You may attribute miracles to Him, but not nonsense. This is no limit to His

---

[4]C. S. Lewis, *The Problem of Pain* (New York: Macmillan, 1962), 26-27.
[5]Lewis, *Problem of Pain*, 27-28.

> power. If you choose to say "God can give a creature free-will and at the same time withhold free-will from it," you have not succeeded in saying *anything* about God: meaningless combinations of words do not suddenly acquire meaning simply because we prefix to them the two other words "God can." It remains true that all *things* are possible with God: the intrinsic impossibilities are not things but nonentities. It is no more possible for God than for the weakest of His creatures to carry out both of two mutually exclusive alternatives; not because His power meets an obstacle, but because nonsense remains nonsense even when we talk it about God.[6]

There you have it: it is impossible, even for God, to give us free will and not give us free will at the same time and in the same way. To say God cannot do something that is intrinsically impossible is not to put God in a box; it is merely to treat nonsense as nonsense, whether the supposed perpetrator of that nonsense is human or divine.

Though it may seem that Lewis, like Aquinas before him, is putting limits on God, what he is really doing is defending, after Aristotle, the ordered creation God made and acknowledging the ordered minds he gave us to perceive and study that order.

---

[6]Lewis, *Problem of Pain*, 28.

2

PLAYING AROUND IN ARISTOTLE'S TOOLBOX

Although Aristotle wrote books with titles such as *Physics*, *Metaphysics*, *Ethics*, and *Politics*, he did not write a book titled *Logic*. Instead, he wrote a series of preliminary studies that have long been referred to collectively as the Organon: Greek for an instrument, or organ, for acquiring knowledge. For Aristotle, logic is not so much a separate discipline as it is a toolbox for engaging with other disciplines. Whether one studies physics, metaphysics, ethics, or politics, he can borrow tools from the toolbox to guide his research and ensure that each step he takes from observation to inference, premise to theory, presupposition to ramification is logical, prudent, and justified.

The six books that make up the Organon are *Categories*, *On Interpretation*, *Prior Analytics*, *Posterior Analytics*, *Topics*, and *On Sophistical Refutations*. Taken together, they provide the mental equipment necessary for initiating and undertaking a systematic and comprehensive study of the world. What Aristotle brought to this study is a remarkable clarity and exactness in terminology and the relationship between claims and conclusions. Socrates and Plato before him labored hard to frame precise definitions of abstract nouns such as *courage*, *justice*, and *goodness*. Aristotle, while continuing their focus on definition, dug down deeper to the very words and concepts out of which proper definitions are forged.

UNPACKING THE GRAMMAR OF LOGIC

Even those who have not studied grammar recognize intuitively the difference between nouns and adjectives. In such phrases as "brown dog," "tall tree," and "musical man," it will be instantly clear to most people that the noun, the object in question, the thing-in-itself, is the dog or the tree or the man. Brown, tall, and musical are not things-in-themselves but descriptors, adjectives that modify the things.

In *Categories*, Aristotle raises this grammatical distinction into a foundation for clear and logical thinking. Dogs, trees, and men are substances (or essences or beings or realities); the words that modify them are accidents that describe but are not essential to their nature. Aristotle distinguishes between one category of substance and nine of accidents: "substance, quantity, quality, relation, place, time, position, state, action, or affection." He then provides a series of examples to illustrate each category (4; 1b25-2a1-3). Here are Aristotle's examples expressed in the form of a list:

substance:	man; the horse
quantity:	two cubits long; three cubits long
quality:	white; grammatical
relation:	double; half; greater
place:	in the marketplace; in the Lyceum
time:	yesterday; last year
position:	lying; sitting
state:	shod; armed
action:	to lance; to cauterize
affection:	to be lanced; to be cauterized

Although all nine accidental categories play a role in Aristotle's philosophy, he generally confines himself to quality, quantity, and, to a lesser extent, relation.

Why are these distinctions important? Because they determine the kinds of questions we can and should ask and those that are irrelevant. Thus, Aristotle follows the passage quoted above with this qualification: "No one of these terms, in and by itself, involves an affirmation; it is by the combination of such terms that positive or negative statements arise. For every assertion must, as is admitted, be either true or false, whereas expressions which are not in any way composite such as 'man', 'white' . . . cannot be either true or false" (4; 2a4-10).

We do not debate whether the person across the street is or is not a man (substance); we can debate, however, whether he is a tall or short man, a smart or foolish man, a winning or a losing man (substance + accident). In the same way, we do not argue whether the color white (an accident of quality) is, in and of itself, true or false; we can, however, debate whether the horse at the end of the street is a white horse, a brown horse, or a gray horse (accident + substance).

Just as Aristotle argues that nouns (substances) and adjectives (accidents) must work together to make statements whose truth or falsity can be debated, so, in the first chapter of *On Interpretation*, he widens his argument to take in the need for nouns and verbs to function in unison:

> As there are in the mind thoughts which do not involve truth or falsity, and also those which must be either true or false, so it is in speech. For truth and falsity imply combination and separation. Nouns and verbs, provided nothing is added, are like thoughts without combination or separation; "man" and "white", as isolated terms, are not yet either true or false. In proof of this, consider the word "goat-stag". It has significance, but there is no truth or falsity about it, unless "is" or "is not" is added, either in the present or in some other tense. (1; 16a9-18)

As a naked noun (substance), *goat-stag* is neither true nor false. Only when it is combined with a verb—a goat-stag is (exists) or a goat-stag is not—does it become a matter for debate and a statement to which the terms *true* or *false* can be properly attached.

Similarly, a verb without a noun attached to it cannot function on its own as a true or false statement:

> Verbs in and by themselves are substantival and have significance, for he who uses such expressions arrests the hearer's mind, and fixes his attention; but they do not, as they stand, express any judgement, either positive or negative. For neither are "to be" and "not to be" the participle "being" significant of any fact, unless something is added; for they do not themselves indicate anything, but imply a copulation [of noun and verb], of which we cannot form a conception apart from the things coupled. (3; 16b19-25)

This may sound like common sense—of course the state of being or not being cannot be adequately discussed unless it is linked to some *thing* that either exists or does not—but that is only because Aristotle, the philosopher of common sense, was the first person to make explicit what people had long known intuitively but were unable to express. Aristotle cared deeply about the meaning of words. Truth and falsehood, virtue and vice, goodness and evil were not relativistic terms for him but expressions of the nature of reality.

SUBSTANCE AND ACCIDENT IN THE CATHOLIC MASS

It should come as no surprise that when the Catholic Church attempted to formulate in words the supreme mystery of the Eucharist—by which ordinary bread and wine are transformed into the body and blood of Christ—she turned to Aristotle for an appropriate language. Here is what she proclaims in the Catechism of the Catholic Church: "By the consecration of the bread and wine there takes place a change of the whole substance of the bread into the substance of the body of Christ our Lord and of the whole substance of the wine into the substance of his blood. This change the holy Catholic Church has fittingly and properly called transubstantiation."[1] Note that it is only the substance, and *not* the accidents, of the bread and wine that are, literally, tran-substantiated during the Mass. In quality and quantity, the bread and wine remain the same; that is why those who participate in Communion are not cannibals, as the ancient Romans often accused them of being.

If one were to ask a devout Catholic whether the consecrated host he holds in his hand is ordinary bread or the body of Christ, he could not give a simple yes or no answer. In its accidents, it is still bread, he must say, but in its substance, it is the body of Christ. Aristotle, I believe, would have found the Catholic doctrine of transubstantiation baffling. Indeed, one might argue that the Catholic use of Aristotle's categories of substance and accident turns Aristotle's law of noncontradiction on its head: for transubstantiation seems to suggest that the consecrated bread and wine can be bread and not-bread, wine and not-wine at the same time. Yet, as paradoxical as it might seem, the categories Aristotle laid down three and a half centuries before Christ was born provided the vehicle that the Catholic Church (via Aquinas) needed to explain a mystery that transcends the normal boundaries of space, time, and logic.

Which is not to say that Aristotle was unable to conceive realities that press the boundaries of what can be stated or thought. In *On Interpretation*, he lays

---

[1]*Catechism of the Catholic Church* (Liguori, MO: Liguori, 1994), 2.2.3.5.1376 (p. 347).

down a series of four statements in which two are positive and two are negative. Here are two of those series:

> Positive statement one: man is just
>
> Negative statement one: man is not just
>
> Positive statement two: man is not-just
>
> Negative statement two: man is not not-just
>
> Positive statement one: every man is just
>
> Negative statement one: not every man is just
>
> Positive statement two: every man is not-just
>
> Negative statement two: not every man is not-just

In both examples, all four of the "two" statements are real in the sense that they can be stated, but only with reference to the "one" statements can we speak in terms of true or false.

As for the "two" statements, their seeming use of negative language (not-man; not-just) does not qualify them as statements that are false rather than true. To the contrary, Aristotle explains,

> Negative expressions, which consist of an indefinite noun or predicate, such as "not-man" or "not-just", may seem to be denials containing neither noun nor verb in the proper sense of the words. But they are not. For a denial must always be either true or false, and he that uses the expression "not man", if nothing more be added, is not nearer but rather further from making a true or a false statement than he who uses the expression "man." (10; 20a31-37)

For the logical, systematic Aristotle to identify statements that can be expressed but that lack true or false content—that are, as it were, simultaneously real and unreal—might seem to threaten a fall into relativism, but that does not prevent Aristotle from exploring the full range of human language and thought.

DOROTHY SAYERS'S ARISTOTELIAN SOLUTION TO THE ORIGIN OF EVIL

Just as the Catholic Church tackled the Christian mystery of the Eucharist by using Aristotle's categories of substance and accident somewhat against him, so a twentieth-century British author named Dorothy Sayers tackled the

Christian mystery of the origin of evil by using Aristotle's meditations on negative phrases such as not-man and not-just somewhat against him. Sayers (1893–1957) is best known as the author of the Lord Peter Wimsey detective series, though she also translated Dante's *Comedy* and wrote a series of radio plays for the BBC on the life of Christ. In her mind-bending tour de force on the nature of the triune God, *The Mind of the Maker* (1941), she addresses the thorny problem of how evil came into our world. If, as the Nicene Creed states, God is the Creator of all things visible and invisible, and if he is all good, then how did evil come into the world? Surely God did not create evil; and yet, if he did not, who did?

To address this question, one that has puzzled theologians and apologists for thousands of years, Sayers turns unexpectedly to Aristotle's discussion of the status of negative statements such as not-man and not-just. "Being (simply by being)," she argues,

> creates Not-Being, not merely contemporaneously in the world of Space, but also in the whole extent of Time behind it. So that though, in the absence of Being, it would be meaningless to say that Not-Being precedes Being; yet, in the presence of Being that proposition becomes both significant and true, because Being has made it so. Or, to use the most familiar of all metaphors, "before" light, there was neither light nor darkness; darkness is not darkness until light has made the concept of darkness possible. Darkness cannot say: "I precede the coming light", but there is a sense in which light can say, "Darkness preceded me."[2]

Like Aristotle, Sayers treats the negative statement Not-Being as something that is both real and unreal. It has no existence in and of itself, and though it can be stated, it cannot be judged as true or false. What reality it has is given it by the existence of Being.

Having established this Aristotelian relationship between the categories of Being and Not-Being, Sayers makes an analogy to Shakespeare's creation of the character of Hamlet and what that creation entails:

> Shakespeare writes [the play] *Hamlet*. That act of creation enriches the world with a new category of Being, namely: [the character] Hamlet. But

---

[2]Dorothy L. Sayers, *The Mind of the Maker* (New York: Harper & Row, 1979), 100-101.

simultaneously it enriches the world with a new category of Not-Being, namely: Not-Hamlet. Everything other than *Hamlet*, to the farthest bounds of the universe, acquires in addition to its former characteristics, the characteristic of being Not-Hamlet; the whole of the past immediately and automatically becomes Not-Hamlet. Now, in a sense, it is true to say that the past was Not-Hamlet before Hamlet was created or thought-of; it is true, but it is meaningless, since apart from *Hamlet* there is no meaning that we can possibly attach to the term Not-Hamlet.[3]

As before, the existence of Not-Hamlet relies completely on the creation of Hamlet; apart from it, it has no existence, though it can be stated in words. Shakespeare the author did not seek to create Not-Hamlet, but his creation of Hamlet brought with it the possibility of Not-Hamlet.

In the same way, Sayers goes on to argue, "the reality of Evil is contingent upon the reality of Good":

> the Good, by merely occurring, automatically and inevitably creates its corresponding Evil. In this sense, therefore, God, Creator of all things, creates Evil as well as Good, because the creation of a category of Good necessarily creates a category of Not-Good. From this point of view, those who say that God is "beyond Good and Evil" are perfectly right: He transcends both, because both are included within His Being. But the Evil has no reality except in relation to His Good; and this is what is meant by saying that Evil is negation or deprivation of Good.[4]

Sayers has Augustine in mind when she writes that Evil is a negation or deprivation of Good; but Augustine was himself influenced in part by Aristotle, who speaks about privation in similar terms in *Metaphysics*—though he speaks in terms of physical-psychological health and disease rather than spiritual-theological good and evil.[5]

Having moved smoothly from Aristotle's categories of Being/Not-Being (real/unreal) to her literary analogy of Hamlet/Not-Hamlet to Aristotle's (via Augustine's) categories of Good/Not-Good, Sayers brings the argument back

---

[3]Sayers, *Mind of the Maker*, 101.
[4]Sayers, *Mind of the Maker*, 102.
[5]"The substance of a privation is the opposite substance, e.g. health is the substance of disease (for disease is the absence of health)" (VII.7; 1032b2-3).

to Hamlet and the implications for the origin of evil that rise up out of the liminal status of Not-Hamlet. "So long as Not-Being remains negative and inactive, it produces no particular effects, harmful or otherwise. But if Not-Hamlet becomes associated with consciousness and will, we get something which is not merely Not-Hamlet: we get Anti-Hamlet."[6] This anti-Hamlet gains consciousness and will when a human actor so misuses his free will as to bring Not-Hamlet into existence as Anti-Hamlet. We cannot lay this misuse at the feet of Shakespeare, though in the act of creating Hamlet he did create the possibility for a (potential) Not-Hamlet and an (actual) Anti-Hamlet. Apart from misuse on the part of the human actor, Not-Hamlet, and thus Anti-Hamlet, would have remained inert, a possibility without a reality.

As with the example from the Catholic Eucharist, it is unlikely that Aristotle could have imagined his categories being used to help resolve a theological quandary about the origin of evil. Nevertheless, the kind of thinking about thinking, backed up by carefully selected terms and qualifications, that he set in motion has long assisted and clarified the attempts of Christian philosophers, theologians, apologists, and critics to make sense of their world, their place in it, and the God who created and sustains it.

---

[6]Sayers, *Mind of the Maker*, 102.

3

MAKING ARGUMENTS THAT MAKE SENSE

In addition to introducing the categories that many philosophers today still use to sort out the substances and accidents of our everyday reality, Aristotle's Organon blessed the world of thought with a dual method for moving logically from claims to conclusions. As Aristotle explains it—and his approach to logic has changed little, if at all, for over two millennia—the logician can either proceed upward from facts, figures, and observations toward a general inference (induction) or proceed downward from self-evident premises and assumptions to a specific conclusion (deduction).

In *Topics*, Aristotle defines induction as "a passage from individuals to universals, for example, the argument that supposing the skilled pilot is the most effective, and likewise the skilled charioteer, then in general the skilled man is the best at his particular task." That is to say, if we observe that skilled pilots, skilled charioteers, skilled carpenters, and skilled blacksmiths are all more effective at their job than their nonskilled counterparts, then we can infer that in other professions the same rule will hold true: that the skilled worker is better at his task than the nonskilled. Aristotle concedes that inductive reason of this kind "is the more convincing and clear: it is more readily learnt by the use of the senses, and is applicable generally to the mass of men." However, he immediately qualifies his concession by arguing that "reasoning [deduction] is more forcible and effective against contradictious people" (I.12; 105a10-19). Although post-Enlightenment thought has increasingly privileged induction over deduction, Aristotle's preference for deduction as the golden road to truth has exerted a powerful influence on philosophy.

VALID AND INVALID SYLLOGISMS

Deductive reasoning generally manifests itself in the form of a syllogism, which Aristotle defines and lists in all its valid and invalid forms in *Prior Analytics*. A syllogism is a three-step proof that begins with a major premise, which is assumed rather than proven; a minor premise, which is an observable fact; and a conclusion, which results from the two premises. Here is an example of a valid syllogism:

Major premise: All men (A) are mortal (B)[1]

Minor premise: Socrates (C) is a man (A)

Conclusion: Therefore, Socrates (C) is mortal (B)

Note that the field of mortality (B) is completely inscribed within the field of mankind (A) and that the field of Socrates (C) is completely inscribed within the field of mankind (A). Given this relationship, it is logically valid to conclude that Socrates (C) is also inscribed fully within the field of mortality (B).

Here is an example of a second, more complicated valid syllogism that makes use of negatives:

Major premise: *None* of the books from the Acme bookstore (A) are new (B)

Minor premise: These books (C) are from the Acme bookstore (A)

Conclusion: Therefore, these books (C) are *not* new (B)

This time, the books from the Acme (used) bookstore (A) do not overlap at all with the field of new books (B). Since the books I possess (C) are from the Acme bookstore (A), then the books (C) must lie *outside* the field of new books (B): that is, they are used.

Here is an invalid syllogism that plays off my initial example:

Major premise: All horses (A) are mortal (B)

Minor premise: Socrates (C) is not a horse (A)

Invalid conclusion: Therefore, Socrates (C) is not mortal (B)

---

[1] In Aristotle's original Greek, this phrase reads "mortal are all men." In keeping with Greek syntax, Aristotle assigns different letters to the parts of his premise: mortal (A) are all men (B). For the sake of clarity, here and elsewhere I will follow standard English syntax: all men (A) are mortal (B).

This syllogism is invalid because the mere fact that Socrates (C) is not a horse (A) does not therefore ensure that he is not mortal (B), since the field of mortality, while it includes horses (A), does not include *only* horses.

Although one rarely encounters this kind of invalid syllogism, there is a type of invalid syllogism that appears often in debates and political rhetoric:

Major premise: All fathers (A) are male (B)

Minor premise: Socrates (C) is male (B)

Invalid conclusion: Therefore, Socrates (C) is a father (A)

Although Socrates was in fact a father, the conclusion that he is a father does not follow logically from the two premises, for the middle term (A) is not properly distributed between B and C. As a result, this type of invalid syllogism is referred to as a syllogism with an undistributed middle.

A more common name for this type of invalid syllogism is guilt by association, since it suggests that the mere fact that two things (fathers, Socrates) share something in common (maleness), proves that they are equivalent to each other. Politicians on the right (or the left) make use of this logical fallacy when they argue that their opponent is a communist (or a fascist) simply because they share one thing (the A of the invalid syllogism) in common with communists (or fascists).

My invalid syllogism can be rendered valid if I so invert the major premise as to properly distribute the middle term (A):

Major premise: All males (A) are fathers (B)

Minor premise: Socrates (C) is male (A)

Valid conclusion: Therefore, Socrates (C) is a father (B)

As odd as it may seem, this syllogism is valid, for it follows logically from the two premises. The problem is that the syllogism, though valid, is now false, for it is not true that all males are fathers. A valid *and* true version of this syllogism would read:

Major premise: All fathers (B) are male (A)

Minor premise: Socrates (C) is a father (B)

Valid conclusion: Therefore, Socrates (C) is a male (A)

In most syllogisms, the minor premise will be a fact that can be observed with the senses. The major premise, however, will generally be an unproven assumption that must be accepted without empirical proof before deduction can begin. Like the law of noncontradiction, the major premise of a syllogism is something that we argue *from*, not *for*. In *Posterior Analytics*, Aristotle explains it thus: "I call the basic truths of every genus [the major premise] those elements in it the existence of which cannot be proved.... The fact of their existence as regards the primary truths must be assumed; but it has to be proved of the remainder, the attributes [by way of a valid syllogism]" (I.10; 76a31-34).

WHY MODERN WESTERN SCIENCE WAS INVENTED BY CHRISTIANS

Needless to say, much of Christian theology and philosophy works by way of deduction, beginning with the premise that God exists, or the Bible is inspired, or man was made in God's image, and then arguing for the proper implications of those primary, assumed truths. Although inductive arguments can be mounted to back up the existence of God or the authority of Scripture or the *imago Dei*, such things tend to function as the starting point of logical argumentation (deduction) rather than the endpoint. Such is the case for the central doctrines of the Trinity and the incarnation. The givens for the first are that the Bible asserts that God is one while also speaking of Yahweh, Jesus, and the Holy Spirit as equally divine; the given for the second is that the New Testament bears witness to Jesus' full divinity and his full humanity. On the basis of these primary truths, syllogisms are mounted to arrive at a conclusion that accounts for the premises.

Secular critics of Christianity, and religion in general, will often dismiss the deductive claims and conclusions of Christian thinkers because they rely on premises or principles or assumptions that are not provable by empirical, inductive means. Ironically, those who dismiss the deductive claims of Christianity on these grounds must also dismiss the deductive claims of modern science itself. That may sound like a ridiculous claim to make, but it is not.

The success of the modern (Baconian) scientific method rests firmly on two premises that cannot be proven by empirical means but must be accepted on "faith" if science it to operate: that the universe is ordered and rational and runs in accordance with discernible laws, and that we can trust our senses to perceive and study and measure those laws. In *For the Glory of God*, sociologist of religion Rodney Stark considers why it is that the scientific method arose in Europe but not in China, India, ancient Greece, or ancient Rome, despite the fact that these cultures all produced great inventors. "Christianity," he explains, "depicted God as a rational, responsive, dependable, and omnipotent being and the universe as his personal creation, thus having a rational, lawful, stable structure, awaiting human comprehension."[2]

The Christian inventors of modern science (Nicolaus Copernicus, Galileo Galilei, Johannes Kepler, Isaac Newton, Robert Boyle, Michael Faraday, and Francis Bacon himself), Stark argues, believed that reason came from God and could thus be used to unveil the secrets of God's rational universe. The Chinese, in contrast, lacked laws of nature because they had no Creator God to lay down those laws. The God of Islam was a creator but an arbitrary one who could not be relied on to act in accordance with human reason and observation. As for the Greeks, they tended to see the cosmos as a living thing with a soul and so were not able to adopt laws to describe the movements of celestial bodies.

If I were to express the rationale and driving engine of Western science in a tight, severely condensed syllogism, one that combines within itself a string of syllogisms that go back to the foundational premise that God is a God of order and rationality and so does not fit exactly Aristotle's A, B, C structure, it would read something like this:

> Major premise: Because they were created by a rational God, the laws of nature are rational and discernible
>
> Minor premise: Because our senses were created by that same rational God, they are able to discern those laws
>
> Conclusion: If we use our senses properly, we can discern those laws

---

[2] Rodney Stark, *For the Glory of God: How Monotheism Led to Reformation, Science, Witch Hunts, and the End of Slavery* (Princeton, NJ: Princeton University Press, 2003), 147. Also see Stark's *The Victory of Reason: How Christianity Led to Freedom, Capitalism, and Western Success* (New York: Random House, 2005). Interestingly, the twentieth-century attempt to reclaim the Christian origins of modern science was initiated in great part by a Hungarian-born American Benedictine priest and physicist named Stanley Jaki (1924–2009). See, for example, his *Bible and Science* (Front Royal, VA: Christendom Press, 1996) and *The Savior of Science* (Grand Rapids, MI: Eerdmans, 2000).

Ironically, in order to work through this syllogism, the fathers of modern science had to deny many of Aristotle's erroneous teachings about the nature of our universe that we will discuss in part two. Still, they would not have been equipped to do so had they not been gifted with a logical method for moving from premises to conclusions.

A second example of a powerful Christian use of the syllogism to argue for a conclusion that Aristotle did not himself share was initiated by a Muslim school of medieval Scholastics known as Kalam.[3] This school formulated what is known as the Kalam cosmological argument, an argument that was revived in the twentieth century by an American Christian apologist named William Lane Craig. Here is how the Kalam cosmological argument is generally expressed:

Major premise: Everything that begins to exist (A) has a cause (B)

Minor premise: The universe (C) began to exist (A)

Conclusion: Therefore, the universe (C) has a cause (B)[4]

The logic here is valid and proves, by way of deductive logic, what was substantiated, by way of empirical science, as the theory of the Big Bang. Though neither alone proves the God of the Bible, both conclusions bear strong theistic implications.

Though Aristotle would surely have conceded the strength of this syllogism, he himself, somewhat unique among philosophers, concluded that *both* God and the universe were eternal—that is, did not have a beginning. I will have more to say about this in part two. For now, I will bring this chapter to a close by praising Aristotle for discovering and clarifying a method of logical thinking that could be used both to empower his own conclusions and to question, and even explode, those conclusions.

---

[3] Although the scientific method did not arise in Islamic countries, Muslim scholars helped make Western science possible by recovering the works of Aristotle, attempting to sync them with monotheism, and passing them on to the West, where they were studied by the Scholastics, particularly Aquinas. The two key Muslim scholars in this transmission were Avicenna (ca. 980–1037) and Averroes (1126–1198), who laid the foundation for the Kalam school. As a tribute to their work, Dante includes Avicenna and Averroes among the virtuous pagans; the only other Muslim he so honors is the Saladin, who was highly respected by such Crusaders as Richard the Lionhearted for his virtue and nobility (see *Inferno* IV).

[4] Slightly adapted from William Lane Craig and J. P. Moreland, eds., *The Blackwell Companion to Natural Theology* (Chichester, UK: John Wiley & Sons, 2009), 102.

4

WHY THINGS MOVE AND CHANGE

Surely the strangest suggestion to come out of the pre-Socratic philosophical world was the one made by Parmenides. Change, he proclaimed, with the riddling bravado of a guru, is an illusion. Being exists, but the category of Not-Being does not. There is no void, no empty space for Being to move around in; there is only Being. All that is, is one. Because all that is, is one, what we call change or motion is an illusion.

To help prove the supremely counterintuitive monistic teaching of his master, who was born around 520 BC, Zeno, who was born around 495 BC, propounded a series of paradoxes to demonstrate that what we perceive as motion is actually an illusion. The best known of these is Achilles and the tortoise. Imagine, if you will, a running race between a humble turtle and the swift-footed hero of the *Iliad*, whose speed is ten times that of his plodding opponent. Surely Achilles will be the winner—unless the tortoise is given a one-hundred-foot start. Why should that head start make a difference?

Because, Zeno argues, in the time it takes Achilles to catch up to the tortoise, the tortoise will have moved forward by ten feet. Achilles then runs ten feet, only to find that the tortoise has moved forward by one. When Achilles runs one foot, he finds the tortoise has run one-tenth of a foot, and so on, ad infinitum. According to Zeno's reductio ad absurdum, the swift-footed Achilles will never overtake the tortoise. The result is a paradox that can only be resolved if we accept Parmenides's contention that motion and change are illusions.[1]

---

[1] See John Mansley Robinson, *An Introduction to Early Greek Philosophy* (Boston: Houghton Mifflin, 1968), 127-39, for an overview of Parmenides's rejection of motion and Zeno's paradoxes that includes a lengthy passage from Plato's *Parmenides*, on which much of our knowledge of this matter rests.

ARISTOTLE AGAINST MONISM

Aristotle, like Plato and Socrates before him, had much respect for Parmenides, but he could not accept his radical monism (all is one), for, if such a theory were true, science would be rendered a useless and meaningless pursuit. Aristotle's major work on science is called *Physics*, but the title is a misleading one. Although Aristotle devotes time to subjects of specific interest to physicists, the title represents a transliteration of the Greek word *physis*—which means simply "nature." Aristotle's goal in *Physics* is to study nature in such a way as to discern its first causes, its principles, and its elements.

I argued at the end of the previous chapter that science arose in the West, rather than in India or China, because the Christian scientists of Europe had faith that our universe was ordered and rational and that our senses could perceive and study that order and rationality—a faith Aristotle shared but in an earlier and less firm and consistent manner. That was not the case in the East, where Hindu and Buddhist mysticism taught, along with (but not because of) Parmenides, that our senses deceive us as to the oneness of everything. This view is most fully explored and defended in the monistic *Bhagavad Gita*, but it is most succinctly summarized in a stanza by American transcendentalist Ralph Waldo Emerson (1803–1882), writing in his most eastern mode:

> If the red slayer think he slays,
> Or if the slain think he is slain,
> They know not well the subtle ways
> I keep, and pass, and turn again.[2]

There is no final distinction between slayer or slain; it is only the deception of our senses that causes us to think so. The truth is that all is one, and change is an illusion that the enlightened must learn to see through.

Aristotle will have none of it, and he makes that immediately clear in the second chapter of *Physics*. To investigate, he argues,

> whether Being is one and motionless [as Parmenides believed] is not a contribution to the science of Nature. For just as the geometer has nothing

---

[2]Ralph Waldo Emerson, "Brahma," lines 1–4, in *Selected Writings of Ralph Waldo Emerson*, ed. William H. Gilman (New York: Signet, 2003), 524.

more to say to one who denies the principles of his science—this being a question for a different science or for one common to all—so a man investigating *principles* cannot argue with one who denies their existence. For if Being is just one, and one in the way mentioned, there is a principle no longer, since a principle must be the principle of some thing or things. . . . We physicists, on the other hand, must take for granted that the things that exist by nature are, either all or some of them, in motion which is indeed made plain by induction. (I.2; 184b25-185a14)

When Aristotle says that the existence of motion and of plurality—the fact that there are many things rather than just one thing—is made plain by induction, he means that our observations of the world tell us so. As always, Aristotle, in opposition to Plato, puts great trust in common-sense knowledge, believing that a good philosopher should pay heed to what is accepted by the people and by the majority of the wise.

Besides, monists play fast and loose with their terminology. That there are separate categories of substance, quality, and quantity gives the lie to the claim that there is only one thing in the universe. Even if we accept substances (man, horse, soul) as part of a single whole, monism cannot account for accidents (white, hot, small), which have no independent existence apart from the substance to which they are attached.

It is absurd to insist that all things are one, just as it is absurd to insist that all things are many. Yet, to say that something can be both one and many, as Aristotle claims (see I.2; 186a3), violates the law of noncontradiction. To resolve this seeming conflict, Aristotle refines his categories. He agrees with the universally held beliefs that nothing comes out of nothing and that accidents fall into opposing pairs: hot and cold, wet and dry, straight and round, and so on. But if one side of the pair is born out of the other, as is also universally believed, how can it do so without turning nothing into something and something into nothing?

The answer relies on a third thing, on a substance that remains constant while the accident changes from one opposing pole to the other. Thus, when a horse (substance) steps into a cold stream on a very hot day, the heat (accident) on its skin disappears to be replaced with cold (the opposing accident); but the horse itself, the one that stepped into the cold stream, remains the same. The same process occurs when a man is instructed in the art of music: he "remains a man and is such even when he becomes musical, whereas what is not musical or is unmusical does not continue to exist, either simply or combined with the subject" (I.7; 190a10-12). This vital distinction between the third thing, the substance that endures (the man who learns), and the binary accident that changes (from unmusical to musical), prevents the law of noncontradiction from being broken. "One part survives, the other does not: what is not an opposite survives (for 'man' survives), but 'not-musical' or 'unmusical' does not survive, nor does the compound of the two, namely 'unmusical man'" (I.7; 190a18-20).

THE PERSISTENCE OF THE SOUL IN HEAVEN OR HELL

Aristotle hastens to add that just as change can be brought about by the addition of something (musicality), so it can be brought about by subtraction, as when a slab of bronze is transformed into a statue by the slow removal of some of its material. The bronze endures as matter, while it changes from being formless to bearing the form of a man. Even so, in what is likely an apocryphal story, Michelangelo is said to have explained his process for making David as one of subtraction: he simply cut away all that was not David until David emerged from the marble.

At the risk of exaggeration, I would suggest that the distinction Aristotle makes here between the horse or man or bronze that endures and the change from hot to cold, unmusical to musical, shapeless to shaped is vital to the Christian spiritual life. The doctrines of heaven and hell insist that the person who spends eternity in heaven or hell is the same person who lived and chose during his years on the earth. His decisions to obey or disobey, believe or disbelieve, accept or reject the law and mercy of God transform him from sinner to saint or child of God to child of wrath, but the person who suffers that change remains the same person. Were this not so, justice would not be served.

Whereas Plato, following in the footsteps of Pythagoras, entertained the theory of reincarnation—though Plato speaks of the transmigration of souls only in his myths, never in the dialectical portions of his dialogues—Aristotle did not. In that respect, his position comes closer than that of Plato to a Christian understanding of the persistence of the individual before and after death. In the midst of our ever-changing world, we remain the same creature created by God, though we can become spiritually strengthened or impoverished by the choices we make.

"What is cast (or casts itself) into hell," writes Lewis in chapter eight of *The Problem of Pain*, "is not a man: it is 'remains.'" It is a "lost soul" that is "eternally fixed in its diabolical attitude."[3] Yet, it remains the person that it was in life. It does not become a bird or quadruped or snake or fish, as it does in the closing section of Plato's *Timaeus*, but retains its individual identity. It has tragically shifted over a lifetime of choices and their consequences from the perfection of the man God intended it to be to the remains of a man who has almost lost himself, but not so much as to become a different species.

ARISTOTLE ON MOTION AND TIME

Who we are persists through time, and it is in analyzing the mystery of time that Aristotle finds an answer to Zeno's paradox of Achilles and the tortoise. Time, Aristotle argues, is not the same thing as change (or movement), though both time and change are continuous. "Time," in fact, "is a measure of motion [change] and of being moved" (IV.12; 221a1). That motion in time can be measured quantitatively, from the beginning to the end of a distance, or quantitatively, from the beginning to the end of a change.

It matters greatly, however, whether the time and the whole motion are finite or infinite. One cannot traverse a finite distance in an infinite time; neither can one traverse an infinite distance in a finite time. But there are two ways in which a line (or time) can be considered finite or infinite. A line can be infinite in its extent or in the number of spatial points into which it can be divided. Time can be infinite in its extent or in the number of temporal points ("nows") into which it can be divided.

If finite and infinite or extension and division are confused, it can lead to a paradox, as it does with Achilles and the tortoise:

> Zeno's argument makes a false assumption in asserting that it is impossible for a thing to pass over or severally to come in contact with infinite things in a finite

---

[3]C. S. Lewis, *The Problem of Pain* (New York: Macmillan, 1962), 125, 127.

time. For ... the time occupied by the passage over the infinite is not a finite but an infinite time, and the contact with the infinites is made by means of moments [both spatial points and temporal nows] not finite but infinite in number. (VI.2; 233a22-31)

Zeno errs in trying to make the running of the race finite while breaking the race itself into an infinite series of points/nows. If Achilles is given infinite time to traverse the infinite discrete points on the line, he will win, and the existence of motion (change) will be vindicated from the monism of Parmenides.

Several chapters later, Aristotle makes his point clearer by stating unequivocally that "time is not composed of indivisible moments any more than any other magnitude is composed of indivisibles" (VI.9; 239b8-9). One cannot arbitrarily divide up time or space in such a fashion, for both are continuous. Aristotle applies this truth to Zeno's paradox of Achilles and the tortoise, which he summarizes thus: "In a race the quickest runner can never overtake the slowest, since the pursuer must first reach the point whence the pursued started, so that the slower must always hold a lead." He then responds, "The axiom that that which holds a lead is never overtaken is false: it is not overtaken, it is true, while it holds a lead: but it is overtaken nevertheless if it is granted that it traverses the finite distance prescribed [not infinite divisible points]" (VI.9; 239b15-17, 25-29).

Time is not atomic; it is not made up of discrete atoms strung out on a line. Time is a continuum that keeps moving on rather than being broken into infinitely divisible nows. Change happens within time, not within a series of nows.

Although, as we shall see in part two, Aristotle identified in the circular motions of the heavenly spheres a kind of change that is infinite, he was unable to locate either motion or rest in a now: "It is impossible ... for anything to be in motion in a present. Nor can anything be at rest in a present" (VI.3; 234a31-32). By so theorizing, Aristotle left something of a riddle for Christian philosophers and theologians. The God who reveals himself in the Bible is not just infinite; he is eternal. As such, he dwells not in the flow of time but in the now of eternity: the "today" of Hebrews 4:7 in which he calls and is ever calling us; the yesterday, today, and forever of Hebrews 13:8 in which he is always the same.

AUGUSTINE ON THE TIMELESSNESS OF GOD

Augustine (354–430), the great philosopher-theologian-bishop whose thought was equally foundational to medieval Catholics and Protestant Reformers, was the first to catch a glimpse of that eternal now that transcends Aristotle's categories while yet seeking to speak in terms of them. For in what other terms can we speak as creatures who live in the continuous stream of time that Aristotle so accurately defines and describes in *Physics*? "For, not in our way," writes Augustine in *The City of God*, "does God look forward to the future, see the present, and look back upon the past, but in a manner remotely and profoundly unlike our way of thinking. . . . He comprehends all that takes place in time—the not-yet-existing future, the existing present, and the no-longer-existing past—in an immutable and eternal present."[4]

In *Confessions*, Augustine develops further the difference between the kind of successive, continuous time that Aristotle describes and the eternal now in which God dwells. A "long time," he explains,

> is long only because constituted of many successive movements which cannot be simultaneously extended. In the eternal, nothing is transient, but the whole is present. But no time [in contrast to eternity] is wholly present. It will see that all past time is driven backwards by the future, and all future time is the consequent of the past, and all past and future are created and set on their course by that which is always present.[5]

Though Augustine does not reference Aristotle in the distinction he makes here, a few chapters later he alludes, I believe, to Aristotle's critique of the paradoxes of Zeno. Here is that critique from *Physics*: "One part of it [time] has been and is not, while the other is going to be and is not yet. Yet time—both infinite time and any time you like to take—is made up of these. One would naturally suppose that what is made up of things which do not exist

---

[4]Augustine, *The City of God*, ed. and abridged by Vernon J. Bourke (New York: Image, 1958), XI.21 (p. 227).
[5]Augustine, *Confessions*, trans. Henry Chadwick (Oxford: Oxford University Press, 2008), XI.11 (pp. 228-29).

could have no share in reality" (IV.10; 217b34-218a3). A few lines later, anticipating his refutation of Zeno, he adds that time "is not held to be made up of 'nows'" (218a8).

Here, most likely in response to Aristotle, is what Augustine writes in *Confessions* about this doubly strange phenomenon of time: Does it exist or not; is it continuous or divisible?

> Whatever part of it [time] has flown away is past. What remains to it is future. If we can think of some bit of time which cannot be divided into even the smallest instantaneous moments, that alone is what we can call "present". And this time flies so quickly from future into past that it is an interval with no duration. If it has duration, it is divisible into past and future. But the present occupies no space.[6]

Ultimately, Augustine can find no simple answer to this earthly dilemma, but then he does not have to. He knows something, by revelation, that Aristotle does not: that God exists in the perpetual now of eternity where time neither fades nor delays, where there is no division but only wholeness, where there is no "shadow of turning" (Jas 1:17).

Aristotle, as we saw above, concluded that there can be neither motion nor rest in a divisible, present moment, a now. In the second-to-last chapter of *Confessions*, Augustine proclaims his faith that God is eternally at work (in motion) and at rest, and his hope that his ever-present motion/rest is a divine foreshadowing of the true Sabbath rest he promises his people: "You, Lord are always working and always at rest. Your seeing is not in time, your movement is not in time, and your rest is not in time. Yet your acting causes us to see things in time, time itself, and the repose which is outside time."[7]

---

[6] Augustine, *Confessions* XI.15 (p. 232).
[7] Augustine, *Confessions* XIII.35 (p. 304).

5

BODY AND SOUL IN DIALOGUE

I SAID IN CHAPTER FOUR that Aristotle did not entertain reincarnation as an option for the afterlife. Part of the reason for that, I would argue, is that he believed that matter and form—and thus body and soul—were bound together in something like an incarnational relationship. Unlike Plato, who held a dualistic view in which body and soul are separate entities and the latter is trapped in the former and yearns to be free of it, Aristotle posited an intimate union between matter and form, body and soul known as hylomorphism: *hylē* and *morphē* in Greek mean, respectively, "matter" and "form."

Aristotle's concept of hylomorphism is central to his influence on Christianity. Indeed, it marks one of the few places where Aristotle's philosophy comes closer to the Christian view of God and man, body and soul than that of Plato. I will, however, need to hold off my discussion of hylomorphism until I can establish exactly what Aristotle meant by matter and form and how he related the two to potentiality and actuality.

FORM AND MATTER

Aristotle's venture into matter and form in *Physics* is prompted by his desire to determine whether the nature of a thing is more closely allied to its matter (its external, visible shape) or its form (its internal, invisible essence). Some people, he concedes, "identify the nature or substance of a natural object with that immediate constituent of it which taken by itself is without arrangement, e.g. the wood is the 'nature' of the bed, and the bronze the 'nature' of the statue" (II.1; 193a9-11). Though Aristotle finds sense in this theory, he concludes that the form "is 'nature' rather than the matter; for a thing is more properly said to be what it is when it has attained to fulfilment than when it exists potentially" (II.1; 193b7-8).

The finished bed or statue only exists potentially in the wood or the bronze (the matter); to achieve its actuality, the form of the bed or statue must be imposed on the matter the way the form of a seal is imprinted on hot wax. In the case of an organic, living substance, whether a tree, horse, or man, the process of completion marks a growth "not into that from which it arose [the seed/matter] but into that to which it tends [the form of the tree, horse, or man]. The shape [form] then is nature" (II.1; 193b18-19).

That which makes a tree a tree, a horse a horse, and a man a man is neither the bark/flesh that clothes it nor the seed/fetus out of which it grew. Such things make up the physical matter of the tree, horse, or man: matter that grows, changes, decays, and dies. In sharp contrast, the spiritual form (or essence, or nature) of the tree, horse, or man is the fixed, unchanging plan or blueprint that gives shape to the matter. Though it may seem to the observer of the natural world that matter precedes form, the truth is exactly the opposite: the form is primary, existing before and within the matter. Matter lacks the power to organize itself. It possesses the potential to be organized, but that potentiality can be rendered real and concrete (actualized) only by the shaping power of the form.

Most Americans who, like me, attended public school were taught that the West evolved along a rough but ascending line from a supernaturalist worldview to a naturalist one, from a focus on the spiritual (actualizing form) to a focus on the physical (potentializing matter). This progressivist myth was born out of the Enlightenment and is untrue to history. While *both* Aristotle and Plato recognized a reality that was higher-deeper than the physical—with an important distinction I will discuss in a moment—most of the pre-Socratic philosophers before them were materialists who sought physical answers for all things and who preferred to pass over who and why questions in favor of what and how questions.

"If we look at the ancients," Aristotle explains,

> physics would seem to be concerned with the matter. . . . But if on the other hand art imitates nature, and it is the part of the same discipline to know the

form and the matter up to a point (e.g. the doctor has a knowledge of health and also of bile and phlegm, in which health is realized, and the builder both of the form of the house and of the matter, namely that it is bricks and beams, and so forth): if this is so, it would be the part of physics also to know nature in both its senses. (II.2; 194a19-26)

It is not enough, Aristotle argues, for a doctor or a builder to concern himself only with the physical fluids of the patient's body he hopes to cure or the physical materials that make up the house he intends to build. An inquiry must be made as well into the true nature, invisible though it may be to the human eye, of the form of health or of the house.

THE SUPERNATURAL VISION OF PLATO *AND* ARISTOTLE

The scientist, just as much as the metaphysician, must be concerned with tangible matter as well as intangible form. If he does not pay attention to both, he will not be able to determine the telos (purposeful end) for which something was made and exists, and if he cannot determine that, he will not be able to grasp the full and true nature of the thing being studied. It is partly true that Aristotle brought philosophy back down to earth, trimming Plato's idealistic wings and grounding philosophy in an empirical focus on this world. But it is also partly false.

Aristotle did not abandon completely Plato's belief that supernatural/metaphysical Forms gave shape, meaning, and purpose to the physical objects and concrete ideas of our world. Instead, he shifted the orientation of Plato's Forms in two specific ways. First, he moved them from their Platonic location outside and above the physical objects and ideas that imitate them to a new residence below and within those objects and ideas. Second, rather than draw a sharp line between form and matter (Plato would say Form and imitation), he united the two in a more intimate and incarnational way.

Aristotle concedes that Plato's theory of the Forms can be applied loosely to mathematics, in which it is somewhat possible to separate abstract principles from the physical properties of bodies on earth. Nevertheless, he takes the "holders of the theory of Forms" to task for trying to "do the same, though they are not aware of it; for they separate the objects of physics, which are less separable than those of mathematics" (II.2; 193b35-36). For Aristotle, scientists cannot arbitrarily divide the form of a thing from the matter to which it is allied; both are needed if the composite (form/matter) object is to move from potentiality to actuality and so achieve its telos.

Aristotle takes up this line of thought again in *Metaphysics*, clarifying as he does his terminology, approach, and basic understanding of what a substance is. "Plato," he explains, "posited two kinds of substance—the Forms and objects of mathematics—as well as a third kind, viz. the substance of sensible bodies" (VII.2; 1028b19-20). As we just saw, Aristotle accepted—somewhat—the objects of mathematics as separable objects. But what of the Forms and the sensible bodies? How are they properly related? To answer this, Aristotle moves his focus from Plato's heavenly Forms, which are removed from this world of change, to what he calls a "substratum . . . of which other things are predicated, while it is itself not predicated of anything else" (VII.3; 1028b36-37).

Where, Aristotle asks, shall we locate this groundless ground of being, this most true and essential substance? Does it inhere in the matter, the form, or a compound of the two? To illustrate the three choices, Aristotle falls back on the same illustration he uses in *Physics*: "By the matter I mean, for instance, the bronze, by the shape the pattern of its form, and by the compound of these the statue, the concrete whole." He then identifies the form as the best candidate: "If the form is prior to the matter and more real, it will be prior also to the compound of both, for the same reason" (VII.3; 1029a3-6). Note that although Aristotle rejects Plato's theory of the Forms, he treats form as a nonsensible thing that is within and prior to matter. Clearly, Aristotle is no materialist who thinks that all there is in the world is matter.

Still, he parts ways with Plato when he treats the *compound* of matter and form as itself a real substance that cannot be severed (or abstracted) into a universal Form and a particular earthly imitation. There are, Aristotle explains, two kinds of substances: "One kind of substance is the formula taken with the matter [the composite object made of form and matter], while another kind is the formula in its generality [Plato's Forms or Ideas]" (VII.15; 1039b21). Whereas the first, the physical matter/form compound, is subject to decay and destruction, the second, the ethereal Platonic Form, remains unchanged. Yes, the Form must exist, but how can it be known apart from a particular and physical compound substance? "Why," Aristotle cries out in frustration, "does not one of the supporters of the Ideas [that is, a Platonist] produce a definition of an Idea? It would become clear, if they tried, that what has now been said is true" (VII.15; 1040b3-4).

ARISTOTLE ON BODY AND SOUL

The dilemma seems to cause Aristotle much distress, but he eventually moves toward a tentative solution to what the pre-Socratic philosophers often referred to as the riddle of the one and the many: Is the nature of reality single, unchanging Being (as it was for Parmenides the monist, for whom everything was form) or ceaseless change from one thing to another (as it was for Heraclitus, for whom everything was matter)? "No one," Aristotle insists, "makes or begets the form [e.g., the universal form that shapes the bronze], but it is the individual that is made, i.e. the complex of form and matter that is generated [e.g., the particular statue]. Whether the substances of destructible things [Plato's Forms] can exist apart, is not yet at all clear" (VIII.3; 1043b18-20).

The solution comes when Aristotle carefully and intentionally unites matter and form with potentiality and actuality as he had done tentatively in *Physics*.

> If people proceed thus in their usual manner of definition and speech, they cannot explain and solve the difficulty. But if, as we say, one element is matter and another is form, and one is potentially and the other actually, the question will no longer be thought a difficulty. . . . The difficulty disappears, because the one is matter, the other form. What, then, causes this—that which was potentially to be actually—except, in the case of things which are generated, the agent? For there is no other cause of the potential sphere's becoming actually a sphere, but this was the essence of either. (VIII.6; 1045a21-34)

The form that gives shape to the matter is there within the matter, but there is often a need as well for an outside agent to effect the union of active actuality (form) and passive potentiality (matter). That outside agent could be God or an artist or the power of heat. That is why it takes a rational builder to draw the potential out of a pile of bricks, wood, and stone by fusing it with the actuating power of the form of the house he is building.

Such are Aristotle's theories on the relationship between matter (potentiality) and form (actuality). In *Physics* and *Metaphysics*, he offers hints that the same relationship between matter and form inheres between the body and the soul. In *On the Soul*, he states the connection plainly:

> If, then, we have to give a general formula applicable to all kinds of soul, we must describe it as the first grade of actuality [form] of a natural organized body [matter]. That is why we can wholly dismiss as unnecessary the question whether the soul and the body are one: it is as meaningless as to ask whether the wax [matter] and the shape given to it by the stamp [form] are one. (II.1; 412b4-8)

For Aristotle, the union between soul and body is not at all like a prisoner trapped within a cage or even a jewel kept in a box for safety. To the contrary, the soul is that which draws out of the body its latent potential so that the two together form a thing that is neither mere form nor mere matter. The soul is prior to the body and contains within itself the blueprint for the actualizing of the body—but neither can achieve full completion apart from the other.

In the next chapter, Aristotle states more carefully the exact relationship between body and soul:

> Since then the complex here is the living thing, the body cannot be the actuality of the soul; it is the soul which is the actuality of a certain kind of body. Hence the rightness of the view that the soul cannot be without a body, while it cannot *be* a body; it is not a body but something relative to a body. That is why it is *in* a body, and a body of a definite kind. (II.2; 414a17-21)

Unlike Plato's Forms, the soul is not a separable thing that can exist on its own. It is true that the soul is not a body, but it is equally true that it *needs* a body—and not just any body but a specific one. The soul actualizes the body, but that body is of a definite, nonrandom kind. Though Plato, like Pythagoras before him, toyed with the idea of reincarnation, Aristotle rejected any notion that an individual soul could move arbitrarily from one body to another. Each soul was united to one and only one particular body.

Had Aristotle stopped here, his words would have been shocking enough, but he develops his theory of the unique pairing of individual souls and particular bodies further, using language that sounds remarkably proto-Christian:

> It was a mistake, therefore, to do as former thinkers [Pythagoras and Plato] did, merely to fit it into a body without adding a definite specification of the kind or character of that body. Reflection confirms the observed fact; the actuality of any given thing can only be realized in what is already potentially that thing, i.e. in a matter of its own appropriate to it. From all this it follows that soul is an actuality or formulable essence of something that possesses a potentiality of being besouled. (II.2; 414a22-28)

This passage should make it clear why reincarnation was not an option for Aristotle. Soul and body are, quite literally, fitted to each other, so much so that it would be unthinkable for a soul to shed one body in order to take on another. The body does not merely contain a generic soul; it is besouled (or ensouled). The union is an intimate and incarnational one.

AQUINAS ON BODY AND SOUL

Aquinas understood well that on the matter of body and soul, Aristotle came far closer to the truth than Plato. In his *Summa*, Aquinas accepts the Aristotelian view that "man is not only a soul, but something composed of soul and body," and rejects Plato's suggestion that man is *"a soul making use of a body."* This paves the way for Aquinas to define the nature of the hylomorphic union that Aristotle defends in *Physics*, *Metaphysics*, and *On the Soul*. The "principle by which we primarily understand, whether it be called the intellect or the intellectual soul, is the form of the body. This is the demonstration used by Aristotle (*De Anima* ii, 2)."[1]

Thus does Aquinas acknowledge, with gratitude, that Aristotle was right about the incarnational relationship between the soul (form-actuality) and the body (matter-potentiality). But the Christian Aquinas does not stop there. He draws out the implications of Aristotle's hylomorphic union for what

---

[1] Anton C. Pegis, ed., *Introduction to Saint Thomas Aquinas* (New York: Modern Library, 1948), I, q. 75, art. 4; I, q. 76, art. 1 (pp. 286-87, 293).

happens to the soul in the period between the death of the body and the final resurrection.

> *Reply Obj.* 5: The soul communicates that being in which it subsists to the corporeal matter, out of which and the intellectual soul there results one being; so that the being of the whole composite is also the being of the soul. This is not the case with other non-subsistent forms. For this reason the human soul retains its own being after the dissolution of the body; whereas it is not so with other forms.
>
> *Reply Obj.* 6: To be united to the body belongs to the soul by reason of itself, just as it belongs to a light body by reason of itself to be raised up. And as a light body remains light, when removed from its proper place, retaining meanwhile an aptitude and an inclination for its proper place, so the human soul retains its proper being when separated from the body, having an aptitude and a natural inclination to be united to the body.[2]

Though Aristotle saw enough of the truth to realize the incompatibility of reincarnation with our incarnational nature as ensouled bodies (or enfleshed souls), he could not have seen so far as Aquinas does here.

For Aquinas, so deep and intimate is the union of soul (form) and body (matter) that even when the soul is released (temporarily) from the body at death, it still bears the imprint of the body whose potentiality it helped to actualize. Though body and soul can be separated, at least temporarily, their hylomorphic union is such that they are one being in a way that is unique from other composites of form and matter.

DANTE ON BODY AND SOUL

Influenced by Aquinas's understanding of the nature of the hylomorphic union, as Aquinas was by Aristotle's, Dante offers a fascinating suggestion about the intermediate state of the bodiless soul in *Purgatory* XXV. Throughout his journey, Dante is able to recognize the dead souls of sinners and saints alike, even though they are not yet in possession of their resurrection bodies. How can that be? The answer to the riddle is given to him not by Virgil but by Statius, a late convert from paganism to Christianity.

---

[2]Pegis, *Introduction to Saint Thomas Aquinas*, I, q. 76, art. 1 (p. 297).

Statius explains that after death, the disembodied soul moves through the air. As it does, the air forms around it a temporary body, but that airy body, though it resembles the original one (for the soul retains a memory of the body), is now shaped in accordance with the spiritual-intellectual state of the blessed or damned soul. The composite that results, shaped exclusively by the formative power of the soul, bears in it the marks of grace or depravity that have been engraved on the soul by a lifetime of choices for good or for ill. Like the picture of Dorian Gray in Oscar Wilde's novel, the fully passive potentiality of the air shows forth the actuality of the soul in all its glory . . . or horror!

For Aristotle and Aquinas, Dante and Wilde, the unique, incarnational fusion of body and soul forms a composite that cannot be easily severed. When questioned about the nature of marriage, Jesus quotes Genesis 2:24 and then adds his own commentary: "For this cause shall a man leave his father and mother, and cleave to his wife; and they twain shall be one flesh: so then they are no more twain, but one flesh. What therefore God hath joined together, let not man put asunder" (Mk 10:7-9). Though the incarnational marriage of husband and wife shall not endure beyond the grave, the incarnational marriage of soul and body will. Aristotle did not know that, for he could not imagine, any more than Plato could, that our body would be resurrected and reunited with our soul.

But the incarnate Word of God, both Christ and the Bible, holds out the miraculous promise to which Job in his despair so desperately clung: "Though after my skin worms destroy this body, yet in my flesh shall I see God" (Job 19:26).

PART 2

HOW TO READ THE HEAVENS AND THE EARTH

6

WHY, WHY, WHY

I SUGGESTED IN THE PREVIOUS CHAPTER that whereas the pre-Socratic philosophers abandoned who and why questions in favor of what and how questions, Aristotle, like Socrates and Plato before him, insisted on asking questions that would return philosophy to its grounding in absolutes that transcend the narrow, ever-shifting limits of our world. While the latter two sought to achieve this goal through definition, dialectic, and myths about beginnings and endings, creation and judgment, the former sought to extend the search for origins into the realm of causation. It is not enough, Aristotle argued, to ask *what* a thing is; we must ask *why* it is as well.

Aristotle's day was not all that different from our own when it came to thinking about causation. Most people, then and now, think only in terms of simple, mechanical cause and effect, rarely in terms of ultimate causation. If someone asks us why the alarm rang at 5 a.m., we are more likely to give a mechanical answer (because the clock reached the set time and went off) than a personal answer (because John has a busy day and needs to get an early start). When it comes to questions about warning signs, we are more likely to dwell on how the sign was printed and put up than on the purpose behind the sign. When it comes to why our body, or our universe, does the things it does, we are more likely to focus on biological, or cosmological, laws than on teleology—on the telos or purpose that either one serves.

THE FOUR CAUSES

In *Physics*, Aristotle identifies and defines four distinct causes that need to be addressed if we are to fully understand the object we are studying.

- [Material cause:] In one sense, then, (1) that out of which a thing comes to be and which persists, is called "cause", e.g. the bronze of the statue, the silver of the bowl. . . .

- [Formal cause:] In another sense (2) the form or the archetype, i.e. the statement of the essence, and its genera, are called "causes". . . .
- [Efficient cause:] Again (3) the primary source of the change or coming to rest; e.g. the man who gave advice is a cause, the father is cause of the child. . . .
- [Final cause:] Again (4) in the sense of end or "that for the sake of which" a thing is done, e.g. health is the cause of walking about. (II.3; 194b23-33)

Whereas most people, past and present alike, tend to confine their inquiries to material and efficient causes, Aristotle pushes us, as he did his fellow Athenians, to press deeper and higher to identify formal and final causes. He does not only push metaphysicians to do so; he pushes physicists (scientists) as well: "The causes being four, it is the business of the physicist to know about them all" (II.7; 198a23).

If an Aristotelian archaeologist of ancient Greece were to set himself the task of identifying the four causes of the Parthenon in Athens, his answer might look like this: the causes of the Parthenon are

1. material cause: the gleaming white Pentelic marble out of which it was built;
2. formal cause: the floor plan of the temple with its specific number of Doric columns and its three steps leading to the sanctuary;
3. efficient cause: the architect Phidias, who also sculpted the great statue of Athena;
4. final cause: to worship their patron goddess Athena and to celebrate Greece's victory over Persia.

Here are three other examples, expressed from a Christian point of view but in keeping with Aristotle's understanding of the four causes. The causes of the earth are

1. material: iron and nickel;
2. formal: 71 percent water and with an atmosphere capable of sustaining organic life;
3. efficient: cosmic gravitational forces;

4. final: to house humanity as the highest of the animal species and the steward of plant and animal life.

The causes of a man are
   1. material: flesh, bone, sinew, organs;
   2. formal: an erect, bipedal mammalian body plan with large brain size and opposable thumbs;
   3. efficient: his parents;
   4. final: to glorify God and enjoy him forever.

The causes of sexuality are
   1. material: the sexual organs of the male and female;
   2. formal: the fittedness of male and female genitalia and of sperm and egg;
   3. efficient: a previous male and female;
   4. final: to procreate the species and strengthen the bond between husband and wife by uniting them as one flesh.

I said a moment ago that most moderns focus on material and efficient causes to the exclusion of formal and final ones. In *Physics*, Aristotle makes it clear that the physicists of his own day were equally quick either to ignore formal and final causes altogether or to subsume them under the heading of material and efficient causes.

> All writers ascribe things to this cause [material or efficient], arguing that since the hot and the cold, &c., are of such and such a kind, therefore certain things *necessarily* are and come to be—and if they mention any other cause [formal or final] (one his "friendship and strife", another his "mind"), it is only to touch on it, and then good-bye to it. (II.8; 198b12-15)

When people, then or now, say nature caused something, they rarely mean the statement in a purposive way. They are not claiming that nature has a telos, but merely that they can identify the natural (mechanical, impersonal) causes that led to it. The simple cause/effect of the efficient cause and the materialistic focus of the material cause are as far as they are willing to go. Even if they reference "friendship/strife" (as the pre-Socratic Empedocles did) or "mind" (as the pre-Socratic Anaxagoras did) as a deeper cause, they give it little space in their "serious" scientific work. They are not interested in a thing's final cause and so do not look beyond (or within) nature for a greater purpose.

DARWINIAN NATURALISM VERSUS INTELLIGENT DESIGN

Whereas Darwinian naturalists such as New Atheist Richard Dawkins see in nature only the *appearance* of design, no actual, conscious purpose, Aristotle was committed to a teleological view of nature—one that perceives in the functions of nature a telos or end that gives order and purpose to all things. It is not enough, Aristotle argues, to say that Zeus sends the rain out of necessity. There must be a purpose beyond necessity: that he sends the rain *in order to* grow the crops. The same holds for the parts of our body. Our teeth are not just accidentally arranged to allow for proper eating. There is design and purpose to their shape, size, and placement.

It is true, Aristotle concedes, that random events occur in our world; nevertheless, purpose and design clearly run throughout nature. A random sequence of efficient causes cannot lead to a purposeful end. Ants and spiders, though they lack intelligence, create complex structures in accordance with a telos. Indeed, Aristotle reasons, "Where a series has a completion, all the preceding steps are for the sake of that. Now surely as in intelligent action, so in nature; and as in nature, so it is in each action, if nothing interferes. Now intelligent action is for the sake of an end; therefore the nature of things also is so" (II.8; 199a9-12). Though materialists then and now would likely accuse Aristotle of making a false analogy between intelligent action and natural (impersonal) action, his point is a strong one that demonstrates his willingness to look beyond simple, mechanical cause and effect to see the bigger picture and the greater design.

In fact, Aristotle argues that the confusion between intelligent design and the naturalistic appearance of design is in great part a linguistic one: "Since 'nature' means two things, the matter and the form, of which the latter is the end, and since all the rest is for the sake of the end, the form must be the cause in the sense of 'that for the sake of which'" (II.8; 199a30-33). The confusion Aristotle here highlights is still very much with us today in our own language and culture. When Dawkins or Carl Sagan or David Attenborough speak of the wonders or mystery of nature, they use rhetoric that seems to ascribe to nature consciousness, purpose, and design, even though they reject such a notion out of hand. The same goes for words such as *universe*, *evolution*, and *chance*. While insisting that such words point only to material (mechanical, impersonal) causes, Darwinists use them *as if* they embodied final (metaphysical, personal) causes as well.

Critics of teleology (final purpose) in nature will often point to mistakes in nature as proof against intelligent design. Aristotle concedes that mistakes occur in both human art and the operations of nature, but that in itself is not proof against design. "If then in art there are cases in which what is rightly produced serves a purpose, and if where mistakes occur there was a purpose in what was attempted, only it was not attained, so must it be also in natural products, and monstrosities [we today would say mutations] will be failures in the purposive effort" (II.8; 199b1-5). Aristotle's point is a simple but powerful one that Darwinian naturalists need to take seriously: the reason we *recognize* mistakes/monstrosities/mutations in art or nature is that we can intuit the design from which they have fallen away. For Aristotle, a thing will naturally follow its purpose and fulfill its telos unless it is acted on by an outside force that intervenes and prevents or twists that purpose/end from being fulfilled.

Though Aristotle did not have access to the Old Testament, his point here makes it seem that he himself intuited that we live in a world that was designed good but that has fallen away from that design. He was at least discerning enough to see that our inability to identify empirically the higher cause (whether formal or final) of a thing does not negate the existence of that cause.

> It is absurd to suppose that purpose is not present because we do not observe the agent deliberating. Art does not deliberate. If the ship-building art were in the wood, it would produce the same results *by nature*. If, therefore, purpose is present in art, it is present also in nature. The best illustration is a doctor doctoring himself: nature is like that. It is plain then that nature is a cause, a cause that operates for a purpose. (II.8; 199b26-32)

The efficient cause is not enough; it needs to be guided by a final cause. Such is clearly the case for human arts such as ship building and doctoring, but it is also the case, and not merely by analogy, for nature. Whether in art or nature, the material cause cannot function alone without the formal cause to give it shape, meaning, and purpose. As we saw in the previous chapter, Aristotle identified a thing's nature with its form rather than its matter.

There *is* a kind of mechanical necessity in nature, but that necessity is not sufficient to organize matter in accordance with a telos.

> The current [naturalistic] view places what is of necessity in the process of production, just as if one were to suppose that the wall of a house necessarily comes to be because what is heavy is naturally carried downwards and what is light to the top, wherefore the stones and foundations take the lowest place, with earth above because it is lighter, and wood at the top of all as being the lightest. Whereas, though the wall does not come to be without these, it is not due to these, except as its material cause: it comes to be for the sake of sheltering and guarding certain things [its final cause]. (II.9; 200a1-7)

Matter is not self-organizing. Though the inanimate stones (the matter) are necessary to produce the wall—that is why Aristotle assigns to matter one of his four causes—they only come to be arranged into the pattern of the wall because they are following a formal blueprint. The force of gravity, as we know it today, is not a sufficient cause for the assembling of stones into the pattern (and purpose) of the wall. To the necessity that impels the matter there must be joined the purpose that pervades the form.

THE MODERN INTELLIGENT DESIGN MOVEMENT

In my overview of Aristotle's defense of formal and final causes, I have used the phrase *intelligent design* several times. Though the phrase is consistent with Aristotle's teleological views, it is also used today to describe a movement in science that has been critical of the antiteleological, naturalistic theories of Darwin and his heirs. Not all the scientists in the intelligent-design movement are Christian, but most are—a fact that has caused their critics to accuse them of creationism in disguise.

Are their accusations justified? Yes and no. They are false because intelligent-design theorists base their conclusions on science and logic, never on biblical analysis or theology. They are true because most of the key players—Phillip E. Johnson, Michael Behe, Stephen C. Meyer, William Dembski, Lee Strobel, Hugh Ross, Thomas Woodward, John Lennox, Jay Richards, and Guillermo Gonzalez—would not have had the moral or intellectual courage to stand up against the entrenched and monolithic influence (in the academy, research labs, media, and museums) of methodological naturalism if they were not believers. Like the pioneers of the scientific method (see chapter three), whose faith in the rationality of God's creation and the reliability of our senses gave them the courage to seek out the laws and principles that underlie the universe, the pioneers of intelligent design have been emboldened by their faith in a personal and active God of order to resist the gatekeepers of Darwinian orthodoxy and seek out scientific evidence for God's providential design in nature.

Rather than give a full history and assessment of intelligent design, I will highlight three components of intelligent design, championed by Behe, Meyer, and Dembski, respectively, that reflect the logical and teleological thought of Aristotle.[1] Darwin claimed that all the complex biological systems we encounter were created by a slow, step-by-step process by which each incremental change was selected by nature (in the purely mechanical sense) for its survival and procreative value. Though this view has been modified to include sudden mutations, the insistence on nonteleological development has not. As Behe has demonstrated, molecular machines such as the bacterial flagella that maintain our bodies could not have evolved by such a step-by-step process. Such machines are irreducibly complex: they serve no useful function until their multiple parts are available and properly assembled. That is to say, a material cause alone cannot account for the flagellum; the matter needs to be arranged by a formal cause. Positing a series of mechanical, efficient causes for each part will not suffice, since there must be a telos (a final cause) to provide an endpoint to guide and select each individual part.

---

[1] See Michael J. Behe, *Darwin's Black Box: The Biochemical Challenge to Evolution* (New York: Free Press, 1996); Stephen C. Meyer, *The Signature in the Cell: DNA and the Evidence for Intelligent Design* (New York: HarperCollins, 2010); William A. Dembski, *The Design Inference: Eliminating Chance Through Small Probabilities* (Cambridge: Cambridge University Press, 1998). Although Behe, Meyer, and especially Dembski all reference Aristotle as one of the first great thinkers to posit design and order in nature, they do not enter into a direct dialogue with him.

What is true of molecular machines is even more true of DNA, as Meyer has demonstrated at great length. Each microscopic, double-stranded DNA molecule in our body—and there are billions of them—contains our full genetic blueprint. As each of the two strands that make up the double-helix structure of the DNA contains that full blueprint, the DNA molecule is able to unwind itself into two identical strands that then replicate themselves. Even if someone could describe and defend a plausible series of random, nonteleological material and efficient causes that might produce the chemical components of the DNA, formal and final causes would be needed to explain the vast amount of front-loaded information that is stored on the material strands of the DNA. Random changes simply cannot produce coherent information.

It is true that each time a strand of DNA replicates itself, a mutation (miscoding) can occur that can lead to small variations in the blueprint. Those small variations *might* be able to lead, through random chance alone, to larger changes within a species. However, even if that could be proven to be the case, what could not have evolved is the irreducibly complex system of replication itself, which must be fully in place for mutation and thus evolution to occur. That this is the case was ironically demonstrated in 1981 when Francis Crick, the naturalistic co-discoverer of the double-helix structure of the DNA, suggested in his book *Life Itself* that aliens might have seeded our planet with DNA (a theory known as panspermia).[2] To claim such a thing is to admit that DNA could not have evolved by natural means but must have been intelligently designed: by aliens rather than God, but designed nonetheless.

In the previous section, I quoted a passage in which Aristotle forges an analogy between the intelligently designed human arts of ship building and doctoring and the seemingly random but actually purposeful operations of nature. Modern intelligent-design theorists often make similar analogies,

---

[2]This irony was repeated in Ben Stein's 2008 documentary *Expelled*, which uncovered attempts by the Darwinian establishment to shut down the discoveries and voices of intelligent-design theorists in schools, universities, and scientific journals. At one point in the documentary, Stein asks New Atheist and committed Darwinist Richard Dawkins how he thinks the information-rich, irreducibly complex DNA could have evolved by blind time and chance. Remarkably, Dawkins suggests that panspermia could have done the job.

causing their critics to accuse them of basing their conclusions on a false analogy between complex human structures and complex natural structures. To answer that legitimate critique, Dembski has forged a careful distinction between complexity and specified complexity. Just because the patterns we see on crystals are complex does not mean that they are of the same order as the complexity in a manmade work of art. We have all seen patterns on hillsides that look vaguely like a human face or a crouching animal. But what if we are hiking in Rapid City, South Dakota, and we look up to see a mountain with four heads carved into it that are not only intricately detailed but match up with the profiles of four presidents we have encountered before in American history textbooks? Such a phenomenon is more than merely complex; it represents a kind of specified complexity that is the hallmark of conscious design.

No natural system or process we know of can produce the specified, information-rich complexity that we encounter in the fine-tuning of the cosmos, the irreducible complexity of the eye, or the front-loaded assembly instructions for the simplest of proteins. There is, as Aristotle knew, design in nature, and it runs all the way down from the immensity of our solar system that makes human life possible to the infinitesimal army of DNA strands—each one holding as much data as a supercomputer—that provides the blueprints for the individual lives we lead beneath the sun.

JOHN PAUL II ON THE NATURE OF THE SEXES

Aristotle's teleology, with its focus on the need for formal and final causes, has strong implications for science, but it also has something to teach our age about the nature of the sexes. In his magisterial *Theology of the Body*, John Paul II (1920–2005) references the same passages from Aquinas and Aristotle that I did in the previous chapter. In his general audience of December 2, 1981 ("The Resurrection and Theological Anthropology"), the pope explained that as

> a result of reflection on the resurrection, Thomas Aquinas neglected in his metaphysical (and at the same time theological) anthropology Plato's philosophical conception of the relationship between the soul and the body and drew closer to the conception of Aristotle. The resurrection bears witness, at

least indirectly, that the body, in the composite being of man as a whole, is not only connected temporarily with the soul (as its earthly "prison," as Plato believed). But together with the soul it constitutes the unity and integrity of the human being. Aristotle taught precisely that, unlike Plato.[3]

In the light of Christ's resurrection, Aquinas was able to judge that Aristotle, not Plato, came closest in his understanding of how body and soul are related. Soul and body do not stand before each other as a prisoner does to his prison guard but in terms of a unity and integrity that persists after death.

This passage comes at the end of a meditation on Mark 12:25, where Jesus teaches that in heaven, in our resurrection state, we will neither marry nor be given in marriage. Moderns who do not recognize the essential nature of masculinity and femininity—that, to put it in Aristotelian terms, our male and female bodies (matter) are incarnationally linked to the masculinity and femininity of our souls (form)—may read this verse as a prophecy that our sexual nature will cease after death. Not so John Paul II.

> The words, "they neither marry nor are given in marriage" seem to affirm at the same time that human bodies, recovered and at the same time renewed in the resurrection, will keep their masculine or feminine peculiarity. The sense of being a male or a female in the body will be constituted and understood in that age in a different way from what it had been from the beginning, and then in the whole dimension of earthly existence. . . . The words Christ spoke about the resurrection enable us to deduce that the dimension of masculinity and femininity—that is, being male and female in the body—will again be constituted together with the resurrection of the body in "that age." . . . The context indicates clearly that in that age man will keep his own human psychosomatic nature. If it were otherwise, it would be meaningless to speak of the resurrection.[4]

The very fact that we will bear resurrection bodies like the one in which Christ appeared to his disciples proves that our heavenly state will be continuous with our earthly. We will retain our psychosomatic (Greek for "soul-body") nature beyond death, not be stripped of the masculine or feminine "peculiarity" with which we were created.

---

[3]John Paul II, *The Theology of the Body* (Boston: Pauline Books & Media, 1997), 240. In his notes, John Paul II identifies his sources as Aquinas's *Summa* 76.1 and Aristotle's *On the Body* II.2.
[4]John Paul II, *Theology of the Body*, 239.

According to Genesis 1:27, a verse John Paul II quotes often in the earlier sections of *The Theology of the Body*, God *created* us male and female, suggesting an incarnational fusion of form (masculine/feminine soul) and matter (male/female body), of a formal cause establishing our dual sexual nature and a material cause rendering that duality concrete and physical. However we understand the fullness of the hylomorphic union, it must include the masculine and feminine natures given to us at creation. Apart from that formal cause, we risk being reduced to animated meat.

7

WHERE DO I BEGIN?

IN THE PREVIOUS CHAPTER, I identified the efficient causes of the earth, a man, and the sexes as, respectively, "cosmic gravitational forces," "his parents," and "a previous male and female." For Aristotle, every efficient cause is a kind of movement that moves something else, but those movements are themselves set in motion by prior movements. Behind the cosmic forces that shaped the earth are other forces that shaped those; behind one's parents are an earlier set of grandparents and great-grandparents. Knowing this, one can construct elaborate series of efficient causes that work like gears in a machine.

INFINITE REGRESS AND THE UNMOVED MOVER

Nevertheless, Aristotle sets ultimate limits to such constructions. If, he writes in *Metaphysics*,

> everything that moves is for the sake of that which is moved, and every movement belongs to something that is moved, no movement can be for the sake of itself or of another movement, but all the movements must be for the sake of the stars. For if there is to be a movement for the sake of a movement, this latter also will have to be for the sake of something else; so that since there cannot be an infinite regress, the end of every movement will be one of the divine bodies which move through the heaven. (XII.8; 1074a25-31)

The concept of infinite regress is as foundational to Aristotle's thought as the law of noncontradiction, the categories of substance, quantity, and quality, or the dictum that nothing can come out of nothing. Though our earthly realm is one of ceaseless change and motion, that motion must have an ultimate starting point. In the absence of such a starting point, we fall into a paradox whereby the origin of motion is endlessly deferred.

In the quoted passage, Aristotle looks to a divine/heavenly body (a star) to initiate the motion. Eventually, however, he argues backward behind the stars until he reaches God, the Unmoved Mover, who initiates *all* motion in the cosmos but is not moved himself. This aspect of Aristotle's philosophy proved compatible with Christianity and functioned, as we will see in a moment, as a strong platform for arguing for the necessary existence of God. But it also garnered nontheistic, nonteleological critics who embraced infinite regress. To my mind, the most formidable of these critics was Baruch Spinoza (1632–1677), a Jewish-Dutch philosopher who was also one of the chief architects of the secular Enlightenment.

SPINOZA DEFENDS INFINITE REGRESS

Though Spinoza claimed to believe in God, his God is utterly impersonal and passionless. Indeed, Spinoza identifies his God fully with nature, a move that, rather than lifting nature up to the status of a formal or final cause, demotes God to nothing more than a material-efficient cause. For Spinoza, there are no final causes, only efficient causes on which we have imposed a divine (or at least metaphysical) telos that does not exist. Men, Spinoza argues in the preface to part four of his *Ethics*,

> are in the habit of calling natural phenomena perfect or imperfect from their own preconceptions rather than from true knowledge. . . . Nature does not act with an end in view [it has no final end]. . . . The eternal and infinite being, whom we call God, or Nature, acts by the same necessity whereby it exists. . . . What is termed a "final cause" is nothing but human appetite in so far as it is considered as the starting-point or primary cause of some thing. For example, when we say that being a place of habitation was the final cause of this or that house, we surely mean no more than this, that a man, from thinking of the advantages of domestic life, had an urge to build a house. Therefore, the need for a habitation in so far as it is considered as a final cause is nothing but this particular urge, which is in reality an efficient cause, and is considered as the prime cause because men are commonly ignorant of the causes of their own urges. . . . As to the common saying that Nature sometimes fails or blunders and produces imperfect things, I count this among the fictions.[1]

---

[1] Baruch Spinoza, *The Ethics and Selected Letters*, ed. Seymour Feldman, trans. Samuel Shirley (Indianapolis: Hackett, 1982), 154.

Note that Spinoza not only parodies Aristotle's example of a wall of a house whose final cause is for the purpose of shelter (habitation) rather than the matter out of which it was built; he also directly criticizes Aristotle's contention that the existence of natural monstrosities points to a proper telos that has, in this case, been frustrated.

For Spinoza, Aristotle's—and Christianity's—final causes are an illusion. They are mere projections of our material instincts and urges. We may have forgotten that we invented them, but they are inventions nonetheless. Those who would reduce Aristotle to an empiricist and materialist who confined true philosophy to the physical world would do well to read Spinoza. Compared to Spinoza's inert, purposeless deity, Aristotle's Unmoved Mover seems downright dramatic.

But let us speak now of that Unmoved Mover and of how Aristotle argues his way back to a necessary first cause of motion. To begin with, Aristotle would have answered "chicken" to the age-old question of which came first, the chicken or the egg. Or, to put it more philosophically, he would have disagreed with Jean-Paul Sartre's contention that existence precedes essence. For Aristotle, essence precedes existence, just as chicken comes before egg, form before matter, soul before body, motion before rest, and actuality before potentiality: "It is clear that actuality is prior to potency [potentiality]. And I mean by potency not only that definite kind which is said to be a principle of change in another thing or in the thing itself regarded as other, but in general every principle of movement or of rest" (IX.9; 1049b5-9).

Could Aristotle have stood before Michelangelo's statue of David, he would have insisted that the actuality (or formal cause) of David preceded the material cause of the marble out of which David was set free. The formula (or blueprint) exists *prior* to the realization of that formula in a particular statue or man: "From the potentially existing the actually existing is always produced by an actually existing thing, e.g. man from man, musician by musician; there is always a first mover, and the mover already exists actually" (IX.8; 1049b23-26). Even in cases where an individual potentiality seems to precede actuality, when that individual is viewed in terms of the greater species level, the actual must always come before the potential. Eggs do not appear out of nowhere; there must have been a primal chicken who laid the first egg. The boy we see on the street can be traced back, eventually, to a primal man who began the movement of generations leading up to the boy's existence. Just as our DNA is front-loaded with preprogrammed information (actuality) that shapes and molds an individual material person (potentiality), so all material objects can be traced back to some type of invisible, preexisting form.

It is clear to me that C. S. Lewis was meditating on Aristotle's *Metaphysics* when he wrote his provocative essay, "The Funeral of a Great Myth." The myth Lewis refers to is a materialistic, antiteleological form of evolution that, like Spinoza, thinks it can explain all things in accordance with infinitely regressive chains of material-efficient causes that work themselves out in the absence of any kind of formal or final cause.

> The basic idea of the Myth—that small or chaotic or feeble things perpetually turn into large, strong, ordered things—may, at first sight, seem a very odd one. We have never seen a pile of rubble turning itself into a house. But this odd idea commends itself to the imagination by the help of what seem to be two instances of it within everyone's knowledge. Everyone has seen individual organisms doing it. Acorns become oaks, grubs become insects, eggs become birds, every man was once an embryo. And secondly—which weighs very much in the popular mind during a machine age—everyone has seen Evolution really happening in the history of machines. We all remember when locomotives were smaller and less efficient than they are now. These two apparent instances are quite enough to convince the imagination that Evolution in a cosmic sense is the most natural thing in the world.[2]

In his argument, Lewis clearly refers back to Aristotle's reductio ad absurdum metaphor of stones that self-organize into a house. His further references to acorns and embryos seemingly evolving into trees and men also rely on examples that Aristotle uses in *Metaphysics* XI.8 (see 1049b19-22). By means of these Aristotelian examples, Lewis, like Aristotle before him, mounts an investigation into causation, asking whether material and efficient causes alone can account for the specified complexity we see around us.

His rebuttal of the great myth is ultimately the same as Aristotle's, though the case Lewis makes for a first mover, for an actuality that precedes

---

[2]C. S. Lewis, *Christian Reflections*, ed. Walter Hooper (Grand Rapids, MI: Eerdmans, 1967), 90.

potentiality, is written in a more vivid and memorable style. The instances that are often held up in support of evolution, Lewis reveals,

> are not really instances of Evolution at all. The oak comes indeed from the acorn, but then the acorn was dropped by an earlier oak. Every man began with the union of an ovum and a spermatozoon, but the ovum and the spermatozoon came from two fully developed human beings. The modern express engine came from the Rocket; but the Rocket came, not from something under and more elementary than itself, but from something much more developed and highly organized—the mind of a man, and a man of genius. Modern art may have "developed" from savage art. But then the very first picture of all did not "evolve" itself: it came from something overwhelmingly greater than itself, from the mind of that man who, by seeing for the first time that marks on a flat surface could be made to look like animals and men, proved himself to exceed in sheer blinding genius any of the artists who have succeeded him. It may be true that if we trace back any existing civilization to its beginnings, we shall find those beginnings crude and savage; but then, when you look closer, you usually find that those beginnings themselves come from a wreck of some earlier civilization.[3]

The nature of reality, Lewis reminds us, is not evolutionary. Before there was an acorn that grew into a tree, there was a fully developed oak that dropped that acorn. The same goes for human embryos and human parents.

Though we see what seems to be evolution in machinery and art, the fact is that both began with a far more highly developed actuality in the mind of a man of genius. The (formal or final) cause of something must be greater than its effect; water does not rise above its source. Entropy, not evolution, is what we more often see in the world. If we do see acorns and embryos grow into oak trees and human adults, that is only because the acorn and the embryo are front-loaded with a prior formula, with a microscopic, information-rich genetic blueprint that bristles with specified complexity.

ARISTOTLE'S SEARCH FOR PURE ACTUALITY

But let us return to Aristotle and see how he develops his thesis to include the teleological dimension of his final cause:

---

[3]Lewis, *Christian Reflections*, 90.

Where Do I Begin?

> The things that are posterior in becoming are prior in form and in substantiality (e.g. man is prior to boy and human being to seed; for the one already has its form, and the other has not), and because everything that comes to be moves towards a principle, i.e. an end (for that for the sake of which a thing is, is its principle, and the becoming is for the sake of the end), and the actuality is the end, and it is for the sake of this that the potency is acquired. For animals do not see in order that they may have sight, but they have sight that they may see. And similarly men have the art of building that they may build, and theoretical science that they may theorize. (IX.8; 1050a4-13)

It is vital that form should precede matter, but that is not enough. There must be a clear and purposeful end, a teleological principle to guide the other causes and ensure that actuality is achieved. Physical eyes did not cause the telos of seeing; the preexisting purpose of seeing caused the potentiality of the eyes to become actualized. Just so, the telos of building existed in the mind before the first builder put his hand to the first tool.

For Aristotle, "It is obvious that actuality is prior in substantial being to potency; and as we have said, one actuality always precedes another in time right back to the actuality of the eternal prime mover. But actuality is prior in a stricter sense also; for eternal things are prior in substance to perishable things, and no eternal thing exists potentially" (IX.8; 1050b3-8). What Aristotle is in search of is pure actuality, an eternal prime (first) mover that stands behind all other substances and actualities and gives them their ultimate form and their initial motion. Apart from that, there can only be infinite regress.

The pre-Socratic materialists of Aristotle's day, like the Darwinian materialists of our own, labor under the same difficulty. If there is no final cause, then material nature does not know where it is going; and if that is the case, then whatever potential is in it can never be actualized. If the design we see in nature is only the appearance of design—as Richard Dawkins insists in all his books and lectures—then nature cannot evolve because it is not evolving *toward* anything. Progress-without-a-telos dooms those who seek it to a search without an end, a quest without a goal. In the absence of an alpha and an omega, a beginning and an end, nature can only stagnate.

What, then, is needed if infinite regress is to be halted, motion initiated, and nature guided? The answer Aristotle offers not only provides a climax to his investigations; it allows him to position himself vis-à-vis Plato and his theory of the Forms.

> If there is something which is capable of moving things or acting on them, but is not actually doing so, there will not necessarily be movement; for that which has a potency need not exercise it. Nothing, then, is gained even if we suppose eternal substances, as the believers in the Forms do, unless there is to be in them [the Forms] some principle which can cause change; nay, even this is not enough, nor is another substance besides the Forms enough; for if it is not to act, there will be no movement. Further even if it acts, this will not be enough, if its essence is potency; for there will not be *eternal* movement, since that which is potentially may possibly not be. There must, then, be such a principle, whose very essence is actuality. Further, then, these substances must be without matter; for they must be eternal, if *anything* is eternal. Therefore they must be actuality. (XII.6; 1071b12-22)

Plato's Forms are not enough because they do not themselves give motion to other things. They are eternal and unchanging, but they do not impart change. If there is a first mover, it must be an eternal initiator of motion and change. It must not simply have the potential to do so, because then it might stop at some point. It must possess in itself the fullness of actuality so that it will never cease initiating the transformation of the potentiality within nature into actuality.

This initiator of all motion that does not himself move, this pure actuality that draws potentiality out of the cosmos, this supreme final and formal cause, is Aristotle's God. It is a God he did not learn about via the special revelation of the Old Testament but one he reasoned himself toward by contemplating the nature of reality, particularly in terms of motion and causation. By so doing, he taught the philosophers and theologians of the Middle Ages—and beyond—how to use their rational abilities to prove the necessary existence of God.

WHAT ARISTOTLE TAUGHT AQUINAS ABOUT GOD

In this matter, Aristotle exerted a particularly strong influence on Thomas Aquinas, who in his *Summa* offers five proofs for the existence of God that are all connected in some way to the need to halt infinite regress. For the sake of space, I will only discuss the first two, which are the ones most closely linked to the dimensions of Aristotle's thought we have been exploring.

For his first proof, Aquinas focuses on the need for an Unmoved Mover to be the initiator and actualizer of all motion:

> It is certain, and evident to our senses, that in the world some things are in motion. Now whatever is moved is moved by another, for nothing can be moved except it is in potentiality to that towards which it is moved; whereas a thing moves inasmuch as it is in act. For motion is nothing else than the reduction of something from potentiality to actuality. But nothing can be reduced from potentiality to actuality, except by something in a state of actuality.[4]

Our senses tell us, contra monists such as Parmenides and Zeno, that the world is in motion, just as our common sense tells us that a thing in motion must have been set in motion by something other than itself. In keeping with Aristotle, Aquinas defines motion as movement from potentiality to actuality, reasoning, also in keeping with Aristotle, that the movement from the first to the second necessitates the presence of something in a state of actuality.

Having established the need for a thing in motion that is possessed of potentiality to be set in motion by something else in a state of actuality, Aquinas moves forward to complete his Aristotelian proof for the existence of a divine Unmoved Mover:

> Thus that which is actually hot, as fire, makes wood, which is potentially hot, to be actually hot, and thereby moves and changes it. Now it is not possible that the same thing should be at once in actuality and potentiality in the same respect, but only in different respects. For what is actually hot cannot simultaneously be potentially hot; but it is simultaneously potentially cold. It is therefore impossible that in the same respect and in the same way a thing should be both mover and moved, *i.e.*, that it should move itself. Therefore, whatever is moved must be moved by another. If that by which it is moved be itself moved, then this also must needs be moved by another, and that by another again. But this cannot go on to infinity [infinite regress], because then there would be no first mover, and, consequently, no other mover, seeing that subsequent movers move only inasmuch as they are moved by the first mover; as the staff moves only because it

---

[4] Anton C. Pegis, ed., *Introduction to Saint Thomas Aquinas* (New York: Modern Library, 1948), I, q. 2, art. 3 (p. 25).

is moved by the hand. Therefore it is necessary to arrive at a first mover, moved by no other; and this everyone understands to be God.[5]

Note that Aquinas, like Aristotle, appeals to common-sense things that all people understand, including that it is impossible, according to the law of noncontradiction, for something to be in the same respect and in the same way both mover and moved. Apart from a first mover that is itself unmoved and that possesses pure actuality, all things, including the universe itself, would be subject to infinite regress.

The actuality of heat that exists in fire is necessary to release the potentiality of heat that is stored in a cold, dry piece of wood. But that source of actuality must be fully actual: that is, it must not contain within itself the potentiality for cold. If it did, it could not be counted on to always draw heat out of a potentially hot substance. In the same way, a thing cannot simultaneously be moved and a mover of itself. It must be moved by something else to set it in motion, just as that which set it in motion must be itself set in motion by something else. But this series cannot go on forever. Just as there must be a source of pure actuality that contains no potentiality for its opposite, so there must be a source of pure motion that does not itself move. That first mover, or Unmoved Mover, which is also pure actuality, is what all people understand to be God.

For his second proof for the existence of God, Aquinas turns to Aristotle's distinction between efficient causes and final causes:

> In the world of sensible things we find there is an order of efficient causes. There is no case known (neither is it, indeed, possible) in which a thing is found to be the efficient cause of itself; for so it would be prior to itself, which is impossible. Now in efficient causes it is not possible to go on to infinity, because in all efficient causes following in order, the first is the cause of the intermediate cause, and the intermediate is the cause of the ultimate cause, whether the intermediate cause be several, or one only. Now to take away the cause is to take away the effect. Therefore, if there be no first cause among efficient causes, there will be no ultimate, nor any intermediate, cause. But if in efficient causes it is possible to go on to infinity, there will be no first efficient

---

[5]Pegis, *Introduction to Saint Thomas Aquinas*, I, q. 2, art. 3 (p. 25).

cause, neither will there be an ultimate effect, nor any intermediate efficient causes; all of which is plainly false. Therefore it is necessary to admit a first efficient cause, to which everyone gives the name of God.[6]

Just as there can be no infinite regress in the realm of motion, so there can be no infinite regress in the realm of causation. A thing in motion cannot also be its own mover; in the same way, a thing cannot be the efficient cause of itself. For a thing to be its own efficient cause, it would have to have existed before it existed, and that is absurd.

To halt infinite regress in motion, there must be an Unmoved Mover that can initiate all motion without itself being moved. To halt infinite regress in causation, there must be a Causeless Cause (or Groundless Ground) that is the ultimate efficient cause of all things without itself being caused by something else. Apart from that Causeless Cause, there can be no causation; the chain breaks down, and all is subjected to futility. That necessary Causeless Cause is also recognized by all as the being we call God.

Just as the Christian Aquinas's argument for the existence of God relies on Aristotle's understanding of motion, causation, and the need for an Unmoved Mover/Causeless Cause of pure actuality, so the Islamic Kalam argument for the existence of God (see chapter three above) relies on that same understanding. Taken together, both give the lie to one of the most persistent atheist arguments against God: If God created us, then who created God? Such a question is finally nonsensical, for it fails to understand that what Jews, Christians, Muslims, *and Aristotle* mean by God is a being of pure actuality that neither comes into being nor is moved, for it is itself the Unmoved Mover and Causeless Cause that gives motion and cause to all other things.

---

[6] Pegis, *Introduction to Saint Thomas Aquinas*, I, q. 25, art. 3 (pp. 25-26).

8

WRESTLING WITH THE STATIC GOD OF DEISM

Although in this book I hold up Aristotle as a (mostly) positive influence on Christianity, I must concede that there is a subtle danger inherent in his vision of God as Unmoved Mover and Causeless Cause. While Aristotle's arguments for the existence of God are helpful for defending the need for a creator—or at least a prime mover—behind us and our universe, they threaten to place on the cosmic throne a static, passive, inert God who is uninvolved and uninterested in the actions and decisions of his creatures.

In this chapter I will begin by celebrating Aristotle for establishing the necessity for a divine first cause as an explanation for the existence, motion, and causality in our world. After that, I will show how those ideas played out in the work of four Christian thinkers (Anselm, Descartes, Leibniz, Pope) who moved slowly but increasingly away from the living, active God of the Bible to posit a God who looks more and more like the impersonal, removed God of Aristotle.

ARISTOTLE AND THE GOD OF THE PHILOSOPHERS

"That actuality is prior is testified by Anaxagoras (for his 'reason' is actuality) and by Empedocles in his doctrine of love and strife, and by those who say that there is always movement, e.g. Leucippus" (XII.6; 1072a4-7). Here, as elsewhere in *Metaphysics*, Aristotle carefully situates himself vis-à-vis the pre-Socratic philosophers. Anaxagoras believed that *logos* ("reason") and *nous* ("mind") exert an organizing power over matter. Empedocles taught that the four elements of earth, water, air, and fire are drawn together by love and torn apart by strife in an eternal dance that creates all the compounds we see in the universe. Leucippus, together with Democritus, was an atomist who believed that all there is in the world are atoms (indivisible bits of matter) and the void; as the atoms move ceaselessly through the void, they occasionally swerve, causing collisions with other atoms that form into the various compounds we see.

While Aristotle treats these theories of his predecessors with respect, particularly their awareness that actuality must *precede* potentiality, he concludes that the principles they put forward still demand a first agent to ensure motion and provide a final and ultimate cause not compromised by the endless cycles of creation and destruction they describe. That first agent, as we have seen, is God, the Unmoved Mover and Causeless Cause. Aristotle describes him as existing in a state of contemplation:

> If, then, God is always in that good state in which we sometimes are, this compels our wonder; and if in a better this compels it yet more. And God is in a better state. And life also belongs to God; for the actuality of thought is life, and God is that actuality; and God's self-dependent actuality is life most good and eternal. We say therefore that God is a living being, eternal, most good, so that life and duration continuous and eternal belong to God; for this is God. (XII.7; 1072b23-29)

If there is a God, then he *must* be living, eternal, continuous, and good. Though he is pure actuality, he *must* be in a perpetually blessed state of rest and contemplation.

Notice I have italicized the word *must*. In terms of his influence on Christianity, Aristotle's thoughts on God have proven to be both a help and a stumbling block to Christian philosophers and theologians. By demonstrating that God's existence can be logically deduced, Aristotle helped clarify Christianity as a rational, coherent worldview that, though it demands faith on behalf of its adherents, can be shown to be logically sound and consistent. By positing God as the necessary endpoint of a series of logical deductions, Aristotle established a dangerous precedent by which God is reduced to the solution of an intellectual riddle—one in which his only job is to start things going.

The name for this philosophical-theological stumbling block (and dead end) is deism. It posits God as a divine watchmaker who creates the watch, winds it up, and then lets it run on its own. Another name for the God of deism is "the God of the philosophers," a removed and impersonal God who makes no moral demands on us, though he may expect us to pay intellectual lip service to his string of logically deduced attributes: omnipotence, omniscience, omnipresence, omnibenevolence, impassibility, and so on. The greatest danger inherent in the God of the philosophers is that God will become for the philosopher a mental construct rather than the dynamic, invasive God of the Old and New Testament.

ANSELM AND THE ONTOLOGICAL ARGUMENT

This danger can be seen in an argument for the existence of God that, though it was not formulated by Aristotle and though it was dismissed by Aquinas (*Summa* 2.2), is strongly Aristotelian in its appeal to deduction, to common sense, and to a chain of reasoning that comes close to being circular and to creating God in our own image, rather than vice versa. I speak of the ontological argument that was first proposed by a true man of God, Saint Anselm, archbishop of Canterbury (1033–1109), but that bears in it the potential of positing a God who does little more than exist.

In his *Proslogion* Anselm works out, in remarkably simple and straightforward language, his ontological argument for the existence of God. After defining God as "a being than which nothing greater can be conceived," and asserting that even a fool who does not believe in God understands the truth of this definition when he hears it, Anselm works out the implications of his definition and assertion:

> Whatever is understood, exists in the understanding. And assuredly that, than which nothing greater can be conceived, cannot exist in the understanding alone. For, suppose it exists in the understanding alone: then it can be conceived to exist in reality; which is greater. Therefore, if that, than which nothing greater can be conceived, exists in the understanding alone, the very being, than which nothing greater can be conceived, is one, than which a greater can be conceived. But obviously this is impossible. Hence, there is doubt that there exists a being, than which nothing greater can be conceived, and it exists both in the understanding and in reality.[1]

---

[1] Saint Anselm, *Basic Writings*, trans. S. N. Deane (La Salle, IN: Open Court, 1962), 53-54.

We are back here to Aristotle's belief that the chicken comes before the egg, form precedes matter, and actuality is prior to potentiality. We are back, as well, to the use of a reductio ad absurdum that invokes the law of noncontradiction to dismiss as absurd a paradox that is created when we take a wrong turn in logic.

Anselm argues that there must be an origin to our conception of God that is greater than our conception (water does not rise about its source). Since a God who exists is necessarily greater and more perfect than one who does not, if God does not exist, then our conception of him is greater than God, which Anselm rejects as absurd. If that God than which nothing is greater can exist in the understanding, he must also exist in reality.

> There is, then, so truly a being than which nothing greater can be conceived to exist, that it cannot even be conceived not to exist; and this being you are, O Lord, our God. . . . For, if a mind could conceive of a being better than you, the creature would rise above the Creator; and this is most absurd. . . . Why, then, has the fool said in his heart, there is no God (Psalms xiv. 1), since it is so evident, to a rational mind, that you do exist in the highest degree of all? Why, except that he is dull and a fool?[2]

To say that we could conceive a being greater than the actual God would not only be illogical; it would be blasphemous. Surely God is greater than our idea of him! If the fool cannot fathom that, it is only because he is a fool!

What saves Anselm's argument from becoming too abstract and relegating God to nothing more than a great idea is the way he so directly and passionately addresses God as "O Lord, our God," in a manner reminiscent of Augustine's *Confessions*. Anselm knows the God whose existence he is attempting to prove logically; that is why he feels the weight of illogicality as heavily as that of blasphemy. One feels the force of this personal knowledge far less strongly in Descartes's *Meditations on First Philosophy*, with God slowly receding into the murky realm of philosophical necessity.

DESCARTES AND THE SLOW SLIDE INTO DEISM

In *Meditation* V, French philosopher, scientist, and mathematician René Descartes (1596–1650) defends Anselm's ontological argument from a criticism

---

[2]Anselm, *Basic Writings*, 54-55.

that was as current in Descartes's day as it is in our own. If my idea of God proves God's existence, the criticism goes, why does my idea of a winged horse not prove the existence of Pegasus? "This objection," Descartes argues,

> rests on a fallacy. Because I cannot think of a mountain without a valley, it does not indeed follow that there is any mountain or valley in existence, but only that mountain and valley, be they existent or non-existent, are inseparably conjoined each with the other. In the case of God, however, I cannot think Him save as existing; and it therefore follows that existence is inseparable from Him, and that He therefore really exists. It is not that this necessity is brought about by my thought, or that my thought is imposing any necessity on things; on the contrary, the necessity which lies in the thing itself, that is the necessity of God's existence, determines me to think in this way. It is not in my power to think God as lacking existence (i.e., to think of this sovereignly perfect being as devoid of complete perfection) in the manner in which I am free to image a horse with wings or without wings.[3]

Descartes is as careful here about his categories as Aristotle. Existence is essential to the idea of God in a way that it is not for mountains and valleys or, even less so, for winged horses. The necessity of existence is as intrinsic to God as it is to Descartes's thoughts about God. Indeed, far from Descartes imposing existence on God, it is God's existence that imposes itself on Descartes.

Note that Descartes speaks, like Aristotle before him, in terms of necessity. God *must* be like this because logic demands it, not because he has revealed himself to be so. The personal connection we saw in Anselm is missing here, not just because Anselm and Descartes are writing different kinds of works but because Descartes is more concerned with clear and distinct knowledge than with the glory or holiness of God. There is something static about a "sovereignly perfect being" that better lines up with the deistic God of the philosophers than the covenantal God who chose a people for himself, led them miraculously out of Egyptian bondage, and revealed to them his law. Descartes does not, as Spinoza *does*, reject this God, but his

---

[3]Monroe C. Beardsley, ed., *The European Philosophers from Descartes to Nietzsche* (New York: Modern Library, 1960), 63.

Meditations tend to abstract and domesticate the I Am who is both a good shepherd and a consuming fire.

LEIBNIZ ON DIVINE PERFECTION

As we move from Descartes to German philosopher, scientist, and mathematician Gottfried Wilhelm Leibniz (1646–1716), the ontological argument becomes more refined and exact, while the God it proves becomes more static and removed, a philosophical marker for the idea of perfection. Like Anselm and Descartes before him, Leibniz was a Christian who was open to working and reasoning within the parameters laid down by Aristotelian logic and metaphysics. In chapter 23 of his *Discourse on Metaphysics*, Leibniz sums up the ontological argument of Anselm and Leibniz and then uncovers a flaw in it, which he takes pains to correct:

> When one reasons in regard to anything, he imagines that he has an idea of it and this is the foundation upon which certain philosophers, ancient [Aristotle and Anselm] and modern [Descartes], have constructed a demonstration of God that is extremely imperfect. It must be, they say, that I have an idea of God, or of a perfect being, since I think of him and we cannot think without having ideas; now the idea of this being includes all perfections and since existence is one of these perfections, it follows that he exists. But I reply, inasmuch as we often think of impossible chimeras, for example of the highest degree of swiftness, of the greatest number, of the meeting of the conchoid with its base or determinant, such reasoning is not sufficient. It is therefore in this sense that we can say that there are true and false ideas according as the thing which is in question is possible or not. And it is when he is assured of the possibility of a thing, that one can boast of having an idea of it. Therefore, the aforesaid argument proves that God exists, if he is possible. This is in fact an excellent privilege of the divine nature, to have need only of a possibility or an essence in order to actually exist, and it is just this which is called self-sufficient being.[4]

Leibniz restates the ontological argument fairly, but he finds Descartes's solution to the winged-horse objection unconvincing. For Descartes's solution to work, Leibniz argues, one must accept that a being like God is possible.

---

[4]Beardsley, *European Philosophers*, 273-74.

Only once that acceptance is made does the rest of the argument follow, allowing God to emerge as a self-sufficient being whose essence and existence are one and the same.

Much more could be said about Leibniz's argument; however, to keep my focus on Aristotle and his birthing, whether intentionally or not, of the God of the philosophers, I will zero in on a single word that plays a vital role here and in all of Leibniz's work: *perfection*. Leibniz begins his *Discourse* by defining God as "an absolutely perfect being" and then maintains throughout that our world, as it reflects God's divine perfections, could not have been made better than it is.[5]

Although I have no doubt of Leibniz's sincere Christian faith or of his belief in the authority of Scripture, his focus on divine perfection as the golden key to metaphysics has the tendency of imposing philosophical necessity on God rather than allowing the active God of the Bible to define himself. Too often, the upshot of this Aristotelian approach is to turn "Who is God?" into "Who must God be?" and so reduce the Creator and Savior of the universe into the one necessary linchpin to hold together a complex philosophical system that demands a source for motion, for causation, and, in Leibniz's case, for perfection.

POPE AND THE TRIUMPH OF DEISM

This Aristotelian reductio, to my mind at least, reaches its fullest embodiment in an epic poem by British poet Alexander Pope (1688–1744) that sums up the Enlightenment's exaltation of reason over revelation, providential design over divine agency, deism over Christianity. Structured in the form of a four-part verse epistle in rhyming couplets, *An Essay on Man* follows an Aristotelian structure that begins by meditating on man's relationship to the universe (similar to *Physics* and *Metaphysics*) and then proceeds to consider man's relationship to himself, society, and the supreme virtue of happiness (similar to *Politics* and *Ethics*).

In the first epistle, Pope expresses his agreement with Leibniz that this is the best of all possible worlds, a perfect expression of God's perfection: "Then

---

[5]Beardsley, *European Philosophers*, 250.

say not man's imperfect, Heaven in fault; / Say rather, man's as perfect as he ought."[6] He then reiterates his belief in divine—or, better, cosmic—perfection with three thundering couplets that end the first epistle on a triumphant note of rational optimism:

> All Nature is but art, unknown to thee;
> All chance, direction, which thou canst not see;
> All discord, harmony not understood;
> All partial evil, universal good:
> And, spite of pride in erring reason's spite,
> One truth is clear, whatever IS, is RIGHT.[7]

This is quite glorious, but the God that superintends this higher art, direction, harmony, and good seems more an idea than a personal being. There is a kind of stoic contentment here that misses out on true Christian joy. Pope calls on his readers to submit to this cosmic order, but it is a rational obedience divorced from love and gratitude.

For Pope, the same divine order runs through man and nature. When we balk against it, we fall guilty of sin and pride, not against a loving God but against a system and the unmoved, causeless, fully actualized Mind that runs it:

> And who but wishes to invert the laws
> Of order, sins against the Eternal Cause. . . .
> All this dread ORDER break—for whom? for thee?
> Vile worm!—oh, madness! pride! impiety! . . .
> Cease, then, nor ORDER imperfection name:
> Our proper bliss depends on what we blame.[8]

The Enlightenment God of the philosophers, like Aristotle's Unmoved Mover, may punish, but that punishment is more legal than covenantal, the result of the breaking of a rational law rather than the betrayal of a sacred trust. The

---

[6] Alexander Pope, *An Essay on Man*, lines 69-70, in *The Norton Anthology of English Literature*, 6th ed., gen. ed. M. H. Abrams (New York: Norton, 1993), 1:2265.
[7] Pope, *Essay on Man*, lines 289-94 (p. 2270).
[8] Pope, *Essay on Man*, lines 129-39, 257-48, 281-82 (pp. 2266-69).

Aristotelian warning that Pope issues in these three couplets is something like, "Don't touch the fire or you will burn your hand." The warning that issues from Yahweh is at once more hopeful and terrible: "Kiss the Son, lest he be angry, and ye perish from the way, when his wrath is kindled but a little. Blessed are all they that put their trust in him" (Ps 2:12).

9

LIVING IN AN ORDERED UNIVERSE

IN THE PREVIOUS TWO CHAPTERS, I praised Aristotle for successfully using reason and logic to prove the existence of a divine Unmoved Mover but then criticized him for establishing a philosophical-theological method that has too often led Christian thinkers toward a deistic God of the philosophers who has nothing to do but exist and superintend the laws of nature that he set in motion. In this chapter and the next, I will praise Aristotle for being the chief architect of a cosmological model that, though it has since proven false, inspired and enriched the Catholic Middle Ages in a mostly positive way, even exerting a beneficent influence on Renaissance Protestant poets such as Spenser, Donne, and Milton.

THE TWO-TIERED COSMOS

Indeed, the ordered, two-tiered, hierarchical cosmos that Aristotle did so much to fashion, shape, and promote is given a poetic last gasp in Pope's *Essay on Man*. In the same first epistle where he celebrates the perfection of God's design, he also describes in memorable detail a mighty ladder that stretches downward from the supreme God to the smallest of insects:

> Vast Chain of Being! which from God began,
> Natures ethereal, human, angel, man,
> Beast, bird, fish, insect, what no eye can see,
> No glass can reach! from Infinite to thee,
> From thee to nothing.—On superior powers
> Were we to press, inferior might on ours:
> Or in the full creation leave a void,
> Where, one step broken, the great scale's destroyed:

From Nature's chain whatever link you strike,
Tenth or ten thousandth, breaks the chain alike. (237-46)[1]

In Pope's vision of the Great Chain of Being, everything has its place, its appointed rung on the cosmic ladder. To disrupt even one rung is to risk chaos. In our own fragmented, unnaturally egalitarian age, we would do well to revive such a vision of universal order, a vision that has social, political, emotional, spiritual, and metaphysical repercussions.

From Aristotle's *Metaphysics*, *On the Heavens*, and *On Generation and Corruption*, as filtered through Cicero's first-century BC "The Dream of Scipio" and the astronomical charts of second-century AD Greco-Egyptian mathematician Ptolemy, the medievals received their complex, two-tiered view of the cosmos. Everything sublunar (below the moon) was in a constant state of change, decay, and death. Above the moon, however, all was perfect, eternal, and unchanging.

At the center of the universe lay the cold, heavy, unmoving earth, which, contrary to Enlightenment propaganda, Aristotle, Cicero, Ptolemy, and the medievals knew was round.[2] Between the earth and the moon, our ever-shifting world was dominated by the dance of the four elements—earth, water, air, and fire—whose collisions formed and continue to form the material compounds on which our world runs. This realm Aristotle called nature (*physis*), and in his *Physics*, he analyzes the changes that hold sway there.

---

[1]Alexander Pope, *An Essay on Man*, lines 237-46, in *The Norton Anthology of English Literature*, 6th ed., gen. ed. M. H. Abrams (New York: Norton, 1993), 1:2269.

[2]In part two of his *For the Glory of God: How Monotheism Led to Reformation, Science, Witch Hunts, and the End of Slavery* (Princeton, NJ: Princeton University Press, 2003), Rodney Stark dispels the Enlightenment myth that the medievals thought the earth was flat. That myth, he shows, was propagated by such key Enlightenment thinkers as Voltaire, Denis Diderot, and Edward Gibbon, who used it to inaccurately dismiss the Catholic Middle Ages as an unscientific age of ignorance and superstition. The myth continues today because nearly all people in the West are taught the erroneous story—partly propagated by a multivolume biography of Christopher Columbus written by the American author of "Rip Van Winkle" and "The Legend of Sleepy Hollow," Washington Irving (1783-1859)—that Columbus thought the earth was round while everyone else in Europe thought it was flat. In matter of fact, all educated people of the time knew that the earth was round. It was Columbus who was mistaken, not about the shape of the earth but about its size. Although the third chief librarian of the Library of Alexandria, Eratosthenes (276-194 BC), had accurately calculated the circumference of the globe, Columbus insisted that the earth was roughly half the size it is. Had Columbus been right, sailing west would have gotten a European traveler to India more quickly. Of course, he was wrong, a mistake that convinced Columbus that he had landed in India instead of the Americas.

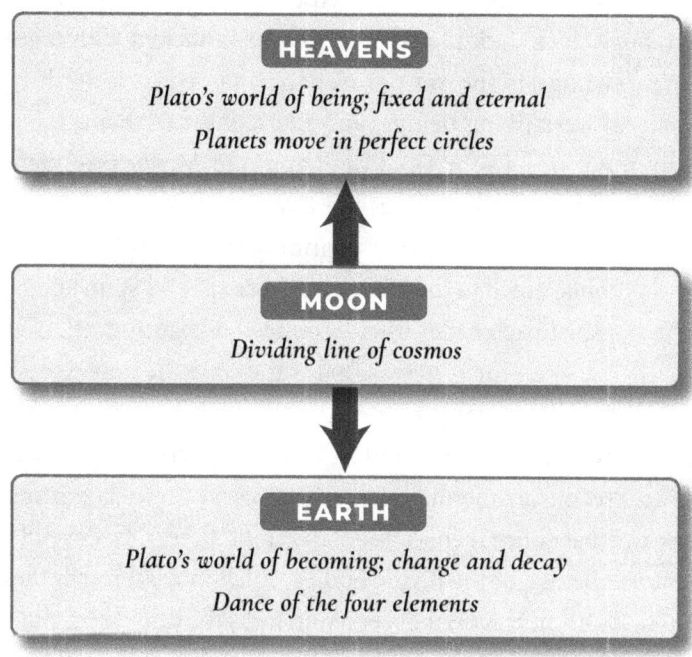

Figure 9.1. Aristotle's two-tiered cosmos, with the moon as the dividing line between the eternal, unchanging heavens and the temporal, ever-changing Earth

THE SEVEN PLANETS AND THEIR INFLUENCES

Above us in the night sky (the heavens), the seven planets whirled swiftly and ceaselessly in perfect concentric circles: Moon, Mercury, Venus, Sun, Mars, Jupiter, Saturn. The earth was not considered a planet, for planet in Greek means "wanderer," and the earth neither moved nor spun. Whereas our sublunary world was composed of the four elements, all of which change and decay, the heavens were made of an eternal, pure, imperishable fifth element (*quintessence* in Latin) called ether (or *aether*). The vast—though not infinite—expanse of the heavens was made of this at once solid and liquid element: both the seven planets and the crystalline spheres in which each was fixed. Of ether too was made the eighth circle of the fixed stars (*stellatum*) that rose above Saturn and that was the home of the constellations. Above that, also of ether, was the ninth sphere: the first mover (*primum mobile*).

These last two spheres, like the seven planets, were fixed in crystalline, forming a huge clockwork mechanism of gears couched within gears. But it was not mechanical in the way our Newtonian universe is mechanical, for all the spheres were living beings, and the highest of them, the primum mobile, spun out of love for God, the Unmoved Mover (see *Metaphysics* XII.7; 1072b3). Between the spheres there was no empty space, no vacuum, so that as each spun, it set the others spinning in a vast spiral cascade from the primum mobile down to the moon. As those spheres spun and hummed and rubbed against each other, they produced a beautiful celestial sound known as the music of the spheres. That is the song the universe sings, but our ears are too dull to hear it.

Because there was no vacuum and all was fixed in crystalline, the spinning of the spheres set off all other motion in the universe. Indeed, Aristotle insists in *Metaphysics* that "since there cannot be an infinite regress, the end of every movement will be one of the divine bodies which move through the heaven" (XII.8; 1074a30-31). In this brief observation lurks the origin of a concept that would sway and fascinate Europeans from late antiquity to the Enlightenment: celestial influence.

Because all motions on earth could be traced back to the movement of one of the spheres, Europeans believed for a long time—and many still believe today—that the arrangements of the planets and stars at the moment of one's birth influence and sometimes determine one's character, choices, and fate. Those same celestial bodies also exert an influence on the earth, drawing out of it certain metals, even as they draw out of men certain personality types. Thus, the influence of the moon and the sun produces silver and gold in the earth and lunacy and wisdom in men, while Venus, Mars, and Jupiter draw copper, iron, and tin out of the earth and make men amorous, martial, and jovial. Although Augustine decisively disproved a doctrinaire belief in horoscopes by pointing out that twins born on the same day do not share the same character and fate (see *City of God* V.2-6), people throughout the Middle Ages and Renaissance continued to believe that the planets and stars under which one was born influenced them in a real way.

Such thinking often gave way to fatalism for the ancients and medievals alike, but the theory of influence established in part by Aristotle did not demand determinism. It is true that the planets and stars shed down their influence, but it is still up to us as volitional agents to receive that influence in a proper way. Thus, the martial influence of Mars, depending on how it is received, can make a man a brave soldier or a merciless killer. Likewise, the amorous influence of Venus can make a woman a faithful spouse or an adulterous lover. The same sun that shines down on the earth makes mud hard and brittle but wax soft and supple. As Dante explains in *Purgatory* XVI:

> The [planetary] spheres *do* start your impulses along.
> I do not say *all*, but suppose I did—
> the light of reason still tells right from wrong;
> And Free Will also, which, though it be strained
> in the first battles with the heavens, still
> can conquer all if it is well sustained.
> You are free subjects of a more immense
> nature and power which grants you intellect
> to free you from the heavens' influence.[3]

CIRCLES WITHIN CIRCLES

Such was Aristotle's poetic vision of a two-tiered cosmos in which the endless revolutions of heavenly spheres initiate motion and influence action on the fixed, terrestrial globe we call home. Plato before him had divided reality into a changeless, perfect Word of Being above, and a changeable, shadowy World of Becoming below. He had spoken too of the spheres, giving each a celestial intelligence to move it along and join its voice to the music of the spheres. But it was Aristotle who worked out the details, who found a "scientific" solution for how the heavens could be perfect and yet in motion.

In the third-to-last chapter of *Physics*, Aristotle makes an argument that is vital to the cosmological model he would pass down to the Middle Ages,

---

[3]Dante, *The Divine Comedy*, trans. John Ciardi (New York: New American Library, 1970), 422. Dante's thoughts on determinism and free will rely heavily on those of Aquinas, which rely heavily on those of Aristotle, whose vision of an ordered cosmos did not abrogate man's free will. Indeed, as we will see in chapter twelve, Aristotle believed we could alter our personality by proper habits. See Michael Ward, *Planet Narnia: The Seven Heavens in the Imagination of C. S. Lewis* (New York: Oxford University Press, 2008), for a compelling argument that the seven Chronicles of Narnia embody the influences of the seven planets, which influences are sometimes received well and sometimes received poorly by the heroes and villains.

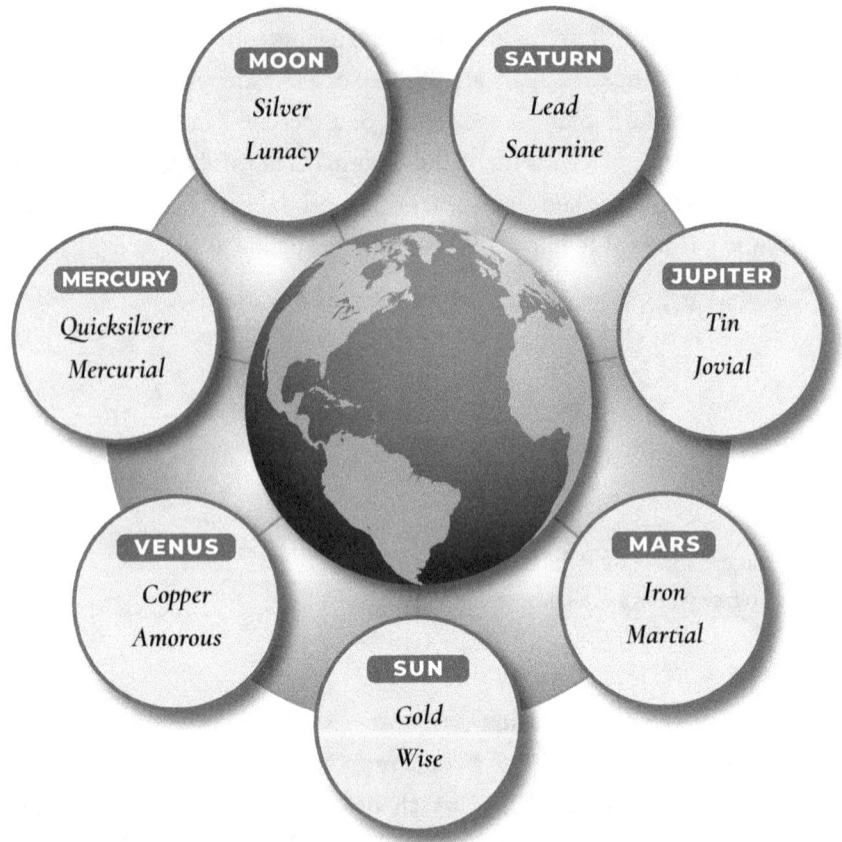

Figure 9.2. The seven planets, which revolve around a circular but stationary earth with their influences, showing what metal they draw out of the earth and what personality type they produce in people. Each planet is encased in a crystalline sphere made of ether; as they rub against each other, they produce a beautiful celestial melody known as the music of the spheres. The planets stretch upward from Moon to Saturn

one he would take up more fully in *Metaphysics* and *On the Heavens*. Though he generally links movement to change and decay, Aristotle here argues "that it is possible that there should be an infinite motion that is single and continuous, and that this motion is rotatory motion" (VIII.8; 261b27-28). If, Aristotle explains, something moves back and forth, or up and down, a line (rectilinear motion), then it will not be a continuous motion. Every time it reverses its course to go back along the same line, it will come to a brief standstill (and end) before beginning again. This is true even if it is moving along a circle, "for, when a thing merely traverses a circle, it may either proceed on its course without a break or turn back again when it has reached the same point from which it started" (VIII.8; 262a16-18).

Not movement in a circle but circular (rotatory) movement is the only kind of motion that is continuous and eternal. Only such movement can achieve the paradox of being simultaneously in motion and at rest, of achieving that perpetual now that Christian thinkers since Augustine have identified with eternity. Only in circular movement is the center

> alike starting-point, middle-point, and finishing-point of the space traversed; consequently since this point is not a point on the circular line, there is no point at which that which is in process of locomotion can be in a state of rest as having traversed its course, because in its locomotion it is proceeding always about a central point and not to an extreme point: therefore it remains still, and the whole is in a sense always at rest as well as continuously in motion. (VIII.9; 265b4-8)

In the second-to-last book of *Metaphysics*, Aristotle repeats his conclusion from *Physics* in simpler terms: "There are other spatial movements—those of the planets—which are eternal (for a body which moves in a circle is eternal and unresting; we have proved these points in the physical treatises [*Physics*])" (XII.8; 1073a30-32). He then explains, somewhat unexpectedly, that the planets that move, fixed in their crystalline spheres, through the heavens are divine: not in the crude sense of the anthropomorphic gods of Homer and Hesiod but in the sense that their motion is eternal and unresting.

Aristotle arrives at this conclusion in part by allegorizing (finding a hidden, spiritual meaning in a story that may or may not be historically true) the lessons he learned from Homer, Hesiod, and the other mythographers of old:

> Our forefathers in the most remote ages have handed down to their posterity a tradition, in the form of a myth, that these [celestial] bodies are gods, and that the divine encloses the whole of nature. The rest of the tradition has been added later in mythical form with a view to the persuasion of the multitude and to its legal and utilitarian expediency; they say these gods are in the form of men or like some of the other animals, and they say other things consequent on and similar to these which we have mentioned. But if one

were to separate the first point from these additions and take it alone—that they thought the first substances to be gods, one must regard this as an inspired utterance. (XII.8; 1074b1-10)

What makes this passage surprising is that church fathers such as Clement of Alexandria (150–215), Origen (ca. 185–ca. 253), and Augustine, inspired in part by the Jewish Philo (ca. 20 BC–ca. AD 50) and the pagan Plotinus (ca. 204–270) and Porphyry (ca. 234–ca. 305), also sought out allegorical truths hidden in the work of pagan poets. While rejecting what was false and often immoral in the tales of the poets, all these thinkers felt assured that a kernel of truth lurked in the myths—that was why they had been preserved and passed down for so many centuries.[4]

HOW CHAUCER AND BOETHIUS ALLEGORIZED ARISTOTLE'S ALLEGORIZING OF THE GREEK GODS

This process of allegorization is what allowed the Christians of the Middle Ages to retain the bulk of Aristotle's cosmological model while stripping it of its deified planets, as Aristotle himself had stripped the deified planets of their anthropomorphic nature. Yet, so powerful was Aristotle's model that the medievals called the planets, as we today continue to call them, by their deified names.[5] Indeed, a Christian poet such as Chaucer (ca. 1342–1400) could even make use of the deified planets by setting one of his poems—"The Knight's Tale" from *The Canterbury Tales*—in a pre-Christian world.

In Chaucer's tale, two cousins named Arcite and Palamon fall in love with Emily, the sister of Hippolyta, queen of the Amazons and wife of Theseus, king of Athens. After many plot complications, the two fight a duel; before they do so, however, the martial Arcite and the amorous Palamon pray for

---

[4] Although the practice of allegorizing myths has been used by pagan and Christian writers alike to good effect, liberal theologians such as Rudolf Bultmann (1884–1976) have used it to treat the miracles of the Bible in an allegorical fashion—extracting a spiritual lesson (a kernel of truth) while denying the historicity of the event. I discuss, from a Christian point of view, the positive and negative aspects of allegorical readings of ancient myths in chapters three and four of my *The Myth Made Fact: Reading Greek and Roman Mythology Through Christian Eyes* (Camp Hill, PA: Classical Academic Press, 2020).

[5] They also used, as we still do today, the same seven planets/gods to name the days of the week. Saturday, Sunday, and Monday are, of course, the days of Saturn, Sun, and Moon. Tuesday through Friday are based on the equivalent Norse gods: Tuesday from Tyr (Mars), Wednesday from Odin (Mercury), Thursday from Thor (Jupiter), Friday from Freia (Venus).

help, respectively, from Mars and Venus: *both* the gods and the planets. Meanwhile, the duel itself is watched over by the planet/god Jupiter, whose dark, saturnine influence—which draws lead out of the earth and brings war, plagues, and disaster to men—casts a pall over the proceedings, leading first to the victory and then to the sudden, accidental death of Arcite.

Into his episodic tale, the Christian Chaucer weaves a pagan dialogue on the nature of fate, fortune, and influence. By so doing, he mimics Boethius's *Consolation of Philosophy*, itself a book written by a Christian but in a pre-Christian mode. As Boethius (ca. 480–524), both the character and the historical author, sits in prison awaiting judgment and execution, he seeks to find what consolation he can from the highest of pagan philosophy: Socrates, Plato, Aristotle, and Cicero, as well as the Stoics, Epicureans, and Neoplatonists. Key to his musings is a meditation on providence and fate. Given the fixed nature of our two-tiered universe, which is set in motion by the primum mobile's love for the Unmoved Mover, it is questionable whether any of us possesses real choice. How can we act apart from the seemingly deterministic nature of our cosmos or from the Causeless Cause who orders all things?

AUGUSTINE AND BOETHIUS ON PROVIDENCE, FATE, AND FREE WILL

Just above I mentioned book V of Augustine's *City of God*. There Augustine concedes that those who believe in divine fate and causation "are perfectly right in believing that God allows nothing to remain unordered and that He knows all things before they come to pass." He then quickly qualifies the statement, arguing that God "is the Cause of all causes, although not of all choices." After discussing the matter at length, Augustine concludes that "our choices fall within the order of the causes which is known for certain to God and is contained in His foreknowledge—for, human choices are the causes of human acts. It follows that He who foreknew the causes of all things could not be unaware that our choices were among those causes which were foreknown as the causes of our acts."[6]

---

[6] Augustine, *The City of God*, ed. and abridged by Vernon J. Bourke (New York: Image, 1958), V.8-9 (pp. 103, 106-7).

Augustine has more to say on this subject, but I will turn my attention back to Boethius and Chaucer since their consciously pre-Christian meditations, which stand at the dawn and sunset of the Christian Middle Ages, offer a clearer window into Aristotle's influence on medieval Christendom.

In book IV of *Consolation of Philosophy*, Boethius takes up the paradoxical relationship between providence and fate, and attacks it with the careful precision of Aristotle, using his language, his logic, and his cosmology:

> Providence is the very divine reason which arranges all things, and rests with the supreme disposer of all; while Fate is that ordering which is a part of all changeable things, and by means of which Providence binds all things together in their own order. Providence embraces all things equally, however different they may be, even however infinite: when they are assigned to their own places, forms, and times, Fate sets them in an orderly motion; so that this development of the temporal order, unified in the intelligence of the mind of God, is Providence. The working of this unified development in time is called Fate.... Providence is the one unchangeable direct power which gives form to all things which are to come to pass, while Fate is the changing bond, the temporal order of those things which are arranged to come to pass by the direct disposition of God. Wherefore everything which is subject to Fate is also subject to Providence, to which Fate is itself subject.[7]

Notice that Boethius writes from the point of view of a two-tiered universe in which the upper part is eternal and unchanging while the lower part is temporal and subjected to change. Whereas providence is the divine reason that arranges and orders all things, fate *is* that arranging and ordering as it manifests itself in time and space. All that lies within the realm of fate is subjected to providence, but providence is not subjected to fate.

I argued in chapter five that Aristotle moved Plato's Forms from above and outside to below and within. Boethius uses Aristotle's binary of center/circumference to express the proper relationship between providence and fate: "As, therefore, reasoning is to understanding; as that which becomes is to that which is; as time is to eternity; as the circumference is to the centre: so is the changing course of Fate to the immovable directness of

---

[7] Boethius, *The Consolation of Philosophy*, trans. W. V. Cooper, in *The Great Books: Seventh Year* (Chicago: Great Books Foundation, 1959), 2:99–100.

Providence."[8] Immovable Providence controls and shapes changeable fate as form does matter in Aristotle's *Physics*. Providence exists in the eternal World of Being and apprehends things directly ("understanding"), while fate is subjected to time and change (becoming) and can only comprehend sequentially ("reasoning").

This distinction between the way providence (God) apprehends eternity (Being) and we comprehend time (becoming) gives Boethius the Aristotelian distinction he needs to resolve the related paradox of God's foreknowledge and human free will. To those who claim that God's foreknowledge of the future necessarily removes our free will, Boethius responds that God, who dwells in eternity, does not actually *fore*see the future:

> If you would weigh the foreknowledge by which God distinguishes all things, you will more rightly hold it to be a knowledge of a never-failing constancy in the present, than a foreknowledge of the future. Whence Providence is more rightly to be understood as a looking forth than a looking forward, because it is set far from low matters and looks forth upon all things as from a lofty mountain-top above all. Why then do you demand that all things occur by necessity, if divine light rests upon them, while men do not render necessary such things as they can see? Because you can see things of the present, does your sight therefore put upon them any necessity? Surely not. If one may not unworthily compare this present time with the divine, just as you can see things in this your temporal present, so God sees all things in His eternal present.[9]

God's knowledge of the future, like our knowledge of the present, is a "now" knowledge, for all is perpetually present in God's eternity. Thus, just as my witnessing of an action happening in the present does not necessarily cause that action, so God's perpetually present knowledge of my own future actions does not necessarily cause those actions.

Aristotle's celestial spheres, on account of their eternal circular movements, are simultaneously in motion and at rest. In a similar but more perfect way, God, the Unmoved Mover, sees all that ever was, is, and will be in a single continuous moment, but without effort, anxiety, or change. For Aristotle,

---

[8] Boethius, *Consolation of Philosophy*, 101.
[9] Boethius, *Consolation of Philosophy*, 128.

God exists in a perpetual state of pure contemplation; if we would find peace, we must imitate his contemplation. We must learn to rest in his providential will and knowledge, for, in Aristotle and Boethius's philosophy and cosmology, to rest in God's providence is to rest in the center of his will.

CHAUCER ON PROVIDENCE, FATE, AND FREE WILL

Given that Chaucer translated Boethius's *Consolation* into Middle English, it should come as no surprise that his characters spend much time reflecting on fate and providence. Early on, when both Arcite and Palamon are in prison, they console themselves, like Boethius before them, by meditating on the fickle nature of fortune:

> Fortune has given us this adversity,
> Some wicked planetary dispensation,
> Some Saturn's trick or evil constellation
> Has given us this, and Heaven, though we had sworn
> The contrary, so stood when we were born.
> We must endure it, that's the long and short.[10]

In just five lines, Chaucer condenses the medieval understanding of fortune, planetary influence, and the determining power of one's horoscope. The solution is not to fight against one's fate but to endure it, partly, it seems, because there is an unseen providence working behind the intrigues of fortune, influence, and horoscope.

Indeed, a little later in the poem, Arcite counsels Palamon not to be too quick to curse fortune, lest he also curse God's overriding providence:

> Alas, why is it people so dispraise
> God's providence or Fortune and her ways,
> That oft and variously in their scheme
> Includes far better things than they could dream?
> One man desires to have abundant wealth,
> Which brings about his murder or ill-health;

---

[10]Geoffrey Chaucer, "The Knight's Tale," 228-33, in *The Canterbury Tales*, trans. Nevill Coghill (Baltimore: Penguin, 1958), 46.

> Another, freed from prison as he'd willed,
> Comes home, his servants catch him, and he's killed.[11]

What seems to us a bad thing, poverty, may preserve us from being murdered for our wealth or rendered ill by our overindulgence. Meanwhile, a seemingly fortunate event, our release from prison, might result in our being murdered when we return home. We must look past fate (good or bad) to perceive providence operating beneath the surface.

As the tale progresses, the narrator, who possesses the Christian revelation that his characters lack, interjects a paean to God's providential foreknowledge:

> Now Destiny, that Minister-General
> Who executes on earth and over all
> What God, from everlasting, has foreseen,
> Is of such strength, that though the world had been
> Sure of the contrary, by Yea and Nay,
> That thing will happen on a certain day,
> Though never again within a thousand years.[12]

By sharing with us, his readers, a wisdom unavailable to his characters, Chaucer helps us to understand that there is a divine providence that transcends our earthly fate, even when we are ignorant of it. God is in control, and he will work out his will, even if it should take a thousand years.

WHAT THE PRE-CHRISTIAN ARISTOTLE KNEW ABOUT CELESTIAL LOVE AND ORDER

However, since his characters lack the special revelation of the Bible, Chaucer has Theseus express this divine order and control in pre-Christian terms, relying on Aristotle's terminology rather than that of the Scriptures:

> "The First Great Cause and Mover of all above
> When first He made that fairest chain of love,
> Great was the consequence and high the intent.
> He well knew why He did, and what He meant.

---

[11]Chaucer, "Knight's Tale," 393-400, in *Canterbury Tales*, 51.
[12]Chaucer, "Knight's Tale," 805-11, in *Canterbury Tales*, 62.

> For in that fairest chain of love He bound
> Fire and air and water and the ground
> Of earth in certain limits they may not flee.
> And that same Prince and Mover then," said he,
> "Stablished this wretched world, appointing ways,
> Seasons, durations, certain length of days,
> To all that is engendered here below,
> Past which predestined hour none may go,
> Though they have power to abridge those days.
> I need not quote authority or raise
> More proof than what experience can show,
> But give opinion here from what I know."[13]

In his speech, which Chaucer patterned closely after several passages from the *Consolation*, Theseus identifies God with Aristotle's "First Great Cause and Mover." But what of his identification of God with love? Surely such an identification necessitates a knowledge of the Bible. Or does it?

Although Theseus, like Aristotle, knows nothing of God's self-sacrificial love that he will show forth most perfectly by giving his Son for the life of the world, he does recognize that all things are connected to God by a golden chain that hangs down from the primum mobile—which spins perpetually out of love for God. Unity and order are not only predicated on God's status as Causeless Cause and Unmoved Mover; they gain their cosmic glue from the love that runs along the Great Chain of Being from the primum mobile to inanimate stones. Aristotle accepted in part Empedocles's belief that love draws together the four elements so that they will collide and form new compounds. Theseus combines Empedocles's notion of love as a uniter with Aristotle's notion of love as the power that moves the spheres. Love thus initiates the unity and the motion that work together to determine the length of days and seasons and the fates of men.

Critics of the Middle Ages have often attacked it for caring only about authority and nothing about experience. Chaucer gives the lie to such a

---

[13]Chaucer, "Knight's Tale," 2129-44, in *Canterbury Tales*, 97.

notion, arguing here that the shape and function of Aristotle's two-tiered, influence-generating cosmos can be grasped by observation and common sense as much as by authority and logic. As we have seen before, Aristotle himself based many of his philosophical theories on his own experience and the shared beliefs of common people.

God's providential order is clear to those who have eyes to see; indeed, the extent of that order and design, in part and in whole, can be deduced from what we observe:

> Since we discern this order, we are able
> To know that Prince is infinite and stable.
> Anyone but a fool knows, in his soul,
> That every part derives from this great whole.
> For nature cannot be supposed to start
> From some particular portion or mere part,
> But from a whole and undisturbed perfection
> Descending thence to what is in subjection
> To change, and will corrupt. And therefore He
> In wise foreknowledge stablished the decree
> That species of all things and the progression
> Of seed and growth continue by succession
> And not eternally. This is no lie,
> As any man can see who has an eye.[14]

Aristotle's God, who dwells in undisturbed contemplation, is the ultimate source of all motion and change in the two-tiered cosmos—both the eternal change of the heavenly spheres and the temporal change of our earthly realm.

In our world, to paraphrase the title of one of Aristotle's treatises, living things are constantly being generated and corrupted. They end and begin, die and are reborn, but the wise foreknowledge of God watches and decrees, establishing the times and the telos for all things. So much was clear to the pagan Aristotle, and that is why Christian thinkers from Augustine to Boethius to Chaucer were willing to learn from his wisdom.

---

[14]Chaucer, "Knight's Tale," 2145-58, in *Canterbury Tales*, 97-98.

10

JOINING THE COSMIC DANCE

ALTHOUGH ARISTOTLE, along with his ancient, medieval, and Renaissance heirs, lived before Sir Isaac Newton discovered and formulated the laws of gravitation, they all lived in a world where most things fall down. Aristotle had eyes to see, and he was well aware that heavy things, such as rocks, descend toward the earth, while light things, such as fire, ascend heavenward. Given his desire to construct a complete system capable of explaining all of nature in a consistent and coherent manner, it should come as no surprise that he included in his system an explanation for why things fall and rise. The solution that Aristotle devised would prove essential to the two-tiered cosmos he bequeathed to the Middle Ages; as such, it deserves a chapter of its own.

WHY THINGS FALL AND RISE

In the previous chapter I discussed the distinction Aristotle makes between circular and rectilinear motion. In the heavenly realms above the moon, where all is simultaneously eternal and continuous, all motion is circular. In our sublunar world, in contrast, things move up and down along a line. In *On the Heavens*, Aristotle clarifies the distinction: "Revolution about the centre is circular motion, while the upward and downward movements are in a straight line, 'upward' meaning motion away from the centre, and 'downward' motion towards it. All simple motion, then, must be motion either away from or towards [rectilinear] or about [circular] the centre" (I.2; 268b21-24).

Of the four elements, it is in the nature (both form and telos) of earth to sink to the center and fire to move away from it, with water tending downward and air upward. Though the elements constantly combine and break apart, each has its own natural level, with earth on the bottom, successive layers of water and air stacked above it, and fire rising to the upper atmosphere. The elements do not gravitate toward their level because they follow abstract laws of nature but because they are impelled to find their proper rung on the cosmic ladder. In that sense, the elements are less like citizens following a legal code than they are like migrating birds seeking their proper home.

Aristotle comes back again and again to the inherent natures of the four elements. Near the end of *On the Heavens*, he tries to reconcile what all people observe with their eyes with the cosmological model he is attempting to construct:

> In accordance with general conviction we may distinguish the absolutely heavy, as that which sinks to the bottom of all things, from the absolutely light, which is that which rises to the surface of all things. . . . Fire, in whatever quantity, so long as there is no external obstacle moves upward, and earth downward. . . . But the heaviness and lightness of bodies which combine these qualities is different from this, since while they rise to the surface of some bodies they sink to the bottom of others. Such are air and water. Neither of them is absolutely either light or heavy. (IV.4; 311a16-25)

Though Aristotle's cosmos has an absolute and intelligible structure, it does contain some relativity and slipperiness. Earth and fire are absolute in their heaviness and lightness; if they are not impeded by an outside force, they will always move to the top or the bottom. Water and air, in contrast, are heavy or light in terms of what element they are near.

I say up and down, top and bottom, but we must remember that for Aristotle heaviness and lightness are defined by their relationship to the center: "That there is a centre towards which the motion of heavy things, and away from which that of light things is directed, is manifest in many ways" (IV.4; 311b29-31).

I belabor this point because Aristotle's belief that earth falls to the center and fire rises away from it necessitates a fixed, central globe as the nodal point from which all things take their "gravitational" movement.

> If it is the nature of earth, as observation shows, to move from any point to the centre, as of fire contrariwise to move from the centre to the extremity, it is impossible that any portion of earth should move away from the centre except by constraint. . . . If then no portion of earth can move away from the centre, obviously still less can the earth as a whole so move. . . . Its [the earth's] shape must necessarily be spherical. (II.14; 296b28-297a9)

As we have seen before, Aristotle's conclusions are based on both observation of the natural world and deductive reasoning as to what the nature of reality *must* be. In no way are his conclusions frivolous or based on an exalted sense of the earth's importance.

Aristotle's goal here, as in most of his works, is to arrive at a synthesis that can explain all we observe with our eyes and reason about with our minds. His attempt to reach that synthesis continues to be relevant, even though his two-tiered cosmos is not true to the reality that was opened to us by the invention of the telescope and other instruments for measuring the universe.

THE FOUR ELEMENTS AND THEIR QUALITATIVE PAIRS

Still, as a testament to Aristotle's powerfully synthetic mind, I would point the reader's attention to his *On Generation and Corruption*, where he codifies with even greater clarity the relationship between the four elements. I mentioned in chapter four that Aristotle studied accidents in terms of opposing pairs. To make clear the proper nature and ordering of the four elements, Aristotle, in keeping with some of the pre-Socratic philosophers, links the four elements to the two qualitative pairs of hot and cold, dry and wet (moist).

> The elementary qualities are four, and any four terms can be combined in six couples. Contraries, however, refuse to be coupled: for it is impossible for the same thing to be hot and cold, or moist and dry. Hence it is evident that the "couplings" of the elementary qualities will be four: hot with dry and moist with hot, and again cold with dry and cold with moist.... Fire is hot and dry, whereas Air is hot and moist (Air being a sort of aqueous vapour); and Water is cold and moist, while Earth is cold and dry. (II.3; 330a30-330b6)

Notice how Aristotle applies the law of noncontradiction to reduce six possible pairings to four. By doing so, he ensures that the four elements will exhaust all potential combinations, yielding a universe that is balanced and efficient. In later chapters, Aristotle uses these combinations to show how it is that one element can morph into another by means of their shared warmth or coldness, wetness or dryness. The movement downward from fire to earth is called condensation; the movement upward, rarefaction.

In Aristotle's cosmos there is neither waste nor inefficiency. Indeed, in *On the Heavens*, Aristotle rejects the possibility of what scientists today

Joining the Cosmic Dance

call the multiverse by insisting that all matter in the universe has been used fully:

> It is evident not only that there is not, but also that there could never come to be, any bodily mass whatever outside the circumference. The world as a whole, therefore, includes all its appropriate matter, which is, as we saw, natural perceptible body. So that neither are there now, nor have there ever been, nor can there ever be formed more heavens than one, but this heaven of ours is one and unique and complete.... There is also no place or void or time outside the heaven. (I.9; 279a6-12)

Aristotle's cosmos was immense—compared to it, our earth was spatially insignificant—but it was not infinite. It was just the right size to make full use of all the matter within it, with nothing left over and with no empty spaces devoid of matter.

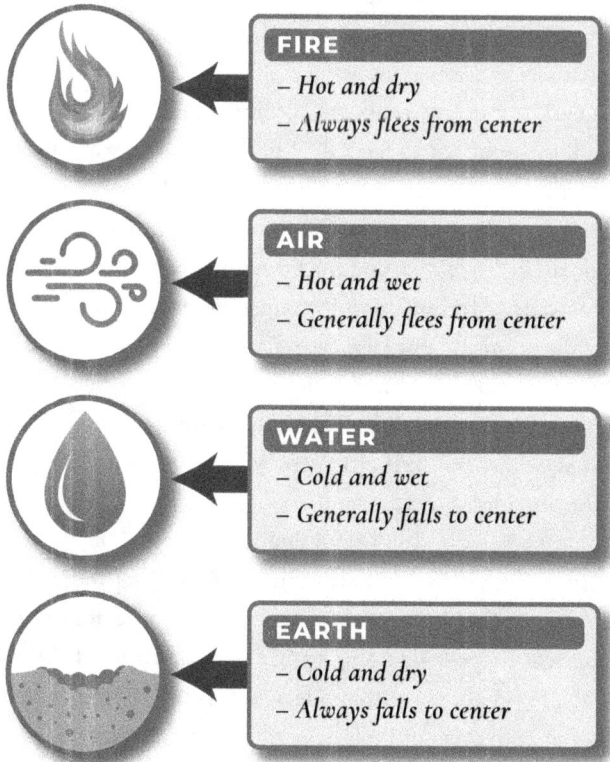

Figure 10.1. The four elements with their qualitative pairs and their relationship to the center. Movement downward from fire to earth is called condensation. Movement upward from earth to fire is called rarefaction

WHAT IT FELT LIKE TO LIVE IN ARISTOTLE'S COSMOS

Such was Aristotle's full vision of the two-tiered cosmos. What, you may ask, did it *feel* like to live in a universe so constructed? I can think of no better way to answer that question than to quote a lengthy passage from a twentieth-century scholar of the Middle Ages who drank deeply from and immersed himself fully in the medieval cosmological model. Here is how C. S. Lewis answers the question in *The Discarded Image* (1964):

> You must go out on a starry night and walk about for half an hour trying to see the sky in terms of the old cosmology. Remember that you now have an absolute Up and Down. The Earth is really the centre, really the lowest place; movement to it from whatever direction is downward movement. As a modern, you located the stars at a great distance. For distance you must now substitute that very special, and far less abstract, sort of distance which we call height; height, which speaks immediately to our muscles and nerves. The Medieval Model is vertiginous. And the fact that the height of the stars in the medieval astronomy is very small compared with their distance in the modern, will turn out not to have the kind of importance you anticipated. For thought and imagination, ten million miles and a thousand million are much the same. Both can be conceived (that is, we can do sums with both) and neither can be imagined; and the more imagination we have the better we shall know this. The really important difference is that the medieval universe, while unimaginably large, was also unambiguously finite. And one unexpected result of this is to make the smallness of Earth more vividly felt. In our universe she is small, no doubt; but so are the galaxies, so is everything—and so what? But in theirs there was an absolute standard of comparison. The furthest sphere, Dante's *maggior corpo* ["largest body," the primum mobile] is, quite simply and finally, the largest object in existence. The word "small" as applied to Earth thus takes on a far more absolute significance. Again, because the medieval universe is finite, it has a shape, the perfect spherical shape, containing within itself an ordered variety. Hence to look out on the night sky with modern eyes is like looking out over a sea that fades away into mist, or looking about one in a trackless forest—trees forever and no horizon. To look up at the towering medieval universe is much more like looking at a great building. The "space" of modern astronomy may arouse terror, or bewilderment or vague reverie; the spheres

of the old present us with an object in which the mind can rest, overwhelming in its greatness but satisfying in its harmony. That is the sense in which our universe is romantic, and theirs was classical.[1]

If we live in a vast, amorphous space with no boundaries or frontiers, no real sense of ascent or descent, and no way to measure relative spaces, then the medievals lived in a mighty cathedral where everything had its proper niche, function, and proportion, and every column and spire lifted the eyes heavenward.

The medieval cosmos was an intimate and harmonious home with a real roof and a real floor. Everyone, from prince to pauper, priest to gravedigger, scholar to farmhand, knew his place within it. There was hierarchy rather than equity, but that hierarchy led to a truer diversity than we have today. Those who live in such an ordered universe—which is what *cosmos* signifies in Greek—are not strangers in a strange land but inhabitants of a peaceable kingdom ruled by a just and benevolent monarch. There *is* danger and peril in such a cosmos, but never the kind of existential dread and despair that the modern feels when he looks out on a dark and uncaring universe without shape, purpose, or scale.

DANTE'S PILGRIMAGE THROUGH ARISTOTLE'S TWO-TIERED UNIVERSE

About a century before Chaucer's British pilgrims set out on their journey for Canterbury, an Italian poet took his own personal journey through the full depth and breadth of Aristotle's two-tiered universe, crossing the threshold between life and death and the frontier between the sublunar world below and the starry heavens above. As he prepares to cross the second, and so move from time to eternity, change to perfection, Dante (1265–1321) learns the spiritual significance latent in Aristotle's philosophical argument that the elements find their proper place in relationship to the center, which is the earth, and the circumference, which is God—though Dante discovers, as he nears the end of his journey, that God is in fact the true center (see *Paradise*, canto 28).

---

[1] C. S. Lewis, *The Discarded Image* (Cambridge: Cambridge University Press, 1964), 98-99.

Thus far in his journey through hell and up the mountain of purgatory, Dante has walked or crawled from level to level, rim to rim. Now, as he stands in the Garden of Eden, which is poised on the top of purgatory, and looks up toward the heavenly spheres, he finds to his great surprise that he is soaring toward the moon. When he asks his guide, in canto 1 of *Paradise*, how it is that he can rise upward like a bird in flight while still encased in his body, the lovely Beatrice gives him a lesson in Aristotelian gravity:

> "The elements
> of all things," she began, "whatever their mode,
>   observe an inner order. It is this form
>   that makes the universe resemble God.
> In this the higher creatures see the hand
>   of the Eternal Worth, which is the goal
>   to which these norms conduce, being so planned.
> All Being within this order, by the laws
>   of its own nature is impelled to find
>   its proper station round its Primal Cause.
> Thus every nature moves across the tide
>   of the great sea of being to its own port,
>   each with its given instinct as its guide.
> This instinct draws the fire about the moon.
>   It is the mover in the mortal heart.
>   It draws the earth together and makes it one.
> Not only the brute creatures, but all those
>   possessed of intellect and love, this instinct
>   drives to their mark as a bow shoots forth its arrows.
> The Providence that makes all things hunger here
>   satisfies forever with its light
>   the heaven within which whirls the fastest sphere.
> And to it now, as to a place foretold,
>   are we too soaring, driven by that bow
>   whose every arrow finds a mark of gold."[2]

Dante agrees with Aristotle that it is natural for fire to find its proper level beneath the moon: not because it is following an abstract law but because it

---

[2]Dante, *The Divine Comedy*, trans. John Ciardi (New York: New American Library, 1970), 99-126 (p. 600).

is like a migrating bird returning to its true home. Dante's universe, like that of Aristotle, is in constant motion as all things seek to find their level and so fulfill their telos.

But Dante is a poet, perhaps the greatest of all poets, and so he makes Aristotle's theories come alive by means of a grand metaphor. All objects in nature, but supremely we humans who have been endowed with reason, are like ships sailing through the sea of space in search of their proper port. Though the power of "gravity" pulls all things down, that which is most true in them impels them to find their station around the Primal Cause, one of Aristotle's titles for God. That God is not only the Lover-Bridegroom of the Bible but the Beloved of Aristotle's system. Just as the primum mobile spins out of love for God, so all things are driven, arrow-like, by a desire to find that golden mark and rest within his pure and perpetual contemplation. For the lower animals, that desire is only instinct; for us in whom God has breathed a rational soul, it is felt as well as chosen.

ASCENDING THE PATH AND STAYING THE COURSE

Indeed, it is precisely because we have free will that we can affect the trajectory of our boat (or arrow) in a positive or negative way. Earth and fire, though their nature draws them up or down, can be deflected from their course by an outside force. We also can be so deflected, but by a mixture of obstructive (external) forces and disordered (inward) desires. For this reason, Beatrice issues Dante both a warning and a hope:

> It is true that oftentimes the form of a thing
>   does not respond to the intent of the art,
>   the matter being deaf to summoning—
> Just so, the creature sometimes travels wide
>   of this true course, for even when so driven
>   it still retains the power to turn aside
> (exactly as we may see the heavens' fire
>   plunge from a cloud) and its first impulse may
>   be twisted earthward by a false desire.
> You should not, as I see it, marvel more
>   at your ascent than at a river's fall
>   from a high mountain to the valley floor.

> If you, free as you are of every dross,
>   had settled and had come to rest below,
>   that would indeed have been as marvelous
> as a still flame there in the mortal plain.[3]

By a misuse of our God-given free will, Beatrice warns, we can drive ourselves off the proper path, the straight road, to God. Or, to put it in the Aristotelian terms to which Dante alludes, we can be like a recalcitrant piece of matter that resists the form that would shape it in accordance with its telos. By refusing to be guided by formal and final causes, we leave ourselves prey to the brute operations of material and efficient causes.

When we turn away from the true course dictated by our proper form and telos, we become as perverse and self-destructive as that fire that, against its nature, falls to the earth in the form of lightning. Did not Jesus tell his disciples when they rejoiced at their power to casts out demons that he himself "beheld Satan as lightning fall from heaven" (Lk 10:18)? In fact, in canto 14 of *Inferno*, Dante himself beholds fire fall down, perversely, in burning flakes to torment the blasphemers, sodomites, and usurers who chose barrenness over a life of service to God.

What Dante does here is to take the up/down cosmology of Aristotle and infuse it with a spiritual meaning. Once Dante has been purged of all sin—not only by working his way up the levels of purgatory linked to the seven deadly sins but also by drinking from the River Lethe so that even the memory of sin is washed away from his mind—he cannot help but soar upward toward God. Indeed, now that he has been purged, it is as natural for him to fly up as it is for a waterfall to flow down. Or, to express the same point in the negative, were he not to fly, he would be like a lighter-than-air flame trapped on the earth, against its nature, its form, and its destiny.

Aristotle's cosmos, as filtered through Boethius and Aquinas, leaps into dramatic life in the vivid imagination of Dante. Dante's vision of the universe is dizzying, with its vertiginous flight upward and its endlessly whirling spheres. But then, Aristotle himself prepared the medievals for that celestial drama in a single line from *On the Heavens*. We tend to think, he writes, "of

---

[3]Dante, *Divine Comedy*, 127-42 (pp. 600-601).

the stars as mere bodies, and as units with a serial order indeed but entirely inanimate; but [we should] rather conceive them as enjoying life and action" (II.12; 292a19-21).

THE TRUE NATURE OF STARS

Though Scripture does not treat the stars and planets as living beings, it does depict the throne room of God as a place of ceaseless angelic activity (see Is 6 and Rev 4), an image that Dante incorporates into canto 31 of *Paradise*. In any case, the medievals *did* allow for angelic intelligences to move each of the spheres, thus injecting a kind of animation into the inanimate spinning of the seven planets, the fixed constellations, and the primum mobile.

C. S. Lewis, that most medieval of modern authors, was clearly moved by the thought of the stars enjoying life and action, for in *The Voyage of the Dawn Treader*, one of the seven Chronicles of Narnia, he introduces us to a living star. Near the end of the novel, our heroes meet a magician named Ramandu, whom they soon discover, to their shock and delight, is a retired star—for, in Narnia, the stars *are* animate. When Eustace Clarence Scrubb, a boy from England whose modern utilitarian education has robbed him of all wonder and imagination, realizes he is talking to a star, he exclaims: "In our world . . . a star is a huge ball of flaming gas." "Even in your world, my son," Ramandu replies, "that is not what a star is but only what it is made of."[4]

Eustace, Aristotle would say, makes a category error in thinking that a star's accidents are the same thing as its substance. It is an error that no true medieval, raised as he was on Aristotelian logic, would have made but one that many a modern makes on a daily basis. Like Eustace, we have lost a sense of wonder before the cosmos; we have killed the heavens, and I am afraid that the modern church has performed the funeral.

It perhaps would not hurt us to look up at the night sky now and then and imagine the stars and planets laughing and besporting themselves as they whirl endlessly in their loving devotion to the Primal Cause.

---

[4]C. S. Lewis, *The Voyage of the Dawn Treader* (New York: Collier Books, 1970), 180.

PART 3

HOW TO BEHAVE

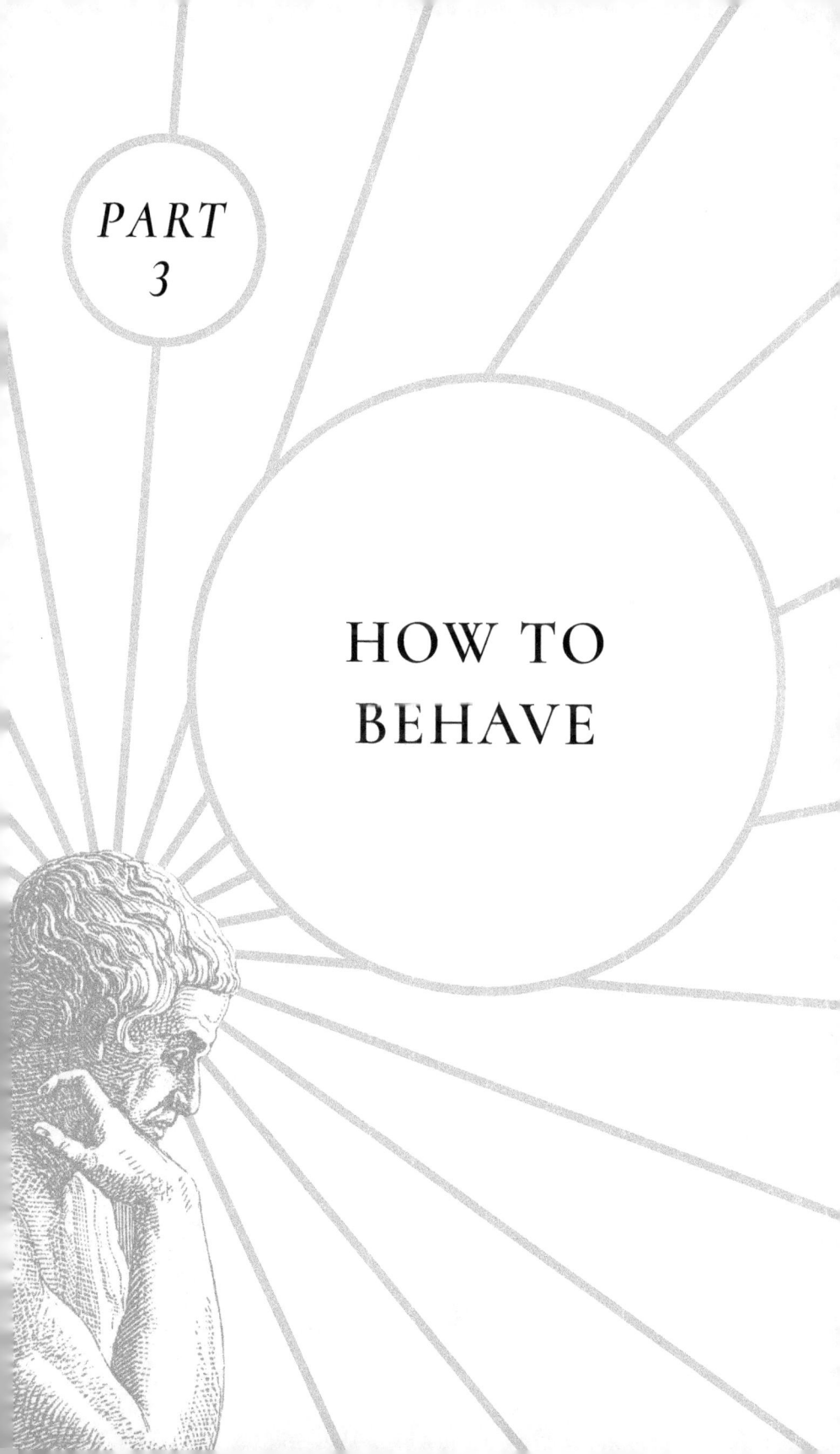

11

STUDYING THE PSYCHE

Psychology means literally "the study of the psyche," and *psyche* is the word that Plato and Aristotle used to signify our soul/mind: that is, the part of ourselves that gives life and motion, thought and feeling, perception and, in humans, reason. Although, as we saw in chapter five, Aristotle held a more incarnational, less dualistic view of soul and body than Plato, he did treat the soul as immaterial and prior to the body. Psychologists who hold, as Spinoza and Sigmund Freud held, a materialist view of reality may speak of the soul, but they do not believe there is any real distinction between soul and body, mind and matter. Our beliefs and actions, feelings and decisions can all be traced back to and explained by a series of efficient and material causes apart from final or formal causes.

ARISTOTLE ON THE SOUL

Not so Aristotle, who saw in the union of soul and body the same relationship that exists between form and matter, actuality and potentiality. If a modern cognitive scientist were to attempt to prove to Aristotle that we do not possess an immaterial (supernatural, metaphysical) psyche on the basis that when our brain is injured, it causes a change to our personality and behavior, he would likely have answered him in the same manner as a Christian. "*Of course* diseases of the brain affect the mind!" he would respond. As hylomorphic (incarnational) beings, our souls and bodies are so intimately joined that what happens to one cannot help but affect the other.

Indeed, in the opening chapter of *On the Soul*, Aristotle takes up this very issue, concluding that there is a two-way traffic between body and soul:

> It therefore seems that all the affections of soul involve a body—passion, gentleness, fear, pity, courage, joy, loving, and hating; in all these there is a

> concurrent affection of the body. In support of this we may point to the fact that, while sometimes on the occasion of violent and striking occurrences there is no excitement or fear felt, on others faint and feeble stimulations produce these emotions, viz. when the body is already in a state of tension resembling its condition when we are angry. Here is a still clearer case: in the absence of any external cause of terror we find ourselves experiencing the feelings of a man in terror. From all this it is obvious that the affections of soul are enmattered formulable essences. (I.1; 403a15-24)

In this difficult passage, Aristotle demonstrates how soul and body mutually affect each other. Thus, when the soul experiences such emotions as fear or courage, love or hate, that experience manifests itself physically in the body. But the relationship can also work in the opposite direction. When the body is tense, perhaps with jaws and fists tightly clenched, the soul feels the fear expressed concretely in the body—even when there is no clear and present physical danger to threaten it. Souls do not simply lie passively within a container of flesh; they are, to use Aristotle's colorful term, "enmattered."

After reviewing the various theories of soul held by Plato and the pre-Socratics, Aristotle reiterates that we are hylomorphic creatures and that one cannot study the soul or body in isolation: it is "better to avoid saying that the soul pities or learns or thinks and rather to say that it is the man who does this with his soul" (I.4; 408b14-15). It is as composite beings that we interface with the world, an aspect of our nature that Aristotle explores by looking at the dwindling of mental ("soulical") powers that accompanies age.

> What really happens in respect of mind in old age is . . . exactly parallel to what happens in the case of the sense organs; if the old man could recover the proper kind of eye, he would see just as well as the young man. The incapacity of old age is due to an affection not of the soul but of its vehicle, as occurs in drunkenness or disease. Thus it is that in old age the activity of mind or intellectual apprehension declines only through the decay of some other inward part; mind itself is impassible. . . . When this vehicle [the body] decays, memory and love cease; they were activities not of mind, but of the composite which has perished; mind is, no doubt, something more divine and impassible. (I.4; 408b20-29)

That our mind/soul becomes cloudy and incapacitated when we are drunk or ill does not prove that our psyche is material. The essential part of us—the form or soul or mind—remains the same, but the decaying of the body through age or infirmity weakens its operations. That is the case because we are not souls trapped in bodies but composite beings.

ARISTOTLE AND AQUINAS ON THE SOUL AFTER DEATH

Yet, at the end of the passage, Aristotle suggests that there is something about the soul-mind (psyche) that will endure past death. The dissolution of the body will dissolve the memories and loves that are so intimately connected to the flesh; nevertheless, some part of us that shares in the impassibility of the divine will remain. Christian theologians such as Aquinas who have been influenced by Plato and Aristotle argue that God is incapable of suffering or feeling pain (what *impassible* means in Latin), a quality that Aristotle gives to the soul after death. When we consider, in chapter fifteen, Aristotle's *Nicomachean Ethics* X, we will see that Aristotle, like Plato, considered the life of contemplation, not of action, to be the highest good for man. As such, it is fitting that Aristotle suggests that what remains after death will be our power to contemplate the divine, a kind of pure thought that is immune from suffering or pain and that has no need of the body.

Although such a vision of heaven is finally incompatible with the Christian doctrine of the resurrection of the body and of the concrete nature of the new heaven and earth, we can see the unshakable influence of Aristotle on Aquinas—who most commonly refers to Aristotle as simply "the Philosopher." In his *Summa* Aquinas, meditating on *Ethics* X and Aristotle's wider philosophy of the soul, comes perilously close to presenting disembodied contemplation of God as the *summum bonum* (Latin for "highest good"). In our mortal life, writes Aquinas, we need

> the body, both for the operation of contemplative virtue, and for the operation of active virtue.... On the other hand, such goods as these are nowise necessary for perfect Happiness, which consists in seeing God. The reason of this is that all suchlike external goods are requisite either for the support of the animal body; or for certain operations which belong to human life, which we perform by means of the animal body: whereas that perfect Happiness which consists in seeing God [known as the beatific vision], will be either in the soul separated from the body, or in the soul united to the body then no longer

animal but spiritual. . . . Since, in this life, the felicity of contemplation, as being more God-like, approaches nearer than that of action to the likeness of that perfect Happiness, therefore it stands in less need of these goods of the body as stated in *Ethic* x. 8.[1]

Aquinas is correct to speak of our resurrection body as a spiritual one (1 Cor 15:44), but the power of Aristotle's logic carries him to the edge of imagining heaven as disembodied souls in perpetual contemplation. If the soul no longer needs the external goods of the body to pursue its contemplation of God, then what need is there for our body to be resurrected at all?

Shall it be said, then, that Aristotle led later Christians astray toward a gnostic view of the body as a thing to be discarded on the way to spiritual enlightenment? I do not believe so. The legacy that Aristotle passed down to Aquinas and to all those influenced by Aquinas was rather one of spiritual growth, an evolution of soul and body that is neither materialistic nor the product of an unguided process of time and chance.

THE SOULS OF PLANTS AND ANIMALS

To understand how this may be, we must consider one of Aristotle's strangest teachings, a teaching that is sure to strike modern ears, especially modern Christian ears, as bizarre and fantastical. Aristotle believed that plants and animals, as well as human beings, had souls. That does not mean that he thought there would be animals in heaven or that plants and animals are moral agents. He meant instead that all living things possess an actualizing form (or soul) that animates the matter of the plant or animal or human.

The lowest form of soul, Aristotle taught his students, is the vegetable soul; it is the force behind life, nutrition, and reproduction. The sensitive animal soul provides all of these but adds to them, in ascending order of complexity, motion, desire, perception, and thought. At the apex is the rational human soul, which has all of the above but with the vital addition of reason and understanding.

The modern evolutionist will be tempted to plot a Darwinian course of evolution from one soul to the next, but that is not the paradigm Aristotle suggests. Indeed, it is fair to say he rejected it, since a proto-Darwinian model

---

[1]Thomas Aquinas, *Summa of the Summa*, ed. and annotated by Peter Kreeft (San Francisco: Ignatius, 1990), I-II, q. 4, art. 7 (pp. 389-90).

was available to him from Democritus and the atomists, who believed that the arbitrary collisions of atoms falling through the void randomly assembled themselves into all the building blocks of life. Had he wanted to construct an evolutionary model, he would have given primacy to plant, animal, and human matter, allowing the matter to evolve souls of increasing complexity. Instead, he makes it clear that the "soul is the cause or source of the living body" in three distinct ways: "It is (a) the source or origin of movement, it is (b) the end [telos], it is (c) the essence of the whole living body" (II.4; 415b8-11).

Aristotle, as I argued in chapter seven, stands (anachronistically) in opposition to Sartre's belief that existence (matter/body) precedes essence (form/soul). Throughout his work, Aristotle insists that our immaterial, nonphysical soul exists prior—in time, in purpose, and in essence—to our material, physical body. In all things, Aristotle explains,

> the essence is identical with the ground of its being, and here, in the case of living things, their being is to live, and of their being and their living the soul in them is the cause or source. . . . Nature, like mind, always does whatever it does for the sake of something, which something is its end [telos]. . . . All natural bodies are organs of the soul. This is true of those that enter into the constitution of plants as well as of those which enter into that of animals. This shows that that for the sake of which they are is soul. (II.4; 415b15-20)

The body exists *for* the soul, and there is a fittedness between the two that does not allow for any kind of transmigration from one to the other. Although there is an upward gradation from vegetable to sensitive to rational souls, each soul/body composite is unique. Again, body exists for soul, and not vice versa—as would be the case if bodies evolved and then, somehow or other, evolved themselves a soul to match.

ARISTOTLE AGAINST EVOLUTION

To demonstrate that I am not putting biblical concepts into Aristotle's mouth or trying to mold him into a special creationist, consider this remarkable passage from *On the Parts of Animals*.

> For the process of evolution [or coming-to-be] is for the sake of the thing finally evolved [or being], and not this [being] for the sake of the process

[evolution or coming-to-be]. Empedocles, then, was in error when he said that many of the characters presented by animals were merely the results of incidental occurrences during their development; for instance, that the backbone was divided as it is into vertebrae, because it happened to be broken owing to the contorted position of the foetus in the womb. In so saying he overlooked the fact that propagation implies a creative seed endowed with certain formative properties. Secondly, he neglected another fact, namely, that the parent animal pre-exists, not only in idea, but actually in time. For man is generated from man; and thus it is the possession of certain characters by the parent that determines the development of like characters in the child. (I.1; 640a18-28)

As in *On the Soul*, Aristotle makes clear that being (essence, form, actuality) precedes becoming (existence, matter, potentiality). Aristotle rejects the materialism of both Democritus and Empedocles to assert that the adult chicken, not the egg, comes first and sets the creative matrix for what will develop, or evolve, into the baby chick.

Although Aristotle does not echo the special creation of Genesis, in which God forms the dust into the first man and then breathes life (soul) into him (Gen 2:7), he does insist that life comes before lifelessness, soul before body, creative, formative activity before passive, unconscious matter. And, it cannot be stressed too strongly, each soul/body composite is singular and unique, not random and arbitrary. That indeed is one of the chief reasons Aristotle cannot accept Plato's Forms. There is no single, abstract definition of Soul (with a capital S), for every soul is fitted to its singular body.

It is, Aristotle argues in *On the Soul*,

absurd in this and similar cases to demand an absolutely general definition [of soul] which will fail to express the peculiar nature of anything that is, or again, omitting this, to look for separate definitions corresponding to each *infima species* [the lowest, most specific species in the chain of classification].... Hence we must ask in the case of each order of living things, What is its soul, i.e. What is the soul of plant, animal, man? (II.3; 414b24-34)

There is no reincarnation in Aristotle, as there is in the myths of Plato, from one human to another; there is especially no reincarnation from the bodies of animal to those of men or vice versa. Vegetable souls cannot evolve into sensitive souls any more than rational souls can de-evolve into sensitive souls. Each pairing of soul and body is its own, unique *infima species*.

It may seem that Aristotle's rejection here of Plato's theory of the Forms offers proof that Aristotle subscribed to a relativistic worldview that sees only particular things in the world, disconnected from anything universal or eternal. In fact, Aristotle held to something far more interesting. He affirmed the existence of what might be called particular universals, souls that are primary and transcendent because they exist prior to and apart from bodies but each of which is fitted hylomorphically to a single body. Although I think and interact with reality as a Platonic Christian, I must concede that on this point, Aristotle comes closer to Christianity than his great master.

PLATO VERSUS ARISTOTLE ON THE PARTS OF THE SOUL

In *Republic* IV, Plato famously depicts the soul as tripartite: having a rational part that is wise, logical, and ordered, an appetitive part that is intemperate, irrational, and disordered, and a spirited part that, when it courageously comes to the proper defense of the rational part, brings harmony to the soul. This internal harmony Plato equates with justice. In *On the Soul*, Aristotle rejects Plato's schema for two major reasons.

> The problem at once presents itself, in what sense we are to speak of parts of the soul, or how many we should distinguish. For in a sense there is an infinity of parts: it is not enough to distinguish, with some thinkers [Plato], the calculative [rational], the passionate [spirited], and the desiderative [appetitive], or with others the rational and the irrational; for if we take the dividing lines followed by these thinkers we shall find parts far more distinctly separated from one another than these, namely those we have just mentioned: (1) the nutritive, which belongs both to plants and to all animals, and (2) the sensitive, which cannot easily be classed as either irrational or rational; further (3) the imaginative . . . and lastly (4) the appetitive. (III.9; 432a22-432b3)

Just as Aristotle posits a multitude of different souls to be fitted to each distinct body, so here he finds the notion of there being only three parts to the soul too limiting to define the multifaceted nature of the human psyche.

That, however, is not the only problem Aristotle has with Plato's tripartite soul. If, Aristotle argues, "the soul is tripartite appetite [or desire] will be found in all three parts" (III.9; 432b7). Appetite/desire cannot be confined to one part of the soul, for appetite/desire affects, for good or ill, all parts of the soul. Indeed, desire is what drives the soul toward or away from something; as such, it is the mover of the soul, which is the mover of the body: "No animal moves except by compulsion unless it has an impulse towards or away from an object" (III.9; 432b16-17).

This is no small matter for Aristotle, who throughout his body of work seeks to identify the cause or origin of motion. The universe, as we saw in chapter nine, is moved by the love of the primum mobile for the Unmoved Mover. As for the soul, it is moved by desire, together with thought and imagination, but desire (or appetite) is the foundational cause and leads to the others:

> For the object of appetite starts a movement and as a result of that thought gives rise to movement.... So too when imagination originates movement, it necessarily involves appetite.... Mind is never found producing movement without appetite ... but appetite can originate movement contrary to calculation, for desire is a form of appetite. (III.10; 433a18-26)

Apart from desire, there is no movement, though desire can give way to thought and imagination. The rational and spirited parts of Plato's tripartite soul may be actual parts, but they cannot move without the desire that Plato confines to the appetitive part.

So far, so good, but Aristotle includes a caveat about the soulical forces of desire, thought, and imagination. Thought, Aristotle writes, "is always right, but appetite and imagination may be either right or wrong. That is why, though in any case it is the object of appetite which originates movement, this object may be either the real or the apparent good" (III.10; 433a26-28). Desire, like imagination, is not always reliable and may be mistaken about its object: whether it is good or bad and whether it exists or not.

Because of this distinction, reason and appetite (desire) can, as they do in Plato's tripartite soul, fall into conflict. "Appetites run counter to one another, which happens when a principle of reason and a desire are contrary and is possible only in beings with a sense of time (for while mind bids us hold back because of what is future, desire is influenced by what is just at hand" (III.10; 433b5-8). In case it is not clear in the passage, the kind of psychomachia (Greek for "soul war") described here can only take place in a human (rational) soul. The same desires that can lead us toward good can lead us astray, especially when we, driven by desire, look only to the present moment and ignore all future consequences.

PUSHING AND PULLING IN THE SOUL AND THE COSMOS

In *Physics*, Aristotle, unaware of the laws of gravitation that would not be discovered for another two millennia, argues that all things in the universe move by pushing or pulling. That is ultimately the reason Aristotle had to construct an elaborate system of concentric spheres fixed in crystal. Only if one heavenly body can push against or be pulled by another heavenly body can motion find its way from the heavenly to the earthly sphere.

In *On the Soul*, Aristotle locates within the soul of each individual person the same forces of push and pull that move the physical bodies of heaven and earth:

> For everything is moved by pushing and pulling. Hence just as in the case of a wheel, so here there must be a point which remains at rest, and from that point the movement must originate. . . . Inasmuch as an animal is capable of appetite it is capable of self-movement; it is not capable of appetite without possessing imagination; and all imagination is either (1) calculative [rational] or (2) sensitive. In the latter all animals, and not only man, partake. (III.10; 433b25-30)

The same desires, and even some of the same imaginings, that move animals also move men, but only man can deliberate over his desires and decide whether to follow desire or reason, the pleasures of the moment or the promises of the future.

If I seem to be belaboring this point, it is only because it is essential not only to Aristotle's view of the soul but to his view of ethics, which will be the focus of the next four chapters. It is out of the struggle between desire and reason, the present and the future, imagination and deliberation that we live and act as moral agents whose decisions and behaviors both emerge from the soul and help to shape it. Paul and Peter both felt that pushing and pulling, that tugging and twisting, in their own attempts to live a life of virtue: "The good that I would I do not: but the evil which I would not, that I do" (Rom 7:19); "He that will love life, and see good days, let him refrain his tongue from evil, and his lips that they speak no guile" (1 Pet 3:10).

12

VIRTUE AS HABIT

Whenever I am asked which of Aristotle's books is the most necessary to read and the most relevant to today, I always answer *Nicomachean Ethics*. As an English professor, I am aware of the historical importance and personal significance of Aristotle's *Poetics*, and I will have much to say of that influential book later. Nevertheless, it is his *Ethics* that has exerted the most profound impact, both on those who specifically identify as Christian and those who celebrate our wider Western tradition. Alongside Plato's *Republic*, Aristotle's *Ethics* has been responsible for forming the Western world's sense of virtue—particularly courage, self-control, wisdom, and justice—and teaching us how one is to live and grow as a moral agent.

THE CHIEF END OF MAN

Before defining the nature and function of virtue, Aristotle pauses to do what he does in nearly all his books: identify the proper end (telos) of virtue, which in this case is equivalent to the chief end, or good, of man. As he does so often, he begins by situating himself in relation to Plato. Unlike his master, Aristotle will not seek out the good of man as something remote and abstract. He will not argue (deductively) *from* the Form of the Good but (inductively) toward an understanding of the chief end of man and of how one should act to best achieve that end.

In *Republic* X (see 595c), Plato says, through Socrates, that though he has loved and revered Homer since he was a boy, his allegiance to philosophy compels him to honor truth above Homer. In imitation of this passage, Aristotle explains why he must forsake Plato's Forms in his pursuit of the chief end, or universal good:

> We had perhaps better consider the universal good and discuss thoroughly what is meant by it, although such an inquiry is made an uphill one by the fact that the Forms have been introduced by friends of our own. Yet it would perhaps be thought to be better, indeed to be our duty, for the sake of maintaining the truth even to destroy what touches us closely, especially as we are philosophers or lovers of wisdom; for, while both are dear, piety requires us to honour truth above our friends. (I.6; 1096a11-16)

Aristotle, like Plato, is not someone who plays with philosophy. Truth matters; it calls for commitment, sacrifice, and a willingness to follow the argument wherever it leads. In this book, Aristotle will sing the praises of friendship like few writers before or after him, and yet he will not allow his friendship with Plato to deter him from the path of truth.

His main reason for parting company with Plato on this point is his desire to offer practical—and *achievable*—advice on how to live a life of virtue: "Even if [as Plato taught] there is some one good which is universally predicable of goods or is capable of separate and independent existence, clearly it could not be achieved or attained by man; but we are now seeking something attainable" (I.6; 1096b33-35). That is why, in sharp contrast to Plato, Aristotle does not measure earthly justice and temperance against ethereal Forms of Justice and Temperance that exist in an inaccessible World of Being. No, Aristotle teaches, actions "are called just and temperate when they are such as the just or the temperate man would do" (II.4; 1105b5-6).[1]

As our role model for just action should be a just man rather than an unattainable ideal, so should the chief end of man be something achievable by all people no matter their trade or situation in life. It should also be something that cannot be taken away by others and that "is always desirable in itself and never for the sake of something else." That something Aristotle identifies as happiness (*eudaimonia* in Greek: "well-being" or "good-spirited"): "For this we choose always for itself and never for the sake of something else, but honour, pleasure, reason, and every virtue we choose indeed for themselves . . . but we choose them also for the sake of happiness, judging that by means of them we shall be happy" (I.7; 1097a34-1097b5).

---

[1] It may be that such Aristotelian reasoning impelled Paul to invite Christians to imitate him as perhaps a more achievable role model than Christ (see, for example, 1 Cor 4:15-16; 11:1; Phil 3:17; 4:9; 2 Thess 3:7-9).

Notice that although Aristotle follows an inductive rather than deductive process to arrive at happiness as the chief end of man, he does, when he arrives there, identify happiness as the universal good toward which human life should aim. Aristotle may have had problems with the Forms as theorized by Plato, but he was no denier of absolutes and transcendentals. Indeed, just before identifying happiness as the chief end, he makes clear that "not all ends are final ends; but the chief good is evidently something final. Therefore, if there is only one final end, this will be what we are seeking, and if there are more than one, the most final of these will be what we are seeking.... Therefore we call final without qualification that which is always desirable in itself and never for the sake of something else" (I.7; 1097a27-34). Happiness is not one of many ends; it is the chief end.[2]

TRAINING THE SOUL IN VIRTUE

What, then, is the nature of this virtue that can help us achieve the universal good of happiness? Aristotle identifies two types of virtue, intellectual and moral, with the first learned through education and the second acquired by habit. It is the second type of virtue that Aristotle focuses on for most of the *Ethics*, but he makes it clear that both types are gained through human effort and training. Although Aristotle was a scientist who explored and classified the unchanging laws of nature, when it came to virtue, he knew that he was dealing with something that was, quite literally, unnatural.

Unlike nature, which follows laws over which it has no control, man chooses whether he will pursue a life of virtue or vice:

---

[2]To keep this book to a reasonable length, I have chosen neither to use Aristotle to rebut all the "isms" that have, at least to my mind, stood in tension with the Christian worldview, nor to provide a full reception history of Aristotle's ideas on the soul, virtue, and other related matters. Had I the time and space, I would set Aristotle in opposition to nominalism (which teaches that words such as *justice* and *wisdom* are particular names rather than universal essences) and deconstructionism (a postmodern school with roots in the Sophists that teaches that words are merely signifiers that cannot be traced back to any universal, eternal, transcendental signifieds). Despite his disagreements with Plato's theory of the Forms, Aristotle believed firmly that words have meaning and can embody real goodness, truth, and beauty. Had I further time and space, I would consider the ever expanding modern theories, beginning with René Descartes, that have been put forward to account for the relationship between body and soul, and trace the many schools of virtue ethics that have followed in Aristotle's wake: from the Stoic ethics of Marcus Aurelius, to the duty ethics (deontology) of Immanuel Kant, to the utilitarian ethics of such thinkers as Jeremy Bentham and John Stuart Mill.

> None of the moral virtues arises in us by nature; for nothing that exists by nature can form a habit contrary to its nature. For instance the stone which by nature moves downwards cannot be habituated to move upwards, not even if one tries to train it by throwing it up ten thousand times; nor can fire be habituated to move downwards, nor can anything else that by nature behaves in one way be trained to behave in another.... The virtues we get by first exercising them, as also happens in the case of the arts as well. For the things we have to learn before we can do them, we learn by doing them, e.g. men become builders by building and lyre-players by playing the lyre; so too we become just by doing just acts, temperate by doing temperate acts, brave by doing brave acts. (II.1; 1103a20-1103b2)

Earth and fire, as we saw in chapter ten, have no choice but to fall toward the center and move away from the center. Only man possesses the ability to resist the force of nature and move in a different direction: either toward or away from goodness and virtue.

A just man is one who acts in a just manner, but he can only *become* a just man by habitually choosing to make just decisions and perform just deeds. Nature may endow us with physical strength or an aptitude for playing the lyre, but we can only transform that endowment or aptitude into the virtue of courage or the skill of lyre playing by exercising that virtue or skill diligently until it becomes a habit, a part of who we are. Being a virtuous man and doing virtuous actions are self-reinforcing activities:

> By abstaining from pleasures we become temperate, and it is when we have become so that we are most able to abstain from them; and similarly too in the case of courage; for by being habituated to despise things that are terrible and to stand our ground against them we become brave, and it is when we have become so that we shall be most able to stand our ground against them. (II.2; 1104a34-1104b3)

This self-reinforcing cycle of virtue marks the polar opposite of a vicious circle, though it can become that if we allow vicious choices and actions to slowly transform us into vicious people. A true education in virtue must begin when one is young by training the child to feel pleasure when he acts virtuously and pain when he acts viciously. In this vital detail, Aristotle agrees fully with what Plato teaches in *Republic* and *Laws*: "We ought to have been brought up in a particular way from our very youth, as Plato says, so as both to delight in and to be pained by the things that we ought; for this is the right education" (II.3; 1104b11-12). For Aristotle, virtue is built up by habit, but it finds its telos in the formation of a certain state of character that, having been properly trained and habituated, naturally chooses virtue over vice and feels proper pleasure at the choice.

C. S. LEWIS'S ARISTOTELIAN VISION OF VIRTUE

Here is how C. S. Lewis expresses and explains the same point in Christian terms in *Mere Christianity*:

> A man who perseveres in doing just actions gets in the end a certain quality of character. Now it is that quality rather than the particular actions which we mean when we talk of "virtue." . . . We might think that, provided you did the right thing, it did not matter how or why you did it—whether you did it willingly or unwillingly, sulkily or cheerfully, through fear of public opinion or for its own sake. But the truth is that right actions done for the wrong reason do not help to build the internal quality or character called a "virtue," and it is this quality or character that really matters. . . . We might think that God wanted simply obedience to a set of rules: whereas He really wants people of a particular sort.[3]

When the prophet Samuel cannot understand why God does not choose the tall and powerful elder son of Jesse as his anointed ruler, God explains to him, "The LORD seeth not as man seeth; for man looketh on the outward appearance, but the LORD looketh on the heart" (1 Sam 16:7).

It is the heart, Lewis explains, that God is most concerned with: not the heart as a source of feeling and emotion but as the center of the will. God wants certain kinds of people who will do virtuous deeds, not people who act virtuously for show while their heart is far away from God. But the only way the heart can become properly focused and attuned to virtue is by performing the right actions in the right way for the right motives. When we obey God, that obedience shapes our hearts in the same way that virtuous behaviors do—when they are done for their own sake rather than for reward or applause.

---

[3]C. S. Lewis, *Mere Christianity* (New York: Macmillan, 1960), III.2 (p. 77).

Lewis, like me, was a firm Christian Platonist, and yet he understood—and I wholeheartedly agree with him—that when it comes to the subject of virtue, Aristotle is an even better guide for the Christian than Plato. Indeed, throughout book III of *Mere Christianity*, which is titled "Christian Behaviour" and which concerns itself with living the Christian life, Lewis relies as much on Aristotle—particularly as filtered through Aquinas and Dante—as he does on the Bible. He does so because, to put the matter boldly and unapologetically, Aristotle got it right! And he got something else right, too.

ARISTOTLE ON MORAL AGENCY

As much an influence on Christian virtue as he was on legal thinking in the West, Aristotle defines with acute ethical clarity and keen psychological insight the precise nature of moral agency. For a human agent to perform an action of true virtue, he "must have knowledge, secondly he must choose the acts, and choose them for their own sakes, and thirdly his action must proceed from a firm and unchangeable character" (II.4; 1105a32-34). To paraphrase James 1:22, a moral agent must be both a hearer and a doer of virtue; he must understand fully the nature of his choice and then put that choice into action. In fact, Aristotle, somewhat sarcastically, compares philosophers who think they will become virtuous merely by studying virtue to "patients who listen attentively to their doctors, but do none of the things they are ordered to do" (II.4; 1105b15-16). Let us not forget James's sobering comparison of nondoing hearers to demons: "Thou believest that there is one God; thou doest well: the devils also believe, and tremble" (Jas 2:19).

"God is not mocked," warns Paul in Galatians 6:7, "for whatsoever a man soweth, that shall he also reap." For Aristotle, as for the Bible, the manner in which a person does something (the means) is as important as the end. Virtue is a complicated thing that calls for intellectual, emotional, and spiritual discernment of a high order. It is easy, writes Aristotle, to "give or spend money; but to do this to the right person, to the right extent, at the right time, with the right motive, and in the right way, that is not for every one, nor is it easy; wherefore goodness is both rare and laudable and noble" (II.9; 1109a26-29).

We who live on this side of Aristotle and Jesus may consider this statement to be an obvious one. But it was not obvious until Aristotle stated it, and it lacked the power to change the world until Jesus preached its proper use in the Sermon on the Mount (Mt 5–7) and exposed its misuse by the hypocritical scribes and Pharisees (Mt 23). Attitudes matter as much as words; motives matter as much as deeds. Whether we act in ignorance or with knowledge, in the heat of passion or after cold calculation, matters as much to God as it does to a human judge. Moral agency is a heavy burden to bear and should not be taken lightly.

As an ethicist of the highest order, Aristotle taught Greece, then Europe, and then the world to attend carefully to whether the deeds of people accused of misconduct were committed voluntarily or involuntarily, freely or as a result of compulsion. He taught us the right questions to ask and the right circumstances to take into account. A modern Supreme Court judge could speak these words, and they would not seem out of place: "Acting by reason of ignorance seems also to be different from acting *in* ignorance; for the man who is drunk or in a rage is thought to act as a result not of ignorance but of one of the causes mentioned, yet not knowingly but in ignorance" (III.1; 1110b24-26). The drunk driver who kills someone in an accident did not do so voluntarily, but he did choose to drink and drive, and that makes him a responsible agent, even if it was the alcohol that impaired his senses and caused him to swerve unwittingly into another car.[4]

ARISTOTLE AND LEWIS ON HOW OUR CHOICES SHAPE OUR CHARACTER

Carefully and systematically, as if he were cataloguing every variety of a plant or animal species, Aristotle works his way through various cases in which ignorance does or does not release a person from moral culpability. Along the way, he makes an incisive distinction between a wish and a choice,

---

[4]The influence of Aristotle's musings on the nature of moral agency can be glimpsed in §2.02 of the Model Penal Code: "A person is not guilty of an offense unless he acted purposely, knowingly, recklessly or negligently, as the law may require, with respect to each material element of the offense." This can be read online at www1.law.umkc.edu/suni/CrimLaw/MPC_Provisions/model_penal_code_default_rules.htm. My thanks to my friend and colleague John Tyler for sharing this link with me. He also shared with me this connection between Aristotelian thought and Anglo-American law: "By the time of Coke, the maxim '*actus non facit reum nisi mens sit rea*' (an act does not make one guilty unless his mind is guilty) had become well ingrained in the common law, and it remains a central precept of Anglo-American criminal law today." Martin R. Gardner, "The Mens Rea Enigma: Observations on the Role of Motive in the Criminal Law Past and Present," *Utah Law Review* (1993): 635-36.

and another between a choice and an opinion, that has both moral and legal implications. Wishes, he explains, are related to ends, while choices are related to means. For example, "We wish to be healthy, but we choose the acts which will make us healthy, and we wish to be happy and say we do, but we cannot well say we choose to be so; for, in general, choice seems to relate to the things that are in our own power" (III.2; 1111b27-29). While wishes can transport us to lands of impossibility, choices rest in our own world of possibilities.

It is the same with choices and opinions. Since opinions, too, can be possible or impossible, they involve issues of right and wrong, truth and falsehood. Not so choice, which involves issues of good and bad, virtue and vice: "By choosing what is good or bad we are men of a certain character, which we are not by holding certain opinions" (III.2; 1112a1-2). It is the choices we make, not the wishes we imagine or the opinions we toy with, that shape our character. Or, to quote Lewis again, who does not have to work hard to take Aristotle's meditations on virtue, choice, and character up a notch into the fuller revelation of Christ and the New Testament:

> Every time you make a choice you are turning the central part of you, the part of you that chooses, into something a little different from what it was before. And taking your life as a whole, with all your innumerable choices, all your life long you are slowly turning this central thing either into a heavenly creature or into a hellish creature: either into a creature that is in harmony with God, and with other creatures, and with itself, or else into one that is in a state of war and hatred with God, and with its fellow-creatures, and with itself. To be the one kind of creature is heaven: that is, it is joy and peace and knowledge and power. To be the other means madness, horror, idiocy, rage, impotence, and eternal loneliness. Each of us at each moment is progressing to the one state or the other.[5]

Aristotle did not develop a doctrine of heaven and hell, but Lewis's extrapolation of what a virtuous or vicious state of character might look like when drawn out to eternity is true to Aristotle's ethical and psychological vision. For Aristotle and Lewis alike, virtue and vice are not things we do but

---

[5] Lewis, *Mere Christianity*, III.4 (p. 86).

WHY VIRTUE AND VICE ARE DIFFERENT FROM KNOWLEDGE AND IGNORANCE

Before closing this chapter, I would like to highlight a key moment in *Ethics* when Aristotle clarifies a major difference between himself and Plato, a difference that to my mind marks one of the few errors in Plato's thought. "The saying [by Plato]," writes Aristotle, "that 'no one is voluntarily wicked nor involuntarily happy' seems to be partly false and partly true; for no one is involuntarily happy, but wickedness is voluntary. Or else we shall have to dispute what has just been said, at any rate, and deny that man is a moving principle or begetter of his actions as of children" (III.5; 1113b14-18). If wickedness is nothing more than a manifestation of human ignorance as to the true nature of virtue and vice, then Aristotle's treatise might just as well be tossed in the fire.

Evil *is* evil precisely *because* we practice it knowingly. If that were not the case, then there would be no need for judges, juries, or prisons. Both morality and the legal system rest on the belief that we are morally responsible agents. If a judge were to determine that we performed a wicked deed in ignorance, he would either set us free, if he thought our ignorance *of the situation* absolved us of guilt, or place us in an asylum, if he thought that our ignorance *of right and wrong* exposed us as a sociopath incapable of dwelling freely among other people.

Again, evaluating ethics is a tricky business that calls for a careful sifting of the evidence to determine when someone deserves our pity and when our blame. Here are two hypothetical cases that Aristotle constructs to make clear the distinction:

- While no one blames those who are ugly by nature, we blame those who are so owing to want of exercise and care.
- No one would reproach a man blind from birth or by disease or from a blow, but rather pity him, while every one would blame a man who

was blind from drunkenness or some other form of self-indulgence. (III.5; 1114a23-31)

Because basic human nature has not changed, these examples could have been written today and understood as readily as they were in the fourth century BC. Or, to be more precise, they can be better understood today because our understanding of blame and pity has been so strongly shaped, *for the better*, by Aristotle's *Ethics*.

In keeping with Aristotle, we can feel opposite emotions toward two people who commit the same terrible deed. Imagine two children run over by a car on two different days and in two different neighborhoods. In the first case, a bank robber attempting to escape from the police drives his car at breakneck speed through a residential area. In the second, a father pulling into his driveway is unable to see that his little girl has broken free from her mother's hand and run to meet her father's car. In both cases, an innocent child is dead, but in the first, we heap blame and righteous anger on the perpetrator, while in the second, we feel only intense sympathy and bewildered pity for the grieving father.

FATE OR FREE WILL?

Are we to say, then, that Aristotle was all right and Plato all wrong on the nature of virtue and vice, knowledge and ignorance, destiny and responsibility? We might as well ask who is right today about the nature of legal (and moral) judgment: Are criminals responsible or not for their misdeeds? Are sinners responsible or not for their sins? Do we blame society or the individual for the crime (or sin) committed? Aristotle is perhaps at his most brilliant in addressing this issue, directing his readers' attention to the case of a sick man who was once morally responsible for his condition but no longer is:

> We may suppose a case in which [a man] is ill voluntarily, through living incontinently and disobeying his doctors. In that case it was then open to him not to be ill, but not now, when he has thrown away his chance, just as when you have let a stone go it is too late to recover it; but yet it was in your power to throw it, since the moving principle was in you. So, too, to the unjust and to the self-indulgent man it was open at the beginning not to become men of

this kind, and so they are unjust and self-indulgent voluntarily; but now that they have become so it is not possible for them not to be so. (III.5; 1114a15-22)

What Aristotle shows us here is that there are many people right now, in this life, who are living in hell. If we are the sum total of our choices, if our character is formed and fixed by the thousand chisel strokes of our myriad good or bad choices, then it stands to reason that we will reach a stage when our character is so fixed that we can no longer change.

Now, if we have chosen consistently the pathway of virtue, we will find freedom and agency as we experience the true happiness that is the proper end of virtue. But if we have, by our own volition, repeatedly chosen the pathway of vice, a time will come when we lose our freedom, agency, and happiness. For, Aristotle warns, "though we control the beginning of our states of character the gradual progress is not obvious any more than it is in illnesses" (III.5;1114b33-1115a2). Aristotle may have been unaware of the Christian doctrine of hell, but he paints a picture here that is as terrifying as any hellfire preacher.

So then, does Aristotle believe that our characters and our destinies are determined by the motion of the stars and the laws of cause and effect or that we choose the people we become and the lives we lead? We might as well ask whether Scripture teaches predestination or free will. The answer is the same: both and neither. As different as they are, the treatises of Aristotle and the books of the Bible take place in a similar space where outside forces guide and control behavior without thereby robbing us of our moral-ethical status as volitional creatures.

Let us not blame Aristotle for failing to resolve with complete clarity a subject the Bible is none too clear on itself. After all, theologians from Augustine and Aquinas, to Luther and Desiderius Erasmus, to Calvin and Jacob Arminius, to Jonathan Edwards and John Wesley disagreed themselves on the proper way to interpret the scriptural view of moral agency.

13

FINDING THE GOLDEN MEAN

For the sake of organizational clarity, I skipped over in chapter twelve what may be Aristotle's best-known and most influential contribution to ethics: the concept of the golden mean. Virtue, for Aristotle, does not represent a list of moral dos and don'ts, as it too often does for Christians. Rather, it is to be defined and understood as the middle point, or mean, between two extremes. Most people understand intuitively that a good-tempered man is someone who does not give way to fits of anger. Fewer realize that he is also not someone who shows a total lack of concern in the face of injustice. The virtue of good temper lies in the mean between its lack (insensibility) and its excess (anger). Jesus' showing patience and mercy to the prostitutes and tax collectors while turning over the tables of the moneychangers in the temple might be an example of just such a mean.

With this missing ingredient, I can now give Aristotle's full definition of virtue: "Virtue, then, is a state of character concerned with choice, lying in a mean, i.e. the mean relative to us, this being determined by a rational principle, and by that principle by which the man of practical wisdom would determine it" (II.6; 1106b36-117a3). As we saw above, Aristotle's measure of virtue is not Plato's Form of Virtue but a virtuous man; it concerns practical choices made by a rational human being that culminate in the formation of a virtuous state of character. What the golden mean—Aristotle simply called it the mean—adds to this definition is a method for determining where we stand on the spectrum between excess and deficiency.

THE SEVEN VIRTUES

Here is how Aristotle applies his measure of the mean to the virtues of courage and temperance:

> The man who flies from and fears everything and does not stand his ground against anything becomes a coward, and the man who fears nothing at all but goes to meet every danger becomes rash; and similarly the man who indulges in every pleasure and abstains from none becomes self-indulgent, while the man who shuns every pleasure, as boors do, becomes in a way insensible; temperance and courage, then, are destroyed by excess and defect, and preserved by the mean. (II.2; 1104a21-26)

Just as true courage is to be found in the midpoint between cowardice (defect) and rashness (excess), so true temperance stands in the gap between the defect of self-indulgence and the excess of boorish asceticism. While this mean should not be confused with ethical relativism, it does allow for some variability based on the specific situation. A Christian might think here of Rahab, who lied to protect the spies, an act that saved the lives of her family (Josh 2:18), earned her a spot in the genealogy of Christ (Mt 1:5), and won her commendation as a hero of faith (Heb 11:31). Context here makes all the difference between breaking one of God's commandments and earning his approval. Just so, to call back my example from the previous chapter, the two men who ran over a child elicited from us opposite responses (blame, pity) because the context of the killing was radically different.

The passage just quoted highlights courage (*fortitude* in Latin) and self-control (temperance), two of four classical virtues—the other two are wisdom (prudence) and justice—that Christian thinkers for two thousand years have identified as the chief virtues of the pre-Christian, Greco-Roman world and that first appear, in full form, in Plato's *Republic* and Aristotle's *Ethics*. In *City of God* XIX.4, Augustine lists and defines the four virtues; earlier, in XIII.21, he even suggests that the four rivers of Eden can be allegorized to represent the classical virtues.

Aquinas lists the same four virtues and links them to different powers of the soul: prudence to the rational, justice to the volitional (will), temperance to the appetitive (concupiscence), fortitude to the spirited (irascible; see

Summa I-II, question 61, article 2). But Augustine and Aquinas are only two of many church fathers who identified the four classical virtues with the highest pagan philosophers: Socrates, Plato, Aristotle, and Cicero, along with the higher Stoics and Neoplatonists.

What distinguishes the four classical virtues from the three theological virtues of faith, hope, and love (charity) is that the latter came by way of special revelation (God speaking directly through Jesus and the Bible), while the former came by way of general revelation (God speaking indirectly through creation, conscience, and reason), from those whom Dante called virtuous pagans. In his treatment of the classical virtues, Aristotle often demonstrates a penetrating ethical insight that at times rivals the moral, though not the theological, teachings of the Bible.

ARISTOTLE AND THE NEW TESTAMENT ON THE TRUE NATURE OF COURAGE AND LIBERALITY

Passion, Aristotle writes, "is sometimes reckoned as courage; those who act from passion, like wild beasts rushing at those who have wounded them, are thought to be brave, because brave men also are passionate; for passion above all things is eager to rush on danger" (III.8; 1116b24-27). Such is the common opinion, but Aristotle disagrees. True courage must be allied with knowledge, or passion will take over and the would-be brave man will sink to the level of an irrational beast. Pugnacious people, too, are "not brave; for they do not act for honour's sake nor as the rule directs, but from strength of feeling." Neither "are sanguine people brave; for they are confident in danger only because they have conquered often and against many foes" (III.8; 1117a8-11). The man of courage acts deliberately, not rashly, knowing what is at stake and what he might lose.

Aristotle is not interested in the appearance of courage or even in the emotions that often accompany it. He is interested in motives, in deliberation, in character. I think he would have understood well Jesus' commendation of the poor widow who put two mites into the temple collection box. In monetary terms her donation was small, but unlike the showy, nonsacrificial giving of the rich, it represented all that she had to live on (see Mk 12:41-44). Jesus saw through the rash protestations of Peter at the Last Supper, as I think

Aristotle would have. Peter said he would die for Christ, but he did not know fully what that meant or what it would involve. Yet, Jesus saw something else in Peter, something Aristotle likely would have missed: that he would find his courage in the end and lead the disciples (see Lk 22:31-34).

In his discussion of liberality, which is closely allied to temperance, Aristotle shows his awareness that "God loveth a cheerful giver" (2 Cor 9:7) and that it "is more blessed to give than to receive" (Acts 20:35): "the liberal man, like other virtuous men, will give for the sake of the noble, and rightly; for he will give to the right people, the right amounts, and at the right time, with all the other qualifications that accompany right giving; and that too with pleasure or without pain; for that which is virtuous is pleasant or free from pain" (IV.1; 1120a24-28). Aristotle further understood that "liberality resides not in the multitude of the gifts but in the state of character of the giver" (IV.1; 1120b7-8). The truly liberal man knows the value of money but does not value it as an end in itself. It does not control him; he controls it.

DANTE ON THE GOLDEN MEAN

As a virtue, liberality lies between the extremes of miserliness (deficiency) and prodigality (excess). Although Aristotle treats prodigality as the less bad of the two extremes, for it is more closely allied to folly than to meanness, he does show how both can ruin the man who indulges in them. In his arrangement of the levels of hell, Dante consciously incorporates Aristotle's understanding of virtue as the mean between the extremes. Thus, in level four of hell (*Inferno* VII), Dante punishes the misers and the prodigals *together*, for both are guilty of the same sin. Though some hoarded their wealth while others wasted it, both showed themselves to be incontinent in terms of the possessions gifted to them by their Creator.

Dante follows the same Aristotelian paradigm in level five (*Inferno* VIII), punishing in the same swamp (Styx) the wrathful and the sullen: those who perverted the virtue of good temper by either overindulging it in the form of wrath or underindulging it in the form of sloth. Like those in the previous level, they are incontinent, for they have twisted a good thing into a bad by taking it to an unhealthy extreme. Aristotle defines "the incontinent man" as one who, "knowing that what he does is bad, does it as a result of passion"

(VII.2; 1145b12-13). That is to say, the incontinent man knowingly does that which harms him by following his desires to a self-destructive excess.

INCONTINENCE AND MALICE

In making such a statement, Aristotle cannot help but bring up again his major ethical disagreement with his master and his master's master: "Socrates was entirely opposed to the view in question, holding that there is no such thing as incontinence; no one, he said, when he judges acts against what he judges best—people act so only by reason of ignorance. Now this view plainly contradicts the observed facts" (VII.2; 1145b25-28). Observation proves beyond a shadow of a doubt that people often act in ways that injure them, even and especially when they know that the behavior is injuring them. Aristotle identifies three scenarios—when we are asleep, mad, or drunk—when we simultaneously know and do not know what is best for us, and then makes the necessary connection to incontinence: "Outbursts of anger and sexual appetites and some other such [incontinent] passions, it is evident, actually alter our bodily condition, and in some men even produce fits of madness. It is plain, then, that incontinent people must be said to be in a similar condition to men asleep, mad, or drunk" (VII.3; 1147a15-18).

Of course, as with the case of the drunk driver in the previous chapter, the drunk man is still liable before the law because he voluntarily caused the drunkenness that led him involuntarily to cause the accident. Judgment, reason, and volition are all involved and make him a responsible agent in his crime. In contrast, "the lower animals are not incontinent . . . because they have no universal judgement but only imagination and memory of particulars" (VIII.3; 1147b4-5). The incontinent man, then, is guilty, but the crime/sin of incontinence is decidedly less bad than other forms of criminality/sin.

Those, Aristotle explains, "who are more given to plotting against others are more criminal. Now a passionate man is not given to plotting, nor is anger itself—it is open; but the nature of [malicious] appetite is illustrated by what the poets call Aphrodite, 'guile-weaving daughter of Cyprus'" (VII.7; 1149b13-16). Just as in our justice system we punish less severely a crime of passion committed in the heat of the moment than a coldblooded murder that was planned beforehand and executed with careful precision, so Aristotle ascribes less guilt and blame to incontinent anger than deceptive malice.

Though guilty of having made choices that transformed him into an incontinent person, when such a person commits a criminal or sinful act, he often does so in a fit of passion, without rationally choosing to do so. Such is not the case for the malicious deceiver who chooses carefully his criminal or sinful course of action. In keeping with this seminal distinction, Aristotle argues that "incontinence is not vice (though perhaps it is so in a qualified sense); for incontinence is contrary to choice while vice is in accordance with choice . . . so too incontinent people are not criminal, but they will do criminal acts" (VII.8; 1151a6-11). The impulsive nonchoice of the incontinent man does not absolve him from guilt, for he is the cause of his incontinent character, but it does render him less guilty than the vicious man who knowingly chooses his crime.

To make even clearer the distinction between the incontinent man and the vicious or malicious or wicked man, Aristotle constructs an analogy that is uncharacteristically vivid and memorable: "The incontinent man is like a city which passes all the right decrees and has good laws, but makes no use of them . . . but the wicked man is like a city that uses its laws, but has wicked laws to use" (VII.11; 1152a20-24). Another way of expressing this is to say that, whereas incontinent people waste away their gifts through their impulsive, passionate behavior, wicked (malicious/vicious) people pervert the gifts given to them as a means to achieve power and domination.

AQUINAS ON THE SINS OF THE FLESH AND THE SINS OF THE SOUL

In Catholic thought, this same distinction is often expressed as the (carnal) sins of the flesh versus the (spiritual) sins of the soul. Although such a distinction has firm and clear roots in the Gospels—where the incontinent prostitutes and tax collectors flock to Jesus while the malicious, self-righteous Pharisees oppose him—it was in great part formulated by Aquinas, who himself was strongly influenced by Aristotle's theories of virtue and vice. In fact, Aquinas replies to the question, "Whether the reason can be overcome by a passion, against its knowledge?" by directly engaging with *Ethics* VII.

After affirming Aristotle's rejection of Socrates's belief that virtue is knowledge and sin is ignorance, Aquinas goes on to argue, in close imitation of Aristotle, how it is possible for an incontinent man to allow his passion to so overcome his reason that he performs an act that he knows will harm him.

> A man who is in a state of passion, [often] fails to consider in particular what he knows in general, in so far as the passions hinder him from considering it.... Even as sleep or drunkenness, on account of some change wrought on the body, fetters the use of reason. That this takes place in the passions is evident from the fact that sometimes, when the passions are very intense, man loses the use of reason altogether: for many have gone out of their minds through excess of love or anger. It is in this way that passion draws the reason to judge in particular, against the knowledge which it has in general.[1]

To be clear, those who allow their passion to overcome their reason are still guilty of sin; it is just that their sin is less severe because it was not done out of malice or with the intent to harm other people. The drunk driver or the half-mad brawler who accidentally kills someone will be sentenced to prison; but his sentence will be shorter than the assassin who coldly plans and executes the murder of an enemy.

DANTE ON THE SINS OF THE FLESH AND THE SINS OF THE SOUL

Influenced by both Aristotle and Aquinas, Dante breaks hell into two levels: upper hell, where the crimes and punishments are lesser, and lower hell, where they are intensified. When Dante, in *Inferno* XI, asks his guide why this is, Virgil responds:

> Have you forgotten that your *Ethics* states
>   the three main dispositions of the soul
>   that lead to those offenses Heaven hates—
> incontinence, malice, and bestiality?
>   and how incontinence offends God least
>   and earns least blame from Justice and Charity?[2]

---

[1] Thomas Aquinas, *Summa of the Summa*, ed. and annotated by Peter Kreeft (San Francisco: Ignatius, 1990), I-II, q. 77, art. 2 (pp. 494-95).
[2] Dante, *The Divine Comedy*, trans. John Ciardi (New York: New American Library, 1970), 92.

How can you ask such a question, Virgil implies, when the answer is so clear in Aristotle! *Of course* the sins of incontinence punished in upper hell (carnality, gluttony, hoarding and wasting, wrath and sloth) are less bad than the sins of malice punished in lower hell (violence and fraud). The former are sins of the flesh, ones that take a good thing to excess, while the latter are sins of the soul, ones that pervert good things to wicked ends.

Furthermore, as Virgil explains a few lines earlier, "Malice is the sin most hated by God. / And the aim of malice is to injure others / whether by fraud or violence."[3] While the sins of incontinent people are turned against themselves, even if they often hurt others in the process, those of malice are consciously directed outward. In judging whether violence or fraud is the greater of the sins of the soul, Dante also relies on Aristotle. The latter is clearly worse, for it most involves the will and most misuses the rational part of our soul. That is why animals can be violent but not fraudulent. To commit fraud, one must possess and then pervert reason. Of those who commit fraud, the worst are the traitors, for they deceive those whom they should love. Although Dante's reasoning here lines up with the Bible, the *kind* of reasoning in which he engages, with its careful distinctions of motive and will, owes an immense debt to Aristotle's *Ethics*.

JOHN DONNE ON FREEING THE CAPTIVE SOUL

A similar kind of Aristotelian reasoning, mingled with the profound theological paradoxes of Christianity, can be found in "Holy Sonnet XIV" of British metaphysical poet John Donne (1572–1631):

> Batter my heart, three-personed God; for You
> As yet but knock, breathe, shine, and seek to mend;
> That I may rise, and stand, o'erthrow me, and bend
> Your force, to break, blow, burn, and make me new.
> I, like an usurped town, to another due,
> Labor to admit You, but Oh, to no end!
> Reason, Your viceroy in me, me should defend,
> But is captived, and proves weak or untrue.

---

[3]Dante, *Divine Comedy*, 90.

> Yet dearly I love You, and would be loved fain,
> But am betrothed unto Your enemy;
> Divorce me, untie, or break that knot again,
> Take me to You, imprison me, for I,
> Except You enthrall me, never shall be free,
> Nor ever chaste, except You ravish me.[4]

Although the pagan Aristotle would have been confused by the first four lines of Donne's sonnet, he would have understood and perhaps even sympathized with the second. Reason, the pre-Christian philosopher knew and believed, should be the captain and guiding light of our soul. Alas, our passions too often lay siege to our citadel of reason, taking it captive and preventing it from fulfilling its true calling.

Donne attributes that siege to spiritual forces, to Satan's attempt to steal us, the bride of Christ, away from our true husband. Aristotle would again have been confused by this aspect of the poem, as he would have been by the resolution in the concluding six lines, but he would have recognized the struggle, the psychomachia, that blunts and weakens the power of the soul, and would have understood the need for drastic measures to free the captive soul from its bondage to self-destructive passion.

Because of the time and place of his birth, Aristotle was ignorant of salvation by grace through faith; nevertheless, he intuited something of the process of sanctification by which our soul is increasingly set free from those sins of malice that would drag it down. That is why, ironically, the same Greek philosopher who can teach Christians little to nothing about redemption can aid those who already know Jesus to foster and practice virtues that will help them conform their souls to the image of Christ.

ARISTOTLE'S BLIND SPOT

I have argued above that Aristotle's insight into ethics often rises to the heights and the profundity of the New Testament. There is one area, however, where Aristotle's notion of virtue comes into conflict with that of Christianity.

---

[4]John Donne, "Holy Sonnet XIV," in *John Donne's Poetry*, 2nd ed., ed. Arthur Clements (New York: Norton, 1992), 115-16.

Living in the shadow of the epics of Homer and the tragedies of Sophocles, Aristotle held up as his ideal the proud man who disdains the petty concerns of the masses, scorning their mean pleasures and their vulgar applause. He is fearless in the face of danger, thinking little of his life, and asks nothing from anyone. What is more,

> It is characteristic of the proud man not to aim at the things commonly held in honour, or the things in which others excel; to be sluggish and to hold back except where great honour or a great work is at stake, and to be a man of few deeds, but of great and notable ones. He must also be open in his hate and in his love (for to conceal one's feelings, i.e. to care less for truth than for what people will think, is a coward's part), and must speak and act openly; for he is free of speech because he is contemptuous, and he is given to telling the truth, except when he speaks in irony to the vulgar. He must be unable to make his life revolve round another, unless it be a friend; for this is slavish, and for this reason all flatterers are servile and people lacking in self-respect are flatterers. Nor is he given to admiration; for nothing to him is great. Nor is he mindful of wrongs; for it is not the part of a proud man to have a long memory, especially for wrongs, but rather to overlook them. Nor is he a gossip; for he will speak neither about himself nor about another, since he cares not to be praised nor for others to be blamed; nor again is he given to praise; and for the same reason he is not an evil-speaker, even about his enemies, except from haughtiness. With regard to necessary or small matters he is least of all men given to lamentation or the asking of favours; for it is the part of one who takes such matters seriously to behave so with respect to them. He is one who will possess beautiful and profitless things rather than profitable and useful ones; for this is more proper to a character that suffices to itself. (IV.4; 1124b23-1125a13)

There is much to commend in this radically self-sufficient man. He neither boasts nor gossips nor speaks ill of others; he pursues objects that are great and noble while treating with contempt any behavior he considers beneath him. He neither follows the crowd nor caters to their flattery; he speaks openly and truthfully with no guile or subterfuge.

Here truly is a man immune to the sins of the flesh: to the carnality, gluttony, prodigality, and sloth of the incontinent masses. He does not steal what is not his, and he does not use his tongue to deceive. Yet, from the

Christian point of view, such a man risks falling into that satanic pride that theologians have long identified as the greatest of sins. Many a man, warns Lewis in *Mere Christianity*,

> has overcome cowardice, or lust, or ill-temper by learning to think that they are beneath his dignity—that is, by Pride. The devil laughs. He is perfectly content to see you becoming chaste and brave and self-controlled provided, all the time, he is setting up in you the Dictatorship of Pride—just as he would be quite content to see your chilblains cured if he was allowed, in return, to give you cancer. For Pride is spiritual cancer: it eats up the very possibility of love, or contentment, or even common sense.[5]

Pride is the spiritual sin of the soul par excellence. Because the proud man considers himself above the sins of the flesh that tempt the masses, he thinks he is righteous and pure. He is in truth motivated by arrogance, but he has so twisted his reason as to convince himself otherwise.

He is like the Pharisee in Jesus' parable who exalts himself about the lowly tax collector (publican) whom he sees lurking, humble and penitent, in the back row of the temple. Here is his boastful prayer: "God, I thank thee, that I am not as other men are, extortioners, unjust, adulterers, or even as this publican. I fast twice in the week, I give tithes of all that I possess" (Lk 18:11-12). Aristotle might see in this disdainful civic leader the noble qualities of the proud man, but Jesus makes it clear that it is not he but the repentant publican who will return home justified (Lk 18:14).

On the subject of ethics, Aristotle saw, from the point of view of Christianity, further and clearer than Plato, but he did have a blind spot that his master did not have. In *Republic* II, Plato contrasts two hypothetical men: one a perfectly unjust man who yet deceives everyone into thinking he is just; the other a perfectly just man who is falsely accused, whipped, tortured, blinded, and impaled on a spike (361b-362a). By the end of *Republic*, Plato makes it clear that the latter man is the happier one, for he is free and just in his soul rather than a prisoner of his own enslaved, unjust, inharmonious soul.

Aristotle will have none of it: "Those who say that the victim on the rack or the man who falls into great misfortunes is happy if he is good, are, whether

---

[5]C. S. Lewis, *Mere Christianity* (New York: Macmillan, 1960), III.8 (p. 112).

they mean to or not, talking nonsense" (VII.13; 1115b18-20). The author of *Ethics* can imagine a fearless warrior who dies heroically on the battlefield or a proud leader who sacrifices his pleasures lest he sink to the level of the incontinent masses. What he could not have imagined, what he could not have found a category for in his system, is a hero who dies on a cross. Plato imagined it and to a degree understood it. But not Aristotle. Such a thought would have transcended his flawless reason and faultless logic.

14

HOW TO WIN FRIENDS AND INFLUENCE PEOPLE

Despite the fact that scores of Christian philosophers and ethicists have focused on the four classical virtues, Aristotle devotes more space in his *Ethics* to the virtue of friendship than to the other four combined. His reason for doing so is made immediately clear:

> Without friends no one would choose to live, though he had all other goods; even rich men and those in possession of office and of dominating power are thought to need friends most of all; for what is the use of such prosperity without the opportunity of beneficence, which is exercised chiefly and in its most laudable form towards friends? Or how can prosperity be guarded and preserved without friends? (VIII.1; 1155a5-10)

Since the chief end of man and the goal of virtue is happiness, and since even the rich and powerful cannot secure that happiness without friends, it stands to reason that friendship is vital and to be carefully cultivated. Aristotle even goes so far as to assert that "when men are friends they have no need of justice, while when they are just they need friendship as well" (VIII.1; 1155a26-27). Friends who trust one another completely do not need to be under the rule of law, but men of good character who follow the law still need friends as the crown of life. Without someone to share one's happiness with, happiness becomes less enjoyable; without someone to help secure one's happiness, happiness becomes less stable.

FRIENDSHIP FOR ITS OWN SAKE

Which is not to say that friendship is merely a means to some other end. Like happiness, true friendship is an end in itself. We enter into it freely and mutually, for its own sake. It is true that some enter into friendship with others for the sake of utility or pleasure, but those are not the kinds of friendships that last: "If the one party is no longer pleasant or useful the other ceases to love him. . . . Perfect friendship [in contrast] is the friendship of men who are good, and alike in virtue; for these wish well alike to each other *qua* good, and they are good themselves. . . . Therefore their friendship lasts as long as they are good—and goodness is an enduring thing" (VIII.3; 1156a19-20, 1156b7-13).

Friendship for Aristotle means far more than work buddies or fraternity brothers going on a hunting trip or having a drink at the pub. To be true friends, both men must be virtuous lovers of the good who see past utility and pleasure to the inner character of the other. It is a good thing if they do activities together—indeed, if they are separated for too long, their friendship may dissolve—but true friendship is founded on something deeper than the mere feelings that often accompany love: "Love may be felt just as much towards lifeless things, but mutual love [friendship] involves choice and choice springs from a state of character; and men wish well to those whom they love, for their sake, not as a result of feeling but as a result of a state of character" (VIII.5; 1157b30-32).

Whereas animals, like humans, feel sexual desire for their mates and parental affection for their young, only human beings engage in friendship. We are drawn by instinct toward our spouses and offspring, but friendship is something we choose freely, not on the basis of a storm of emotions but on the basis of reason and virtue. That may make the matter of friendship seem one of cold calculation, but it was not so for Aristotle. He may seem at times to be almost robotic in his systematic thinking and his insistence on categorizing everything, but he was also a man of passion and feeling who understood, perhaps better than many poets, our deep need for friendship.

CAN MEN AND WOMEN BE FRIENDS?

In fact, remarkably and quite unexpectedly, Aristotle, who, like Plato, speaks of friendship exclusively in male terms, concedes that friendship is possible between a husband and a wife whose marriage bond rests on considerations of utility and pleasure:

> Between man and wife friendship seems to exist by nature; for man is naturally inclined to form couples—even more than to form cities, inasmuch as the household is earlier and more necessary than the city, and reproduction is common to man and to the animals. With the other animals the union extends only to this point, but human beings live together not only for the sake of reproduction but also for the various purposes of life; for from the start the functions are divided, and those of man and woman are different; so they help each other by throwing their peculiar gifts into the common stock. It is for these reasons that both utility and pleasure seem to be found in this kind of friendship. But this friendship may be based also on virtue, if the parties are good; for each has its own virtue and they will delight in the fact. And children seem to be a bond of union (which is the reason why childless people part more easily); for children are a good common to both and what is common holds them together. (VIII.12; 1162a16-29)

Just as many Americans have had instilled in them negative stereotypes of the Middle Ages as dark, backward, and bigoted, so most have had instilled in them a false belief that all men of the past considered their wives to be nothing more than chattel, goods and property to be used at whim. The *Iliad* and *Odyssey* alone should give the lie to this, as they present Hector and Andromache and Odysseus and Penelope as mature, faithful couples who share mutual affection. That hundreds of generations of readers have understood and identified with them substantiates that they represent recognizable realities and not merely exceptions to a general rule.

The passage I have just quoted from Aristotle offers further proof that there *were* men in ancient Greece who considered their wives to be true partners. Were it not so, Aristotle's description would have made little sense to his contemporaries. It is true that the ancient world would have to wait for Christianity to accord to women the same intellectual, emotional, and spiritual value as men—something neither Plato nor Aristotle would have understood or accepted—but that does not take away from the fact that at least some degree of mutual friendship and respect was possible and actually existed between some husbands and wives.

As I have noted before, Aristotle, unlike Plato, based much of what he wrote on common opinions held by either wise counselors or the majority of people. There is no doubt marriages in ancient Greece, as they still are in most parts of the world, were arranged with utility in mind, but that does not mean such marriages did not produce strong bonds of friendship between the spouses. Divorce rates are, after all, lower in places where marriages are arranged than in places where they are chosen on the basis of (feelings of) love.

Aristotle did not have to read Genesis 3 to understand that human marriage was something higher than the mating of animals. Both human and animal "marriage" are essential to procreation and to the rearing of young, but among humans, marriage is qualitatively, not just quantitatively, different than it is among the beasts. As we will see in part four, Aristotle was a keen social scientist who studied carefully the constitutions of his fellow Greek city-states. Yet, despite his commitment to the polis as natural to man, Aristotle understood that the family is "earlier and more necessary than the city." It is natural for humans to bond together, but the familial bond is even more essential than the political one. Just as there can be no full and secure happiness without the bonds of friendship to undergird it, so there can be no full and secure state without the bonds of family to ground it.

THE COMPLEMENTARITY OF THE SEXES

It is a good thing, Aristotle makes clear, for the friendship of husband and wife to be cemented by utility and pleasure, as well as by the common bond of their shared children. But the friendship can go deeper than that if both are good, virtuous people. Indeed, since men and women, husbands and wives complement rather than duplicate each other, their union can be one that combines their specific strengths and virtues. When it does, Aristotle promises, when husband and wife recognize and celebrate their differences, it will bring delight rather than strife. Real friendship, Aristotle makes clear, is based on equality, but that equality, at least between the sexes, should not be confused with sameness. Marriage partners are not interchangeable, and that is a good thing.

Where true, unhealthy inequality, as opposed to proper, healthy complementarity, exists, most friendships will not last, whether they are between two male friends or a husband and a wife:

> Such incidents happen when the lover loves the beloved for the sake of pleasure while the beloved loves the lover for the sake of utility, and they do not both possess the qualities expected of them. If these be the objects of the friendship it is dissolved when they do not get the things that formed the motives of their love; for each did not love the other person himself but the qualities he had, and these were not enduring; that is why the friendships also are transient. But the love of characters, as has been said, endures because it is self-dependent. (IX.1; 1164a6-13)

This advice, offered by a Greek philosopher of the fourth century BC, could just as well have been given by a modern marriage counselor. Our needs and desires as human beings have changed little over the last twenty-four centuries.[1]

We must not think that because Aristotle speaks here about balance and exchange that he is reducing friendship to a business partnership or trying to quantify love and chart its progress on a graph. There is a logic to love and friendship, just as there is to science, politics, poetics, or any of the other myriad subjects Aristotle wrote about. The real question here is one of endurance: What lasts and what is ephemeral? What relies on things that dissolve and what on things that remain? Like courage, true friendship rests on a proper and complete knowledge of the situation; it does not build its house on sand. If two people enter their friendship (or their marriage) with opposing expectations, they cannot expect it to last.

When society sees such an unequal friendship break up, they will often target their blame based on the knowledge of the one injured: "When a man has deceived himself and has thought he was being loved for his character, when the other person was doing nothing of the kind, he must blame himself; when he has been deceived by the pretences of the

---

[1] Though he has yet to publish a book on the subject, Canadian psychologist and author Jordan Peterson speaks often online about what attracts men to women and women to men, and how they can complement each other in a healthy way. John Gray, author of *Men Are from Mars and Women Are from Venus* (San Francisco: HarperCollins, 1992), while continuing to speak and write about the complementarity of the sexes, has updated his theories to take into account the pressures of the modern world in *Beyond Mars and Venus: Relationship Skills for Today's Complex World* (Dallas: BenBella Books, 2017). Gary Smalley's *Making Love Last Forever* (Nashville: Thomas Nelson, 1996) and Patrick Morley's *The Man in the Mirror* (Brentwood, TN: Wolgemuth & Hyatt, 1989) both offer advice that accords well with Aristotelian common sense.

other person, it is just that he should complain against his deceiver" (XI.3; 1165b7-11).

Self-deception, like incontinence, does not simply happen to a person. The one who gives himself over to willful ignorance, like the one who gives himself over to unregulated passion, is a responsible agent in his own ruin. If the injured party ignored every warning sign that his friend (or wife) only wanted him for his money, he has only himself to blame. If the friend was a master deceiver and pulled the wool over his or her friend's eyes without his consent, then we can pity him, though we will certainly not want to emulate him.

Such firm, common-sense advice Aristotle offers in abundance over the course of books VIII and IX, but there are a few places where he transcends such practical advice to touch on issues from which Christians committed to a New Testament ethic can learn and be challenged—if not, in fact, convicted.

WHEN FRIENDS BETRAY

Jesus exhorts his disciples to love their enemies (Mt 5:44), but what does that exhortation mean when it comes to our friends? If a friend betrays and deceives us, do we continue to be his friend? Yes, we can love him in the sense that we pray he will return to God and be blessed, but should we retain him as a friend? If there is nothing we can do to call him to repentance, while he often succeeds in pulling us down to a state of incontinence, should we continue to associate with him? These are very real and exceedingly difficult choices that most Christians will have to make at some point in their lives. Paul offers some good advice: "Therefore if thine enemy hunger, feed him; if he thirst, give him drink: for in so doing thou shalt heap coals of fire on his head" (Rom 12:20); but that does not quite provide us with the guidance we need for dealing with a friend who betrays us or continually tempts us to ungodly behavior.

Enter Aristotle, who, though he would likely have balked at the bald command to love his enemies, does address the issue in a surprisingly "Christian" way:

> If one accepts another man as good, and he turns out badly and is seen to do so, must one still love him? Surely it is impossible, since not everything can be loved, but only what is good. What is evil neither can nor should be loved; for it is not one's duty to be a lover of evil, nor to become like what is bad; and we have said that like is dear to like. Must the friendship, then, be forthwith broken off? Or is this not so in all cases, but only when one's friends are incurable in their wickedness? If they are capable of being reformed one should rather come to the assistance of their character or their property, inasmuch as this is better and more characteristic of friendship. But a man who breaks off such a friendship would seem to be doing nothing strange; for it was not to a man of this sort that he was a friend; when his friend has changed, therefore, and he is unable to save him, he gives him up. (XI.3; 1165b13-23)

Christians are often instructed to "love the sinner but hate the sin," a phrase that acknowledges not only that the evildoer is something different from his evil deeds but that it is *not* a good thing to love evil. Aristotle goes so far as to state that it is *impossible* to love evil. To love evil is to become evil, for we become what we love. I do not think any church father could have said it as clearly as that!

But what are we to do with friends whom we thought were good but who later revealed themselves to be bad? The answer is that it depends. If they "are incurable in their wickedness," we should distance ourselves from them; if "they are capable of being reformed," then we should persist in our friendship. For it is, Aristotle argues, "better and more characteristic of friendship" to come to the assistance of a friend in need whom we can help. We *are* justified, we have the "right," to end a friendship when the friend has become something totally different from what he once was. Still, Aristotle urges us to stick with the friendship unless we are "unable to save him."

In the next chapter, Aristotle takes up the same basic issue but from a different angle. This time he focuses on incontinent men who destroy themselves and then seek out friends who will help them forget their misery, their heavy weight of regret, and their faction-rent soul. Such a "bad man," Aristotle warns, "does not seem to be amicably disposed even to himself, because there is nothing in him to love; so that if to be thus is the height of wretchedness, we should strain every nerve to avoid wickedness and should endeavour to be good; for so and only so can one be either friendly to oneself or a friend to another" (IX.4; 1166b25-29).

Not only should we be wary of such friends; we should beware lest *we* become such a person. If our incontinence leads us to hate ourselves, we will be incapable of loving others or of being their friend. Again, we cannot love wickedness, either in others or in ourselves. Virtue is the only secure foundation for friendship or for happiness. Such a philosophy does not contradict the practical advice of Proverbs to keep one's distance from evil and foolish men (see Prov 1:10-16; 2:12-15; 4:14-17; 23:9), but it does fall short of the self-sacrificial love revealed in Christ and the New Testament (see Rom 5:8).

LEWIS ON THE JOYS AND DANGERS OF FRIENDSHIP

Although I have already quoted at some length from the work of C. S. Lewis, I am afraid I must turn to him one more time. Lewis, together with his friend J. R. R. Tolkien, the author of the Lord of the Rings and a committed Catholic who knew well his Aristotle and his Aquinas, was an apologist for friendship in an age that was dismissive at best and suspicious at worst of male friendship.

In his strongly Aristotelian chapter on friendship in *The Four Loves*, Lewis explains why it is that the ancient, not to mention the medieval and Renaissance, world shared Aristotle's high view of friendship. "To the Ancients," Lewis explains,

> Friendship seemed the happiest and most fully human of all loves; the crown of life and the school of virtue. The modern world, in comparison, ignores it. . . . Affection and Eros were too obviously connected with our nerves, too obviously shared with the brutes. You could feel these tugging at your guts and fluttering in your diaphragm. But in Friendship—in that luminous, tranquil, rational world of relationships freely chosen—you got away from all that. This alone, of all the loves, seemed to raise you to the level of gods or angels.[2]

Moderns, including Christian ones, might find it odd that Lewis speaks of friendship in such spiritual terms, but there is an aspect of friendship that

---

[2] C. S. Lewis, *The Inspirational Writings of C. S. Lewis* (New York: Inspiration, 1991), 244-45.

does seem to lift us up toward the angels. While erotic love drives us to bear children and affection to rear them, friendship is something we choose. It is in that sense a more rational kind of love, one that inspires us to rely less on animal instinct and more on goodness and virtue.

Still, though Lewis praises friendship as highly as Aristotle, he does caution his readers that there was something of which Aristotle was ignorant, something a Christian must always bear in mind. "Friendship (as the ancients saw) can be a school of virtue; but also (as they did not see) a school of vice. It is ambivalent. It makes good men better and bad men worse."[3] While friendship can empower a group of men to stand bravely and self-sacrificially against tyranny, it can also shield them from feeling proper remorse when they run roughshod over those not in their circle. The same bond of brotherhood that holds the arm of the medieval knight steady in combat can dull his heart and deafen his ears to the plight of peasants caught in his path and that of his comrades.

This darker side of friendship can be glimpsed in "What I Believe" (1938), an essay written by E. M. Forster (1879–1970), celebrated English author of *A Passage to India*, *Howard's End*, and *A Room with a View*. "I hate the idea of causes," writes Forster,

> and if I had to choose between betraying my country and betraying my friend, I hope I should have the guts to betray my country. Such a choice may scandalise the modern reader, and he may stretch out his patriotic hand to the telephone at once and ring up the police. It would not have shocked Dante, though. Dante places Brutus and Cassius in the lowest circle of Hell because they had chosen to betray their friend Julius Caesar rather than their country Rome.[4]

Although Forster is not altogether fair to Dante—who punishes those who betray their country in the same circle of hell, albeit slightly higher up—he accurately exposes a strong, devil-may-care commitment to friendship over other ties that can be traced from Aristotle, to the aristocrats of Rome, to Dante's literary circle, to the eccentric geniuses who bonded together to

---

[3] Lewis, *Inspirational Writings*, 25.
[4] E. M. Forster, *Two Cheers for Democracy* (New York: Harcourt, Brace & World, 1951), 68.

create the Renaissance, to the French Jacobins whose revolutionary dreams tore their country to pieces.

As with his proud man, Aristotle's virtuous friends, in the absence of Christian humility, can quickly become haughty and disdainful. It is a noble thing to be lifted up to the rational realm of the angels, but we must beware lest we fall, like Satan, into pride.

15

THE GOOD LIFE

READ ANY BOOK ON THE PHILOSOPHY of Aristotle, and it will highlight an important distinction Aristotle makes between three different kinds of thinking: theoretical (or intellectual, or contemplative), practical, and productive. In part five, we will focus on the third, which Aristotle takes up in *Rhetoric* and *Poetics*. The second has been the subject of the last three chapters and will guide our discussion of *Politics* in part four as well. I have already considered the first in detail in parts one and two; however, in book VI of *Ethics*, Aristotle clarifies the distinction between theoretical and practical thinking in a way that is worth highlighting here.

THE PRACTICAL AND THE THEORETICAL

Intellectual (theoretical) and moral (practical) virtue both arise from the soul, but they do so by means of different powers and with a different end and measure in view.

> What affirmation and negation are in thinking, pursuit and avoidance are in desire; so that since moral virtue is a state of character concerned with choice, and choice is deliberate desire, therefore both the reasoning must be true and the desire right, if the choice is to be good . . . of the intellect which is contemplative, not practical nor productive, the good and the bad state are truth and falsity respectively. (VI.2; 1139a21-29)

As we have already seen, practical virtue is something we choose by subjecting desire to reason. Whether in ethics (which focuses on individual choices) or in politics (which focuses on the choices that guide and guard the relationship between people joined together in a polis), the choices we make cause us either to pursue and succumb to our instincts or to avoid and transcend them. When the proper balance is struck between reason and passion, knowledge and desire, the individual or the polis thrives, goodness triumphs, and happiness is achieved.

In the case of intellectual virtue, and the theoretical thinking that fuels it, the choice is not between good actions and bad actions but between affirmation and negation, truth and falsity, that which is in accord with the nature of reality and that which is not. Theoretical thinking does not lead to practical decisions of moral behavior; neither does it lead to works of art or other objects of beauty. It leads instead to contemplation as an end in itself, to insight into the way the universe works, physically *and* metaphysically.

BRIDGING THE DIVIDE BETWEEN SCIENCE AND PHILOSOPHY

To the modern mind, science and philosophy do not belong in the same category. Aristotle thought differently. The reason his *Physics* and *Metaphysics* are of a piece is because both, Aristotle believed, "follow [deductively] from first principles." Yet, "the first principle from which what is scientifically known follows cannot be an object of scientific knowledge, of art, or of practical wisdom; for that which can be scientifically known can be demonstrated, and art and practical wisdom deal with things that are variable" (VI.6; 1140b32-35). The universal, self-evident truths from which theoretical thinking begins cannot themselves be proved by science. They also cannot be proved by practical or productive thinking, for those deal with actions and objects in our variable world of change, not with absolutes that are fixed and eternal.

To arrive at that special wisdom that is the origin and end of theoretical thinking, Aristotle explains, there "must be intuitive reason combined with scientific knowledge—scientific knowledge of the highest objects which has received as it were its proper completion" (VI.7; 1141a18-20). Not by reason, action, or craft but by intuition do we apprehend transcendent truths. As I argued in chapter three, the reason science grew up in the West is that nearly all the early modern scientists were Christians who accepted on faith that (1) the universe is ordered and rational because it was made by an ordered and rational God, and (2) we can trust our God-given senses to perceive, study, and measure that cosmic order because we are made in his image.

Our post-Enlightenment world teaches that science (physics) is based on fact and observation while religion (metaphysics) is based on revelation that cannot be proved. Aristotle knew nothing of such a false dichotomy. When he set himself to contemplate the full nature of reality, he engaged *both* his intuition of first principles and his reason. Indeed, in that mix of intuition and reason that he called theoretical thinking, he found his greatest happiness. To act virtuously or lead others to virtue (practical thinking) and to create lasting works of art (productive thinking) were both good and admirable, but they did not represent, for Aristotle, the *summum bonum*.

That is why, after devoting nearly all of *Ethics* to explicating the exact nature and practice of virtue, Aristotle surprises us in his third-to-last chapter with an overwhelming vision of the highest state of happiness for man. I will dedicate the rest of this chapter to opening up that vision and mining its wisdom, wisdom that had a profound impact on the Middle Ages and that was reclaimed in the twentieth century by a highly original German Christian philosopher who deserves to be better known.

ARISTOTLE ON THE LIFE OF CONTEMPLATION

Though most modern readers, Catholic or Protestant, religious or secular, will find it surprising, Aristotle concludes unhesitatingly that contemplation is the highest and happiest form of life, for, "firstly, this activity is the best (since not only is reason the best thing in us, but the objects of reason are the best of knowable objects); and secondly, it is the most continuous, since we can contemplate truth more continuously than we can *do* anything" (X.7; 1177a19-22). If three essential criteria for happiness are that it should engage our highest faculty, guide us toward objects that are the best, and allow us to do so for long, uninterrupted periods of time, then contemplation, the activity most closely allied to theoretical thinking, must be the happiest.

To these criteria Aristotle adds several more that elevate the life of contemplation to the highest ideal one can strive for:

> The activity of philosophic wisdom is admittedly the pleasantest of virtuous activities; at all events the pursuit of it is thought to offer pleasures marvellous for their purity and their enduringness, and it is to be expected that those who

> know will pass their time more pleasantly than those who inquire. And the self-sufficiency that is spoken of must belong most to the contemplative activity.... This activity alone would seem to be loved for its own sake. (X.7; 1177a23-35)

Pleasure, purity, enduringness, knowledge, self-sufficiency—all of these are promised and provided by a life devoted to contemplation. The pleasures it gives are far less mingled with pain than the pleasures provided by passion or art, military conquest or political success. After spending all of books VIII and IX celebrating the virtues of friendship, Aristotle praises the life of contemplation as one that, though enhanced by friends, does not rely on them. A man who contemplates in solitude can achieve the heights of happiness, a happiness that itself seeks no other end but itself.

Of course, there *is* one thing necessary for the unhindered pursuit of theoretical thinking, and that thing is leisure—which itself must be supported by the kind of political and economic stability that Aristotle discusses in his *Politics*. Only once one has sufficient leisure can he devote large swaths of time to contemplation. It is for that reason that Aristotle boldly proclaims that "we are busy that we may have leisure, and make war that we may live in peace" (X.7; 1177b4-5). Aristotle has nothing but praise for the courageous soldier who defends his polis and wins glory for himself, but he nevertheless privileges peace over war. In fact, he treats as the only final justification for war its ability to create the necessary matrix for enjoying peace. In the same way, Aristotle insists that leisure does not exist for the sake of work but work for the sake of leisure.

CONTEMPLATING THE DIVINE

In chapter nine, I mentioned that Aristotle's God, the Unmoved Mover of *Physics* and *Metaphysics*, lives in a state of pure and perpetual contemplation and that we find peace when we imitate his contemplation. Here, Aristotle goes further to suggest that our ability to engage in such a life offers proof that we partake in some small degree of the divine nature:

> Such a life would be too high for man; for it is not in so far as he is man that he will live so, but in so far as something divine is present in him; and by so

much as this is superior to our composite nature is its activity superior to that which is the exercise of the other kind of virtue. If reason is divine, then, in comparison with man, the life according to it is divine in comparison with human life. But we must not follow those who advise us, being men, to think of human things, and, being mortal, of mortal things, but must, so far as we can, make ourselves immortal, and strain every nerve to live in accordance with the best thing in us. . . . For man, therefore, the life according to reason is best and pleasantest, since reason more than anything else is man. (X.7; 1177b26-1178a7)

This passage, written by a pagan without access to the biblical teaching of the *imago Dei*, is nothing short of a miracle. Aristotle works his way, by a mingling of intuition and reason, toward an understanding that there is something divine in our nature, something that transcends the limits of our mortality and comes close to making us immortal. We may be hylomorphic beings composed of body and soul, but that which is the best part of us, the reason that is lodged in our soul, exalts us heavenward.

Rather than invoke the Unmoved Mover, as he does in *Physics* and *Metaphysics*, Aristotle invokes here the gods, whom he takes for granted people believe in. Yet, like Plato before him, Aristotle rejects any notion that the gods behave the way they do in Homer or Hesiod or the tragedians. He counts it absurd that the gods would partake in acts of courage, temperance, or justice, since they do not participate in the affairs and transactions of men. Everyone, Aristotle insists, supposes that the gods live and are active, but what do they do?

If, he reasons, "you take away from a living being action, and still more production [that is, practical and productive thinking], what is left but contemplation [theoretical thinking]? Therefore the activity of God, which surpasses all others in blessedness, must be contemplative; and of human activities, therefore, that which is most akin to this must be most of the nature of happiness" (X.8; 1178b20-24). Though the gods (or God) do not need courage, temperance, or justice, Aristotle suggests, they do practice the virtue of wisdom in the form of contemplation as an eternal end in itself. When we mimic that activity, we become most like them and thus most happy.

Although Aristotle disagreed with Plato about the exact nature of the Forms, both philosophers agreed that the life of contemplation was the best and that the proper object of that contemplation was those things that do not change. This belief, that the life of contemplation was higher than that of action or production, was shared by most medieval thinkers, in particular Boethius, Aquinas, and Dante.

BOETHIUS AND AQUINAS ASCEND THE LADDER OF CONTEMPLATION

Consolation of Philosophy begins with the imprisoned Boethius being scolded by Lady Philosophy for abandoning contemplation for poetic pleasure and the productive thinking that accompanies it. He describes Lady Philosophy as a mature and majestic woman with eyes of fire and a crown on her brow. She wears a fine robe of her own weaving that includes a strange device along the hem: "On the border below was inwoven the symbol Π (Pi), on that above was to be read a Θ (Theta). And between the two letters there could be marked degrees, by which, as by the rungs of a ladder, ascent might be made from the lower principle to the higher."[1]

Pi and theta are the letters that begin, respectively, the Greek words for "practical" and "theoretical." The meaning of the device is that man is meant to ascend the ladder of wisdom from practical thinking (activity, virtue) to theoretical thinking (contemplation). While the sentiment squares with Platonic philosophy, Boethius's presentation of it is strongly Aristotelian, as it is, to an even greater degree, in Aquinas. I have already shown, in chapter eleven, that Aquinas fully agreed with Aristotle's contention, in *Ethics* X.8, that the life of contemplation is the highest and lifts us toward the divine—so much so that he comes perilously close to describing our soul as disembodied in its achievement of the beatific vision (a phrase that is Platonic but squares with *Ethics* X.7-8).

Aquinas asks whether happiness is linked to the speculative (theoretical) or practical intellect and then supports the former by listing three Aristotelian criteria: (1) man's "highest power is the intellect"; (2) "contemplation

---

[1] Boethius, *The Consolation of Philosophy*, trans. W. V. Cooper, in *The Great Books: Seventh Year* (Chicago: Great Books Foundation, 1959), 2:2.

is sought principally for its own sake"; (3) "in the contemplative life man has something in common with things above him, viz. with God and the angels . . . [but] in things pertaining to the active life, other animals also have something in common with man, although imperfectly."[2] Such Aristotelian reasoning on the nature of happiness and the good life was one of the factors that led medievals to place such a high premium on the life of contemplation as lived by monks, nuns, friars, and other mystics. That is not to say that such beliefs were unbiblical, but they do bear the firm imprint of Plato and Aristotle.

DANTE ON THE ACTIVE AND CONTEMPLATIVE LIFE

This privileging of the contemplative life over the active is perhaps best illustrated in Dante's *Comedy*, where, in a scene that directly imitates the opening of *Consolation of Philosophy*, Dante has Beatrice, who is in part an allegory for the contemplative life, scold him for turning his eyes away from her example and chasing after false muses who caused him to wander away from his true path upward (see *Purgatory* XXX). To drive home the point, Dante bookends his meeting with Beatrice with a gentler interaction with Matilda, who helps him drink from the River Lethe to erase his memory of sin and who functions as an allegory for the active life (cantos 28-29, 31).

That Dante intends Matilda to represent the active and Beatrice the contemplative life is made clear in canto 27, where Dante has a dream in which he encounters Leah in a garden singing about herself and her sister Rachel, the two wives of Jacob whom we meet in Genesis 29. In the song, Leah, like Matilda, embodies the active life, while Rachel, like Beatrice, embodies the contemplative:

> Say I am Leah if any ask my name,
> > and my white hands weave garlands wreath on wreath
> > to please me when I stand before the frame
> of my bright glass. For this my fingers play
> > among these blooms. But my sweet sister Rachel
> > sits at her mirror motionless all day.

---

[2]Thomas Aquinas, *Summa of the Summa*, ed. and annotated by Peter Kreeft (San Francisco: Ignatius, 1990), I-II, q. 3, art. 5 (pp. 379-80).

> To stare into her own eyes endlessly
>   is all her joy, as mine is in my weaving.
>   She looks, I do. Thus live we joyously.³

The way Dante describes the dichotomy between Leah and Rachel makes them not only reflections of Matilda and Beatrice but of Martha and Mary as well (see Lk 10:38-42). While Martha, who shares Leah's predilection for the active life, serves Jesus by bustling around in the kitchen and attending to the food, Mary, who shares Rachel's predilection for the contemplative life, sits at the feet of Jesus and meditates on his words.

The modern who reads Leah's song, or the passage in Luke 10, might be tempted to accuse Rachel and even Mary of being self-centered, overly passive, and useless to society. Why do these women not get up and *do* something, rather than sit there in a trance? Dante, like Aristotle, Boethius, and Aquinas before him, would disagree. In fact, by seamlessly weaving together figures from his own day (Matilda and Beatrice) with two sets of sisters from the Old and New Testament (Rachel and Leah, Mary and Martha) and the culminating vision of Aristotle's *Ethics*, Dante champions the superiority of the contemplative life over the active as both a classical and a biblical ideal.

PIEPER ON LEISURE

But Dante lived and died seven centuries ago. Has the modern world produced any recent Christian writers to defend the contemplative life as better than or at least equal in goodness to the active life? It has. His name was Josef Pieper (1904-1997), and his work has deservedly seen a steady revival in America over the last few decades. In *Leisure, the Basis of Culture* (1948), Pieper, a Thomist who drew extensively on Plato and Aristotle, sought to turn the eyes of post-World War II Europe back to Aristotle's teaching that "we are busy that we may have leisure." Rather than focus, as the medievals did, on religious orders, Pieper took a wider approach, calling the modern world to task for trading in the virtues of contemplation for a culture and ethos of total work.

---

³Dante, *The Divine Comedy*, trans. John Ciardi (New York: New American Library, 1970), 523.

Pieper begins his analysis and critique by pointing out that the Greek word Aristotle uses for leisure is *scholē*. Not having available to him a word for "busy" or "work," Aristotle had to make do with *a-scholē* (the Greek *a-* is equivalent to "un" in English). Hence, a more literal translation of Aristotle's statement would yield, "We are *not-at-leisure* in order to *be-at-leisure*." As for the word *scholē*, Pieper explains, it "is the origin of Latin *scola*, German *Schule*, English *school*. The name for the institutions of education and learning means 'leisure.'"[4]

Then, connecting what Aristotle says about leisure in *Ethics* X.7 to what he says about liberal as opposed to servile education in *Politics* VIII.1-3 and assessing its impact on the premodern world, Pieper concludes: "The Christian concept of the 'contemplative life' (the *vita contemplativa*) was built on the Aristotelian concept of leisure. Further, the distinction between the 'Liberal Arts' and the 'Servile Arts' has its origin precisely here."[5] Whereas farmers, craftsmen, and other workers received a servile (technical) education that emphasized skills over character (productive thinking), the gentlemen of the leisured classes were given a liberal arts education meant to free (liberate) their minds for the purpose of virtue (practical thinking) and contemplation (theoretical thinking).

In the wake of the Enlightenment and the Industrial Revolution, the distinction between workers and "scholastics" (students trained in the liberal arts) was broken down, and all were expected to justify themselves by work. Thus, while the modern worker is allowed and even encouraged to take vacations, he is to do so as a means of rest so that he can work all the harder when he returns to the office. The same dynamic applies whether the worker is an engineer or a professor, an electrician or a priest.

In sharp contrast, Aristotle, one of the hardest-working philosophers of all time, believed that it was for the sake of the vacation that we work at all. Now, by defending Aristotle's understanding of work and leisure against that of the modern world, Pieper knew that he would be criticized by those who confuse vacations with frivolity and leisure with laziness.

---

[4]Josef Pieper, *Leisure, the Basis of Culture*, trans. Gerald Malsbary (South Bend, IN: St. Augustine Press, 1998), 4.
[5]Pieper, *Leisure, the Basis of Culture*, 5.

He knew as well that by being an apologist for leisure he would risk invoking the wrath of Christians who equate leisure with the deadly sin of sloth.[6]

Anticipating such a critique, Pieper argues that sloth (*acedia* in Latin: "idleness, spiritual torpor") does not manifest itself as a yearning for leisure but a rejection of who God created us to be. An indulgence in sloth causes us to surrender our true dignity and potential. "The opposite of *acedia* is not the industrious spirit of the daily effort to make a living, but rather the cheerful affirmation by man of his own existence, of the world as a whole, and of God."[7] The modern workaholic who uses endless busyness to shield himself from having to meditate on God's purpose for his life is in far greater danger of sloth than the man who reads a book of poetry under a tree and opens his mind to the beauty of the words and the power of the images. Just as the purpose of the Sabbath was not to draw the Israelites away from meaningful work but to draw them closer to God, so the true purpose of festivals is not, by means of unrestrained license, to drag us downward toward the beast but, by means of intimate fellowship and refined joy, to lift us upward toward the angels.

WORK, PRAYER, AND JOY

A focus on leisure, festival, and the liberal arts, far from vitiating our spirit and vigor, makes us more human, more fully alive to the telos for which God created us. Writing in mid-twentieth-century Europe, Pieper was sharply aware of what happens when a totalitarian work state comes to view its citizens as proletarians, as faceless cogs in an industrial machine that demands quantifiable work of all its laborers, whether their collar be blue or white. Leisure rescues us from the horrors of mass identity. It restores to us our soul, our uniqueness, our individual purpose. It broadens our dignity beyond the useful and impels us not to control but to know. We seek leisure, and the contemplation that accompanies it, because we are human; when we do so, we become less like Camus's Sisyphus—whom Pieper defines as a worker

---

[6]Most of what I say in this paragraph and the following appears in my essay, "Wise Passiveness: Pieper and Wordsworth on the Liberal Arts," *Modern Age* 56, no. 3 (Summer 2014): 75-80.
[7]Pieper, *Leisure, the Basis of Culture*, 29.

"chained to his labor without rest, and without inner satisfaction"—and more like refined ladies and gentlemen.[8]

Between the modernist, progressive, ultimately Marxist philosophy of work and the Platonic-Aristotelian, Judeo-Christian philosophy of leisure, there stretches a great gulf. According to the former, even thinking itself is a form of work. Knowledge is to be gained by an active pursuit, defined by effort and confined within the spatiotemporal limits of our world. According to the latter, true insight and wisdom come from a passive, intuitive reception of truth. Our mind, having been prepared by relaxation and tranquility rather than assertion and struggle, grasps—or, better, is grasped by—the eternal moment. To achieve such a vision does take effort, but it is not directed toward narrow utilitarian or vocational ends, and its goal is not to reduce, calculate, and quantify. It seeks not facts but truth, not analysis but synthesis, not to figure out but to understand, not to master but to know, not to do but to be.

There is a sense in which the leisure advocated by Aristotle, Aquinas, and Pieper resembles Western Stoicism and Eastern Buddhism's call to detach oneself from the restlessness of the world and seek inner harmony and balance. But there is this vital difference: the Platonic-Aristotelian, Judeo-Christian, medieval-Catholic understanding of leisure ever dwells in the presence of joy—and not just joy in the abstract but the joy of touching an eternal, transcendent truth that can be both studied and known. There is something metaphysical and supernatural that lies outside ourselves and our world, and that something can be apprehended only by those who prepare their hearts and minds to seek after the beatific vision.

---

[8]Pieper, *Leisure, the Basis of Culture*, 55. In her essay "Why Work," Dorothy Sayers, writing in the same Aristotelian mode as Pieper, has this to say about work:

> The habit of thinking about work as something one does to make money is so ingrained in us that we can scarcely imagine what a revolutionary change it would be to think about it instead in terms of the work done. To do so would mean taking the attitude of mind we reserve for our unpaid work—our hobbies, our leisure interests, the things we make and do for pleasure—and making that the standard of all our judgments about things and people. We should ask of an enterprise, not "will it pay?" but "is it good?"; of a man, not "what does he make?" but "what is his work worth?"; of goods, not "can we induce people to buy them?" but "are they useful things well made?"; of employment, not "how much a week?" but "will it exercise my faculties to the utmost?"

Dorothy Sayers, *Letters to a Diminished Church* (Nashville: W Publishing Group, 2004), 132-33.

To quote again Aristotle's uncanny intuition about the final destiny of man: "We must not follow those who advise us, being men, to think of human things, and, being mortal, of mortal things, but must, so far as we can, make ourselves immortal, and strain every nerve to live in accordance with the best thing in us."

The anonymous medieval Russian monk who wrote *The Way of a Pilgrim* would have agreed, for he, like countless Eastern Orthodox Christians from the early fifth century to today, devoted many long hours of his life to praying continuously the Jesus prayer: "Lord Jesus Christ, Son of God, have mercy on me, a sinner." This prayer, which is taken from the prayer of the publican in the New Testament (Lk 18:13), can be prayed by anyone, young or old, rich or poor, employed or unemployed. Contemplation of God can begin today by anyone, no matter their income, no matter their education.

PART 4

HOW TO GET ALONG WITH OUR NEIGHBORS

16

THE POLITICAL ANIMAL

Before moving on to *Politics*—which Aristotle wrote to follow directly after and bring to completion his arguments in *Ethics* as he wrote *Metaphysics* ("after physics") to follow and complete *Physics*—I would like to consider two chapters from *Ethics* that set the stage for *Politics*. In those chapters (*Ethics* VIII.10-11), Aristotle pauses in the midst of his lengthy discussion of friendship to examine three different kinds of constitutions and how each bears the potential within it to go bad.

THE INEVITABLE DECLINE OF POLITICAL SYSTEMS

In *Republic* VIII, Plato discusses the various constitutions of his day in the form of a slowly corrupting, downward spiral from the best type of constitution to the worst. As Plato describes it, aristocracy degrades into timocracy, which degrades into oligarchy, which degrades into democracy, which degrades into tyranny. To increase the intensity of this series of political declensions, Plato dramatizes it as if it were a tragic cycle written by Aeschylus or Sophocles. In Plato's version of the fall of a great and noble house, an aristocratic father is succeeded by a timocratic son, an oligarchic grandson, a democratic great-grandson, and a tyrannical great-great-grandson.

Aristotle, while maintaining the same basic political systems, arranges them in a different, more hopeful manner. Instead of positing a steady decline from aristocracy to tyranny, he posits three good systems—monarchy ("rule by one"), aristocracy ("rule by the best"), and timocracy ("rule by honor")—each of which has the potential to degrade into a corrupt version of itself: monarchy into tyranny, aristocracy into oligarchy, timocracy into democracy. Interestingly, Aristotle argues that the best form (monarchy) degrades into the worst form (tyranny), while the least good form (timocracy) degrades into the least bad form (democracy).

THE STATE AS FAMILY WRIT LARGE

Because Aristotle constructs this political classification system in the context of friendship, he naturally connects each form of government to a relationship within the family. He begins by noting, "The association of a father with his sons bears the form of monarchy, since the father cares for his children; and this is why Homer calls Zeus 'father'; it is the ideal of monarchy to be paternal rule." Of course, such a relationship can become corrupted, as it does, Aristotle argues, "among the Persians [where] the rule of the father is tyrannical; they use their sons as slaves" (VIII.10; 1160b24-28). Aristotle does not allow the potential for a father's love for his children to morph into despotic rule to tarnish the proper use of patriarchal rule within the family and state. In fact, Aristotle's analogy and his insistence, as we saw in chapter fourteen, that "the household is earlier and more necessary than the city" (VIII.12; 1162a18) suggests that a culture where fathers routinely tyrannize their children will give birth to a tyrannical political structure.

Aristotle next moves on to aristocracy, comparing its good and degenerate forms to a proper and improper relationship between a husband and wife:

> The association of man and wife seems to be aristocratic; for the man rules in accordance with his worth, and in those matters in which a man should rule, but the matters that befit a woman he hands over to her. If the man rules in everything the relation passes over into oligarchy; for in doing so he is not acting in accordance with their respective worth, and not ruling in virtue of his superiority. Sometimes, however, women rule, because they are heiresses; so their rule is not in virtue of excellence but due to wealth and power, as in oligarchies. (VIII.10; 1160b33-1161a2)

To put this in modern terminology, Aristotle describes the proper relationship between a husband and wife as being equal but not egalitarian; their joint rule of the home rests on complementarity rather than sameness, on an honoring of each spouse's spheres and their proper authority within that sphere.

Things go wrong when the husband tries to dominate both his sphere and that of his wife, or the wife tries to dominate both her sphere and that of her husband. Mutual honor and respect should exist between husband and wife; when it does, there is hope that the same honor and respect will be shared by the various ruling members of the aristocracy. When that honor and respect is violated, factions and cliques grow up within the ruling body, and aristocracy ("rule by the best") gives way to oligarchy ("rule by the few"). Those few, both then and now, tend to be the money men of trade and industry.

As for timocracy, Aristotle finds it reflected in the proper relationship between older and younger siblings:

> The association of brothers is like timocracy; for they are equal, except in so far as they differ in age; hence if they differ much in age, the friendship is no longer of the fraternal type. Democracy is found chiefly in masterless dwellings (for here every one is on an equality), and in those in which the ruler is weak and every one has licence to do as he pleases. (VIII.10; 1161a3-9)

Brothers share an equality that is slightly different from that of husband and wife, for the siblings are at once more equal, in that they do not rule over separate spheres, and less equal, for elder brothers will tend to have more power than younger ones. This can be managed unless the brothers grew up in a masterless home where they did not learn proper obedience from their father and so demand a flat equality that leads to chaos. Thus rule by the majority of honorable citizens degrades into democratic mob rule and the collapsing of all natural distinctions and hierarchies.

PROPER HIERARCHY IN THE FAMILY AND STATE

To each of these relationships and their corresponding constitutions, Aristotle assigns a certain kind of friendship.

> By nature a father tends to rule over his sons, ancestors over descendants, a king over his subjects. These friendships imply superiority of one party over the other, which is why ancestors are honoured. The justice therefore that exists between persons so related is not the same on both sides but is in every case proportioned to merit; for that is true of the friendship as well. The friendship of man and wife, again, is the same that is found in an aristocracy; for it is in accordance with virtue—the better gets more of what is good, and each gets what befits him; and so, too, with the justice in these relations. The friendship of brothers is like that of comrades; for they are equal and of like age, and such persons are for the most part like in their feelings and their character. Like this, too, is the friendship appropriate to timocratic government;

for in such a constitution the ideal is for the citizens to be equal and fair; therefore rule is taken in turn, and on equal terms; and the friendship appropriate here will correspond. (VIII.11; 1161a18-29)

The modern reader should discern in this remarkable passage the perfect fusion of two disciplines: sociology and political science. Aristotle not only understands keenly the dynamic of family relationships and the dynamic of political relationships; he sees how they intertwine and reinforce each other.

It is a good and proper thing, Aristotle would teach our overly egalitarian world, for fathers to rule over sons, kings over subjects, and ancestors over descendants. This arrangement does not mark the opposite of justice but a hierarchy of merit that brings meaning and stability—as long as it is not corrupted. The same is true for the aristocratic friendship that exists between husbands and wives when each honors their own virtue and skills and those of their spouse. This system, in its political form, can be just as effective as monarchy, though it tends to be less stable. The friendship that exists between brothers can also be transferred into the political realm if the citizens who rule are truly comrades and respect each other's equal worth; but with more rulers, there comes the increased risk of anarchy and the breakdown of order.

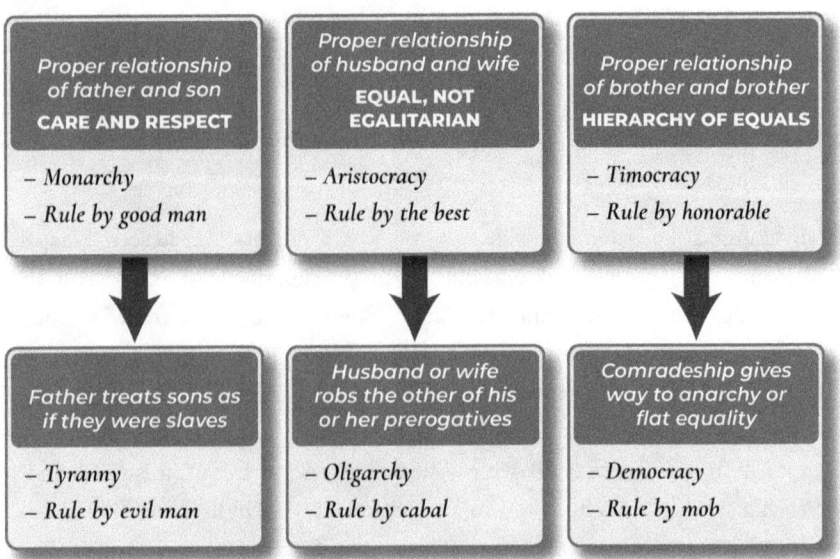

Figure 16.1. Proper familial relationships produce good governing structures. But both can devolve into degraded forms

THE GENESIS OF THE POLIS

Just as Aristotle asserts, in *Ethics* VIII.12, that "the household is earlier and more necessary than the city," and draws connections, in *Ethics* VIII.10-11, between monarchy, aristocracy, and timocracy and the relationship between father and son, husband and wife, and brother and brother, so he begins book I, chapter 2 of *Politics* by grounding the genesis of the polis in the prior institution of the family.

> He who thus considers things in their first growth and origin, whether a state or anything else, will obtain the clearest view of them. In the first place there must be a union of those who cannot exist without each other; namely, of male and female, that the race may continue (and this is a union which is formed, not of deliberate purpose, but because, in common with other animals and with plants, mankind have a natural desire to leave behind them an image of themselves), and of natural ruler and subject, that both may be preserved. For that which can foresee by the exercise of mind is by nature intended to be lord and master, and that which can with its body give effect to such foresight is a subject, and by nature a slave; hence master and slave have the same interest. (I.2; 1252a24-1252b1)

It is not the state (or polis) that creates the family but the family that lays the foundation out of which the state grows. The family itself begins with the necessary relationship of husband and wife as propagators of the next generation, hence forming the family. A modern American writer might stop here, but Aristotle goes on to add to the nuclear family of parents and children a number of servants or slaves, thus forming what the ancient Greeks called an oikos: a household that functions as an economic unit (*oikos* is the root of our word *economics*, which means, literally, the "laws of the household").

Although the master of the oikos is free and the slave is not, all work together to form the household unit that Aristotle treats as foundational to all social, economic, and political life. Unlike in the nondemocratic East, Aristotle goes on to add, where there is no distinction between women and slaves—for *all* are slaves—in Greece, husband and wife work alongside each other as free citizens. The slaves are enslaved, it is true, but they are a part of the oikos and serve an integral function within it. That is not to say that Aristotle was an abolitionist, but it is to say that he ascribed the slave a vital place within the oikos.

ARISTOTLE ON SLAVERY AND THE SEXES

Which leads me to an aspect of Aristotle that I very much wish I could skip over: his views on slavery. Though I would be overjoyed to find in Aristotle a rational argument against slavery, no such argument is made. Still, Aristotle *does* offer something unique to his age: a *defense* of slavery. Rather than simply accept slavery as a brute fact of nature or reduce the slave to the level of a beast of burden, Aristotle explores the possibility that some people are slaves by nature. After all, Aristotle reasons, for an oikos, and a polis, to run efficiently and to allow for a leisured class to pursue the life of the mind (contemplation), laborers are necessary. Who is to perform this labor? For Aristotle, slaves perform that function (labor) in the oikos that allows the master to pursue the good life and achieve his end.

"Is there," Aristotle asks, "any one thus intended by nature to be a slave, and for whom such a condition is expedient and right, or rather is not all slavery a violation of nature?" He then answers his own question: "There is no difficulty in answering this question, on grounds both of reason and of fact. For that some should rule and others be ruled is a thing not only necessary, but expedient; from the hour of their birth, some are marked out for subjection, others for rule" (I.5; 1254a19-23). Aristotle's point here is not to say that the slave is a nonhuman but that his proper telos is to labor and to be guided in that labor by a master. In fact, Aristotle argues further that both master and slave are happier and healthier when they fulfill their proper functions.

Such reasoning cuts across the grain of modern thought, for modern thought, in *both* its religious and atheist modes, rests on the Judeo-Christian belief that all people are created in the image of God and thus possess equal value, worth, and dignity. Still, Aristotle's reasoning—which I do not fully endorse but which I seek to understand and learn from—does not necessarily reject the basic value of all people. It seeks, rather, to discern natural hierarchies and so determine the most effective relationship between man and nature, man and man, and man and himself.

> It is clear that the rule of the soul over the body [man and himself], and of the mind and the rational element over the passionate, is natural and expedient; whereas the equality of the two or the rule of the inferior is always hurtful. The same holds good of animals in relation to men [man and nature]; for tame animals have a better nature than wild, and all tame animals are better off when they are ruled by man; for then they are preserved. Again, the male is by nature superior, and the female inferior; and the one rules, and the other is ruled; this principle, of necessity, extends to all mankind [man and man]. Where then there is such a difference as that between soul and body, or between men and animals (as in the case of those whose business is to use their body, and who can do nothing better), the lower sort are by nature slaves, and it is better for them as for all inferiors that they should be under the rule of a master. For he who can be, and therefore is, another's and he who participates in rational principle enough to apprehend, but not to have, such a principle, is a slave by nature. Whereas the lower animals cannot even apprehend a principle; they obey their instincts. And indeed the use made of slaves and of tame animals is not very different; for both with their bodies minister to the needs of life. (I.5; 1254b5-25)

Aristotle's discussion of relationships within the oikos, and thus within the polis, is framed by the relationship between soul and body, which, as we have seen before, is equivalent to that between form and matter, actuality and potentiality. In a virtuous man and thus a happy man, the soul rules the body, while the rational part of the soul rules the irrational part.

This is how it should be in the inner life; so should it be in the external life. The slave has a stronger body for work, and the master a stronger virtue for civic life. It is better for the natural slave to be ruled by a good master than to live the life of a homeless nomad. In this state, the slave will live longer and better. In the same way, domesticated animals are healthier and live longer lives under a good master than in the wild.

I am aware that it is not easy for modern people, myself included, to read such arguments, especially given the history of slavery and racism in our country. But we must recall that Aristotle not only lived before Christ but in an age that had no tractors or other machines. Hunter-gatherers living in nomadic tribes might be able to eke out a subsistence living, but those who gathered into cities—from the Latin *civitas*, the same root as the word *civilization*—often needed slave labor to maintain their culture. All the ancient civilizations, from the Egyptians to the Babylonians, the Assyrians to the Carthaginians, the Greeks to the Romans, the Aztecs to the Mayans, had slaves, as did the settlers of the New World, who exploited slaves to dig for gold and to grow sugarcane and cotton. During the Industrial Revolution in Europe and America, those who worked in mines and factories lived lives that were almost as dire as those of slaves. While, again, I do not endorse Aristotle's views on slavery, he should at least be commended for so transcending the thought of his age as to see the slave as a human being.[1]

Just as modern readers will find Aristotle's thoughts on slavery hard to digest, so will they balk at his insistence, in the long passage quoted above, that the male is superior to the female. We must, however, take this insistence in the context already established earlier in this chapter: (1) that women are not equivalent to slaves, and (2) that husbands and wives serve complementary, aristocratic functions that are both of value. Furthermore, we must remember that, though there is evidence to suggest that some primitive (that is, tribal rather than town- or city-dwelling) matriarchies have existed, the belief that the man should be the head of his wife and that he should protect and lead her has been consistent throughout nearly all cultures and religions.[2]

To insist that our modern, radically egalitarian vision of the sexes is the correct one, and that everyone before 1960, including Aristotle and the church fathers, was wrong if not sexist, is to blind ourselves to the past and to our shared human nature. Indeed, as Brad Wilcox and Nancy Pearcey have

---

[1] In part four, titled "God's Justice: The Sin of Slavery," of *For the Glory of God: How Monotheism Led to Reformation, Science, Witch Hunts, and the End of Slavery* (Princeton, NJ: Princeton University Press, 2003), sociologist Rodney Stark reminds his readers that there was no slavery in medieval Catholic Europe. Though the medieval serfs were often poorly fed and clothed, they were not slaves; in fact, feudal obligations existed between lords and serfs. It was the discovery of the Americas that brought slavery back to a Christian world that had abolished it, at least in Europe proper. Its resurgence would call for new generations of crusading Christians—William Wilberforce in England; the abolitionists in America—to eliminate the evil of slavery.

[2] See Heide Goettner-Abendroth's *Matriarchal Societies: Studies on Indigenous Cultures Across the Globe* (New York: Peter Lang, 2013) and *Matriarchal Societies of the Past and the Rise of Patriarchy: West Asia and Europe* (New York: Peter Lang, 2022).

demonstrated, there is strong statistical evidence to show that most wives are happier and more fulfilled in a strong family led by a soft patriarch who guides and protects, making decisions that will benefit the family as a whole.[3]

FROM OIKOS TO POLIS

But let us return to the oikos and to Aristotle's dual argument that out "of these two relationships between man and woman, master and slave, the first thing to arise is the family," and that the "family is the association established by nature for the supply of men's everyday wants" (I.2; 1252b9-13). It is only after an area is populated by several such independent, self-sufficient households that the economic-social-political process begins that will result in the formation of a polis such as Athens:

> When several families are united, and the association aims at something more than the supply of daily needs, the first society to be formed is the village. And the most natural form of the village appears to be that of a colony from the family, composed of the children and grandchildren, who are said to be suckled "with the same milk." ... Every family is ruled by the eldest, and therefore in the colonies of the family the kingly form of government prevailed because they were of the same blood. As Homer says: "Each one gives law to his children and to his wives." For they lived dispersedly, as was the manner in ancient times. Wherefore men say that the Gods have a king, because they themselves either are or were in ancient times under the rule of a king. For they imagine, not only the forms of the Gods, but their ways of life to be like their own. (I.2; 1252b14-27)

If the movement to establish complete equity between the sexes is a recent one, the attack on the headship of the father as inherently negative and oppressive is even more so. What Aristotle describes here is, quite literally, patriarchy: Greek for "rule by the father." For Aristotle, it is the most natural form of rule in the home as well as the village and, if the poets are correct, among the gods as well.

---

[3]See W. Bradford Wilcox, *Soft Patriarchs, New Men: How Christianity Shapes Fathers and Husbands* (Chicago: University of Chicago Press, 2004); Nancy Pearcey, *The Toxic War on Masculinity: How Christianity Reconciles the Sexes* (Grand Rapids, MI: Baker, 2023). It should be noted here that order and hierarchy in the familial, social, and political spheres need not walk hand in hand with slavery!

In Genesis and Job, Abraham, Isaac, Jacob, and Job each serves as the father, head, and priest of his oikos (see Gen 13:1–14:20; 28:1-5; 46:1-7; Job 1:1-5). Each of the tribes of Israel descends from a patriarchal head, and, though the offices of priest, king, and prophet become separated, they are reunited in Jesus, who is the head of his bride, the church. Aristotle's household rules are reiterated in Ephesians 5:21–6:9 and Colossians 3:18–4:1, with the husband called to love his wife as Christ does the church in a self-sacrificial way that transcends Aristotle's pagan ethos without dismantling the natural ordering within the oikos that Aristotle defends. The call in 1 Peter 3:7 for the husband to give his wife honor "as unto the weaker vessel" accords well with the role of the true patriarchal father as defender and guardian.[4]

As the family extends into a village tribe, it is natural that it should be ruled by the chief patriarch, a figure such as Jacob, whose name is changed by God to Israel and who oversees the growing branches of his tribal family. This arrangement, for Aristotle, gives way to kingship, or monarchy, which he considered the best form of government—though it can, as we saw earlier, devolve into the worst form: tyranny. The family writ large, the village offers greater stability and self-sufficiency to its members. That is why Aristotle calls it a colony of the family.

As growth continues, the final leap is taken, and the scattered villages come together to form an even stabler, more self-sufficient polis, one that can enable its citizens to best pursue virtue and happiness.

> When several villages are united in a single complete community, large enough to be nearly or quite self-sufficing, the state [polis] comes into existence, originating in the bare needs of life, and continuing in existence for the sake of a good life. And therefore, if the earlier forms of society are natural, so is the state, for it is the end of them, and the nature of a thing is its end. (I.2; 1252b27-32)

As in all of Aristotle's works, the nature of a thing is what it grows into when it reaches its perfection, its end, its completion and consummation. We are

---

[4]Please be assured that when I use the word *patriarchy*, I do not mean the toxic patriarchy advocated by sexists such as Andrew Tate but the soft patriarchy advocated by Wilcox and Pearcey. That patriarchy was practiced in the Old Testament does not on its own make the case for male headship, since the patriarchs of Genesis practiced polygamy. It is, rather, 1 Cor 11:3 that makes the case, since it links headship not to a cultural norm but to the eternal relationship between Father and Son within the Trinity.

meant for the polis; it is our proper telos. That is why we cannot achieve true virtue or happiness apart from it.

The polis cannot be an unnatural arrangement imposed artificially on man, for it springs out of the most natural of all human groupings: the family. If the family is a right and proper institution, then so must be the village and the polis.

POLIS AS TELOS

That leads us to what may be the best-known phrase to come down to us from the works of Aristotle: "Man is by nature a political animal." But what did Aristotle mean by the phrase? The answer is found in *Politics* I.2, in the paragraphs that follow directly after those in which Aristotle traces the movement from family to village to polis (state).

> Hence it is evident that the state is a creation of nature, and that man is by nature a political animal. And he who by nature and not by mere accident is without a state, is either a bad man or above humanity; he is like the "Tribeless, lawless, heartless one," whom Homer denounces—the natural outcast is forthwith a lover of war; he may be compared to an isolated piece at draughts. (I.2; 1253a2-6)

Only a bad man or a saint can live apart from a polis. We hylomorphic creatures whose bodies connect us to the animals and whose souls connect us to the gods are not meant to live isolated and alone. It is true that the accidents of life will often cut us off temporarily from community, but the man who by nature avoids all political connections is either a beast who wants discourse of reason or an angel who needs no human fellowship.

To adapt Aristotle's vivid metaphor slightly, the man without a polis is like a chess piece without a chessboard: an object without function or telos. In the Greek tragedies Aristotle knew and loved, characters, such as Oedipus, who committed taboo crimes would be exiled from their polis, dooming them to a barbaric life without tribe or law or hearth. Such people will naturally become lovers of war, for they are at enmity with all and at peace with none.

Though it is true, Aristotle concedes, that some animals form themselves into groups, those groups bear little resemblance to a human polis:

> Now, that man is more of a political animal than bees or any other gregarious animals is evident. Nature, as we often say, makes nothing in vain, and man is the only animal whom she has endowed with the gift of speech. And whereas mere voice is but an indication of pleasure or pain, and is therefore found in other animals ... the power of speech is intended to set forth the expedient and inexpedient, and therefore likewise the just and the unjust. And it is a characteristic of man that he alone has any sense of good and evil, of just and unjust, and the like, and the association of living beings who have this sense makes a family and a state. (I.2; 1253a7-17)

Some animals have the ability to make sounds when they experience pleasure or pain, but man alone has the gift of speech, by which he can articulate judgments of good and evil, justice and injustice, virtue and vice. By *speech*, Aristotle means language, the origin of which is as mysterious to the secular scientist as is the origin of consciousness. Both are key aspects of what it means to be human, as is our unique but natural propensity to gather together in families, villages, and states.

Thus far Aristotle has made it clear that family comes before village, as village comes before polis. It is vital to remember this, for in the next paragraph Aristotle seems for a moment to contradict this very point:

> Further, the state is by nature clearly prior to the family and to the individual, since the whole is of necessity prior to the part; for example, if the whole body be destroyed, there will be no foot or hand, except in an equivocal sense, as we might speak of a stone hand; for when destroyed the hand will be no better than that. But things are defined by their working and power; and we ought not to say that they are the same when they no longer have their proper quality, but only that they have the same name. The proof that the state is a creation of nature and prior to the individual is that the individual, when isolated, is not self-sufficing; and therefore he is like a part in relation to the whole. (I.2; 1253a18-27)

The reason this paragraph does not contradict Aristotle's earlier assertion that the oikos (household) is earlier and more necessary than the polis is that his use of the word *prior* here is not a reference to time. The polis is prior to the family in the sense that the soul is prior to the body or the form to the matter or the actual to the potential.

Rather than indicate that the polis precedes the oikos chronologically, Aristotle means here to posit the polis as the telos, the end toward which the institutions of family and village point and reach their fulfillment. We have value as individuals, but our telos, in the sense of function, is ultimately defined and fulfilled by our relationships within the polis. When we are not connected to a polis, we may seem to be alive, but we are like a stone hand that has the appearance of a living hand but is unable to perform any function linked to a living hand. A hand cut off from a body ceases to be a telos-driven hand.

We can find a parallel, though not an exact copy, of this concept in the New Testament, where each believer is honored as an individual saved by Christ but is also a member of the body of Christ. Apart from the diverse members that make up that body, we cannot live out the fullness of our calling (see 1 Cor 12:12-31). Just so, Jesus speaks of believers as branches who must be connected to the vine; when they are not, they become unfruitful and are thrown in the fire (see Jn 15:1-8). Though the body of Christ is not a political unit or even a civic arm of the state, it orients the individual believer and allows him to make use of his God-given gifts the way a chessboard does a king, knight, or bishop.

BEWARE THE MAN WITHOUT A POLIS

Having established the necessary and organic relationship between individual and polis, Aristotle concludes his second chapter by contrasting the political (civilized) man with one who is unpolitical and therefore uncivilized.

> But he who is unable to live in society, or who has no need because he is sufficient for himself, must be either a beast or a god: he is no part of a state. A social instinct is implanted in all men by nature, and yet he who first founded the state was the greatest of benefactors. For man, when perfected, is the best of animals, but, when separated from law and justice, he is the worst of all. (I.2; 1253a28-33)

Note that Aristotle says here plainly what he hints at earlier: that a man without a polis is either a beast or a god. There is nothing natural about Jean-Jacques Rousseau's noble savage, for nature implants in all of us a social instinct that we can only fulfill by being part of a civil (political) society.

Note as well that, though the natural social instinct predates chronologically the formation of the polis, we only reach perfection when we are a member of that polis. That is why Aristotle says that the man who first founded the polis was a great benefactor. Though the man who did so was driven by a natural instinct for civil society, civil society was unable to commence until he established the polis. I would compare this to one of the mysteries of the Holy Scriptures. Although the Bible is the eternal Word of God, it had to be written down by inspired authors and collected and authorized by an inspired church. Thus the church gave us the Bible, but it is the Bible, the eternal Word of God, that created the church. The concept of the lone Christian unconnected to any church is very much a modern one.

In the history of the church, many such lone Christians have ignited heresies and cults that continue to plague us today. For Aristotle, the man without a polis is a savage, unholy animal driven to violence by unrestrained lust and gluttony. Thankfully, that is not the whole story. Though man in his savage state is the worst of beasts, man, when he is perfected—we might say domesticated—by the just laws of a just polis, is the best of all animals. The special capacities we have to think, reason, and communicate are, when channeled by a proper administration of justice, capable of building things of wisdom and virtue. Sadly, those same capacities that allow for such goodness, truth, and beauty make us all the more dangerous and destructive when they are not ordered by civil laws.

17

A CRITIC AND A DEFENDER OF ARISTOTLE

If I may alter my organizational structure for a moment, I would like to devote this chapter to two thinkers, the first from the eighteenth century and the second from the twentieth, who reacted to and interacted with Aristotle's *Politics* in opposing ways. The first is an anti-Christian deist who played a decisive role in nudging Europe away from her Judeo-Christian as well as her Greco-Roman heritage: Swiss philosopher Jean-Jacques Rousseau (1712–1778). The second is a Scottish philosopher who, shortly after publishing his strongly Aristotelian *After Virtue* (1981), crossed the Tiber to become a Catholic of strong Thomistic sensibilities: Alasdair MacIntyre (b. 1929). By considering these two thinkers in sequence, we can better gauge the long influence of Aristotle on the political, social, economic, and anthropological thought of the West. We can also see how Aristotle, without intending to, helped restore to these fields a perspective that is more compatible with Christianity than the secular thought of the Enlightenment.

ROUSSEAU ON THE ORIGIN OF THE STATE

In his *Discourse on the Origin and Basis of Inequality Among Men* (1754), Rousseau spins a tale of the genesis of civil society that simultaneously mimics and deconstructs Aristotle's development from family to village to polis. Indeed, the work bears as its epigram the following sentence from Aristotle's *Politics*: "We must look for the intentions of nature in things which retain their nature, and not in things which are corrupted" (I.5; 1254a36).

In the context of *Politics* I.5, this sentence signifies that we should pattern social, political, and economic relationships on the relationship that exists between the soul and the body of a healthy and virtuous man, not a corrupted and vicious one. In Rousseau, however, the sentence is twisted—whether unconsciously or intentionally, I will not speculate—to present the polis itself as a corruption of the "natural," primitive state of man. Whereas Aristotle traces a natural and good procession from family to village to polis, affirming throughout the centrality of private property (see chapter eighteen below), Rousseau sees in the rise of private property and civil society the cause of most of the evil in the world.

Consider how he begins part two of his *Discourse*:

> The first man who, having enclosed a piece of land, took it into his head to say, "This is mine," and found people simple enough to believe him, was the true founder of civil society. The human race would have been spared endless crimes, wars, murders, and horrors if someone had pulled up the stakes or filled in the ditch and cried out to his fellow men, "Do not listen to this imposter! You are lost if you forget that the fruits of the earth belong to everyone, and the earth to no one."[1]

Apart from private property, one of the chief purposes of the family, village, and polis—to protect and preserve private property—is eliminated.

The biblical commandment "Thou shalt not steal" would have no more meaning in a world without property than "Thou shalt not commit adultery" would have in one without marriage. There would have been little reason for Aristotle to write his *Ethics* or his *Politics* if private property did not exist, for the proper rules of ethical and civil behavior are in great part linked to our ability and willingness to respect the property of others while being generous with our own. But then, these are not concerns for Rousseau, for, in addition to rejecting private property as a bad invention of civil society, he argues that sin (Christian)/vice (Aristotle) is not inherent in man's nature but is itself another bad invention of civil society.

THE NOBLE SAVAGE

"On first consideration," Rousseau writes in part one, "it would seem that men in the state of nature, having no kind of moral relations or recognized duties

---

[1]Jean-Jacques Rousseau, *The Essential Rousseau*, trans. Lowell Bair (New York: New American Library, 1974), 173.

among themselves, could not have been either good or evil, and had neither virtues nor vices."[2] Rousseau may seem here to be affirming Eden and the fall, but he is not. His "men in the state of nature" is not a reference to prelapsarian Adam and Eve but to the "noble savage," a myth mostly invented and aggressively propagated by Rousseau, though he does not use that exact phrase in his work. The noble savage is a primitive man who has no need for family, village, or state. He is a radically autonomous individual free from original sin and from all social, political, economic, and moral restraints.

Near the end of part two, Rousseau returns to his noble savage and contrasts him with political/civilized man—*polis* translates into Latin as *civitas*; hence, political and civilized are etymologically synonymous—in a manner that turns Aristotle on his head:

> Savage man and civilized man differ so greatly in the depths of their hearts and in their inclinations that what constitutes the supreme happiness of one would reduce the other to despair. Savage man is steeped in peace and freedom; he wants only to live and remain idle; not even the ataraxia [calm serenity] of the Stoic can approach his profound indifference to every other object. Civilized man, on the other hand, is always active and restless, always sweating and tormenting himself to find still more laborious occupations. He continues working to the end, and even hastens his death to place himself in a situation that will permit him to live, or renounces life to acquire immortality.[3]

There is no doubt that many modern men in cities live just such lives of savage torpor and quiet desperation, as British and American Romantics such as William Wordsworth and Henry David Thoreau writing in the wake of Rousseau pointed out. Still, Rousseau's argument is too simplistic and reductive; it overromanticizes unstructured rural life and overdemonizes city life. It also takes for granted that there is no part of us that is immortal or divine.

It is true that the patriarchs of Genesis, like the liberated Israelites of Exodus, Leviticus, Numbers, Deuteronomy, Joshua, and Judges, lived partly nomadic lives with no city to call their own. But the former lived in the

---

[2] Rousseau, *Essential Rousseau*, 163.
[3] Rousseau, *Essential Rousseau*, 199.

perpetual hope that they would be granted a Promised Land to possess as their own, while the latter lived under a revealed law code with God as their king as they awaited the fulfillment of that hope. Christians look forward to the new Jerusalem—a sort of mingling and perfecting of Eden and Jerusalem—while obeying now the higher law of grace and believing that families and communities are good things through which we learn and practice morality and charity.

Aristotle was neither a primitivist nor an anarchist nor a communist. He believed that property rightly used was a good thing, that laws (both moral and civil) promote human flourishing, and that city life, springing as it does out of the family, is natural and proper to man.

MACINTYRE TO THE RESCUE

Just when it seemed that Rousseau's vision of the noble savage had won, and that Aristotle's foundational vision of man as a political animal whose telos and function are inextricably linked to civil society had gone out of fashion, *After Virtue* took the English-speaking world of moral and political philosophy by storm. In it, MacIntyre warns the West of the rise of emotivism: "the doctrine that all evaluative judgments and more specifically all moral judgments are *nothing but* expressions of preference, expressions of attitude or feeling, insofar as they are moral or evaluative in character."[4]

MacIntyre then proceeded to link this new form of moral relativism to a new understanding of the self as radically autonomous, unbounded by any limits, categories, or definitions. "This democratised self which has no necessary social content and no necessary social identity can then be anything, can assume any role or take any point of view, because it *is* in and for itself nothing."[5] Since the Enlightenment, of which Rousseau was a chief architect, man has increasingly defined himself in opposition to civil society rather than, as for Aristotle, in terms of his role within the family, tribe, and/or polis. Nothing binds or constrains him within a web of duties and responsibilities.

---

[4] Alasdair MacIntyre, *After Virtue: A Study in Moral Theory* (Notre Dame, IN: University of Notre Dame Press, 1981), 11.
[5] MacIntyre, *After Virtue*, 31. On this subject, also see Carl Trueman, *The Rise and Triumph of the Modern Self: Cultural Amnesia, Expressive Individualism, and the Road to Sexual Revolution* (Wheaton, IL: Crossway, 2020).

Whereas, MacIntyre argues, pre-Enlightenment man lived within limits that defined his function, "the emotivist self, in acquiring sovereignty in its own realm lost its traditional boundaries provided by a social identity and a view of human life as ordered to a given end."[6] As we saw in chapter ten, when we allow ourselves to be deflected from our proper course by misdirected desires and a recalcitrant refusal to be shaped by our proper form/telos, we become perverse and self-destructive. This disordering of our proper wants and boundaries manifests itself as an extreme personal freedom that is more license than liberty, anarchy than autonomy, individualism than individuality. Any degree of accountability to any form of authority is cast off, leaving us truly alone and adrift.

MacIntyre found in both Aristotle and the Catholic-Protestant tradition a triple allegiance to "untutored human nature, man-as-he-could-be-if-he-realised-his-*telos* and the moral precepts which enable him to pass from one state to the other." Unfortunately, "the joint effect of the [Enlightenment's] secular rejection of both Protestant and Catholic theology and the scientific and philosophical rejection of Aristotelianism was to eliminate any notion of man-as-he-could-be-if-he-realised-his-*telos*."[7]

Both the high pagan classical and Catholic medieval traditions that connect Aristotle to Aquinas shared

> at least one central functional concept, the concept of *man* understood as having an essential nature and an essential purpose and function.... According to that tradition to be a man is to fill a set of roles each of which has its own point and purpose: member of a family, citizen, soldier, philosopher, servant of God. It is only when man is thought of as individual prior to and apart from all roles that "man" ceases to be a functional concept.[8]

Apart from our roles within the multiple enclaves of civil society, we not only cease to have a purpose; we cease to be human. To be liberated from our social and functional identity is to be liberated from our own humanity: to become an angel or a beast.

---

[6]MacIntyre, *After Virtue*, 32.
[7]MacIntyre, *After Virtue*, 52.
[8]MacIntyre, *After Virtue*, 56.

RESTORING THE PROPER TELOS OF MAN

As MacIntyre defended Aristotelian functionalism (man is by nature a political animal), so he defended Aristotelian teleology (all things in nature, including and especially man, have a telos that directs their movement and growth).

> For the middle ages mechanisms were efficient causes in a world to be comprehended ultimately in terms of final causes. Every species has a natural end, and to explain the movements of and changes in an individual is to explain how that individual moves toward the end appropriate to members of that particular species. The ends to which men as members of such a species move are conceived by them as goods, and their movement towards or away from various goods are to be explained with reference to the virtues and vices which they have learned or failed to learn and the forms of practical reasoning which they employ. Aristotle's *Ethics* and *Politics* (together of course with the *De Anima*) are as much treatises concerned with how human action is to be explained and understood as with what acts are to be done. Indeed within the Aristotelian framework the one task cannot be discharged without discharging the other.[9]

Neither Aristotle nor Aquinas, nor most of the great philosophers and theologians who stand between them, artificially separated politics from ethics, physics from metaphysics, science from virtue, factual from spiritual. All were oriented toward natural ends and could be explained in terms of final causes. Theoretical and practical were all of a piece.

To say that man is by nature a political animal is inseparable from saying that he is a virtuous animal. To say that his function within the polis is ordered toward a telos is identical to saying that his body is to obey the telos established by his soul. Morality can only exist within such a functionalist-teleological framework. If we abandon Aristotle, MacIntyre argues, we have nowhere to turn but to Friedrich Nietzsche's "central thesis: that all rational vindications of morality manifestly fail and that *therefore* belief in the tenets of morality needs to be explained in terms of a set of rationalisations which conceal the fundamentally non-rational phenomena

---
[9]MacIntyre, *After Virtue*, 78-79.

of the will."[10] Either ethics and politics share the same secure foundation of natural teleology and human functionality, or they can be justified only by nonrational instincts and an amoral will to power.

If we are to hold back the socially and morally destructive forces of emotivism, the autonomous individual, and the antihumanistic Enlightenment split of facts and values, then we must turn back to Aristotle and the classical tradition out of which he emerged. "In all those cultures, Greek, medieval or Renaissance," MacIntyre explains, "where moral thinking and action is structured according to some version of the scheme that I have called classical, the chief means of moral education is the telling of stories." For Aristotle, that scheme and those stories came out of the epics of Homer. In those epics, as in the heroic sagas of Iceland and Ireland, every "individual has a given role and status within a well-defined and highly determinate system of roles and statuses. The key structures are those of kinship and of the household. In such a society a man knows who he is by knowing his role in these structures; and in knowing this he knows also what he owes and what is owed to him by the occupant of every other role and status." That is why, in such societies, courage "is important, not simply as a quality of individuals, but as the quality necessary to sustain a household and a community."[11]

Far more rests on Aristotle's key claim that "man is by nature a political animal" than we might at first think. In ontological terms, we are contingent beings, for our human and mortal life relies on the divine and immortal life of God. We are, however, contingent in the moral sense as well, for virtue is defined by and manifests itself in terms of our function within a particular oikos or polis. So it was in the heroic age celebrated by Homer; so it was with greater force during that golden age of Athens that birthed and nurtured Aristotle: "The common Athenian assumption then is that the virtues have their place within the social context of the city-state. To be a good man will on every Greek view be at least closely allied to being a good citizen."[12]

Once again we see that Aristotle's *Ethics* and *Politics* are as intimately and necessarily linked as his *Physics* and *Metaphysics*. Just as Aristotle allows for

---

[10]MacIntyre, *After Virtue*, 111.
[11]MacIntyre, *After Virtue*, 114-15.
[12]MacIntyre, *After Virtue*, 127.

no physical vacuum in the latter two books, so he allows for no moral vacuum in the former. Virtue has both content and context. Aristotle, MacIntyre insists, did not compartmentalize fact and value, public and private the way we do in our post-Enlightenment world: "Notice how on an Aristotelian view law and morality are not two separate realms, as they are for modernity.... According to Aristotle then excellence of character and intelligence cannot be separated. Here Aristotle expresses a view characteristically at odds with that dominant in the modern world."[13] What is needed today in our fragmented world is a resynthesis of reason and virtue, the theoretical and the practical, logos (word) and praxis (action). Only by such means can we restore the full dimensions of our humanity and ground virtue in a foundation less slippery than that of emotivism and the autonomous self. MacIntyre does not exaggerate when he warns that we must choose Aristotle or Nietzsche.

WHAT THE PRE-CHRISTIAN ARISTOTLE MISSED

Still, MacIntyre does highlight two areas in which Aristotle's pre-Christian vision prevents him from soaring as high as he might. Though he connects his philosophical system to an eternal Unmoved Mover, that divine First Cause lacks personality and agency. "The impersonal unchanging divinity of which Aristotle speaks, the metaphysical contemplation of which furnishes man with his specific and ultimate *telos*, can itself take no interest in the merely human, let alone in the dilemmatic; it is nothing other than thought timelessly thinking itself and conscious of nothing but itself."[14]

The Aristotelian God who is loved and desired does not himself love or desire. He offers himself up as an object of contemplation, but we cannot know him, and he seems uninterested in knowing us. Aristotle would likely have agreed that we see now dimly in a mirror, but I do not think he harbored any hope that we would one day know the Unmoved Mover face to face. He would likely have agreed as well that we see now only in part, but I cannot imagine that the promise that we will one day be known in full even as we are fully known would have meant anything to him (see 1 Cor 13:12).

---

[13]MacIntyre, *After Virtue*, 143, 145.
[14]MacIntyre, *After Virtue*, 148.

MacIntyre makes clear that the statement in 1 Corinthians 13:13, that the greatest of these is love (or charity), would have likewise made no sense to Aristotle, since there "is no word in the Greek of Aristotle's age correctly translated 'sin', 'repentance' or 'charity.'" The reason this is important is that the Christian drama of sin, repentance, and charity, which treats evil as an antagonist, makes possible the Christian genre of man as a pilgrim on a quest that is difficult but that promises redemption, reconciliation, and divine charity at and as its end. In contrast, MacIntyre argues, "Aristotle takes the *telos* of human life to be *a certain kind of life*; the *telos* is not something to be achieved at some future point, but in the way our whole life is constructed."[15]

This distinction between the Aristotelian and the Christian does not rob the former of the truth of its position; it merely points out that there is greater dynamism, struggle, and consummation in the latter. Only in the latter is life "informed by an idealized view of the world as an integrated order, in which the temporal mirrors the eternal. Every particular item has its due place in the order of things. This is that intellectual vision of total system which finds its supreme expression in Dante and in Aquinas."[16]

This great truth MacIntyre learned from Aristotle, as Aquinas and Dante had learned it before him. What makes MacIntyre's achievement the more impressive is that, whereas Aquinas and Dante lived in a world that already accepted the truths discerned by Aristotle, MacIntyre succeeded in restoring Aristotle to a social and academic world in flight from our Judeo-Chistian *and* our Greco-Roman past.

---

[15] MacIntyre, *After Virtue*, 162-63.
[16] MacIntyre, *After Virtue*, 164-65.

18

THE BLESSINGS AND DANGERS OF PRIVATE PROPERTY

THE *REPUBLIC* IS A DIALOGUE replete with sudden revelations, unexpected twists and turns, and audacious leaps of logic. The most memorable of these surprises, however, must be Plato's descent into the downright scandalous. While arguing for the censorship of myths that depict the gods as licentious and arbitrary, Socrates (ironically?) suggests that his guardian class of philosopher-kings should hold all things in common, including their wives. In the utopian scheme Socrates propounds in *Republic* V, procreation will be based not on the intimate, lifelong bond of husband and wife but on a practical political need to produce the most eugenically fit offspring.

ARISTOTLE TAKES PLATO TO TASK

I, for one, have tried to dismiss Plato's community of women as a form of grand satire, a sort of reductio ad absurdum on the difficulty of eliminating greed from the ruling class and preventing them from building their own personal dynasties. Whether or not Plato was being sarcastic, his star pupil was convinced that he was not. In *Politics* II, Aristotle takes up Plato's indecent proposal with deadly seriousness and explains why such a system is both unnatural and unworkable. To be honest, even if Plato was writing with his tongue firmly in his cheek, I do not think Aristotle the concrete thinker would have gotten the joke.

Still, I am grateful Aristotle took Plato seriously, for it provoked him to mount a seminal defense of private property that modern proponents of socialism and wealth redistribution, whether secular or Christian, would do well to heed. "The members of a state," Aristotle explains,

> must either have (1) all things or (2) nothing in common, or (3) some things in common and some not. That they should have nothing in common is clearly impossible, for the constitution is a community, and must at any rate have a common place. . . . But should a well-ordered state have all things, as far as may be, in common, or some only and not others? For the citizens might conceivably have wives and children and property in common, as Socrates proposes in the *Republic* of Plato. Which is better, our present condition, or the proposed new order of society? (II.1; 1260b38-1261a9)

With his signature clarity, Aristotle offers three options for organizing a state: either the citizens share all things in common, nothing in common, or a mixture of the two. The second option is obviously untenable, for they must at the very least share the city itself in common. But is it therefore incumbent on a state to follow Socrates's model in *Republic* and have the rulers share their property, their wives, and their children?

Aristotle quickly and definitively answers no to this question. It is not just that Socrates's communal scheme for his rulers is impractical; it defeats the very purpose and telos of the polis:

> I am speaking of the premise from which the argument of Socrates proceeds, "that the greater the unity of the state the better." Is it not obvious that a state may at length attain such a degree of unity as to be no longer a state?—since the nature of a state is to be a plurality, and in tending to greater unity, from being a state, it becomes a family, and from being a family, an individual. . . . We ought not to attain this greatest unity even if we could, for it would be the destruction of the state. Again, a state is not made up only of so many men, but of different kinds of men; for similars do not constitute a state. (II.2; 1261a15-25)

The polis, Aristotle insists, is not a complete unity but an aggregate: a unity in diversity, an *e pluribus unum*. To try to make it into a unity is to try to turn it into a household or even an individual. Pure equality and the breakdown of all private property, Aristotle makes clear, will destroy the very polis it tries to build.

WE CARE FOR THAT WHICH IS OUR OWN

Besides, even if unity *were* the goal of the polis, a community of wives where nobody knows whose son is whose will not bring about any real unity. It will only result in a lowest-common-denominator world of disinterest and neglect.

> For that which is common to the greatest number has the least care bestowed upon it. Every one thinks chiefly of his own, hardly at all of the common interest; and only when he is himself concerned as an individual. For besides other considerations, everybody is more inclined to neglect the duty which he expects another to fulfill; as in families many attendants are often less useful than a few. (II.3; 1261b33-37)

The view that Aristotle describes here is neither optimistic nor pessimistic; it is simply realistic, grounded in a common-sense understanding of human psychology. We care more for that which is our own, whether that own be our property or our family. There is nothing intrinsically selfish about this, though we can fall into the twin vices of hoarding or wasting if we neglect the golden mean. Rather than make us care for all things and people equally, Aristotle explains, a community of wives and children will lead to a watery sort of fraternity in which family feelings are diluted like a little wine in too much water. "Of the two qualities which chiefly inspire regard and affection—that a thing is your own and that it is your only one—neither can exist in such a state as this" (II.4; 1262b22-24). When all wives and sons are held together communally, it will not strengthen our affections but reduce them to mediocrity.

The same goes for diligence, industry, and hard work. When people share property,

> those who labor much and get little will necessarily complain of those who labor little and receive or consume much. . . . There is always a difficulty in men living together and having all human relations in common, but especially in their having common property. The partnerships of fellow-travelers are an example to the point; for they generally fall out over everyday matters and quarrel about any trifle which turns up. (II.5; 1263a12-20)

Communal property, far from bringing people together to build society, causes resentment and petty legal disputes. People with secure private property will labor together in a limited way to cultivate some communal land, but if they lose their own property, their incentive to participate in communal work will quickly fade.

PRIVATE PROPERTY IS NOT THE ROOT OF EVIL

Something of even greater importance will fade as well: virtue. Moral goodness is closely allied to private property. Where there is compulsion, as there is in communism, there can be no virtue, for we can only be liberal with that which we own. If all wives were held in common, Aristotle argues, the virtue of "temperance toward women" would be annihilated. Likewise for "liberality in the matter of property. No one, when men have all things in common, will any longer set an example of liberality or do any liberal action; for liberality consists in the use which is made of property" (II.5; 1263b10-14).

Advocates for the abolition of private property, whether they lived in Aristotle's day, Rousseau's day, or our own, claim that communal ownership of lands and goods will lead to benevolence and brotherhood. All "the evils now existing in states, suits about contracts, convictions for perjury, flatteries of rich men and the like," they promise, will end, for such things "arise out of the possession of private property." But they are and have always been wrong about such matters. "'These evils," Aristotle insists, "are due to a very different cause—the wickedness of human nature. Indeed, we see that there is much more quarrelling among those who have all things in common, though there are not many of them when compared with the vast numbers who have private property" (II.5; 1263b19-26).

This passage is truly remarkable, showing that Aristotle, unlike Plato, had a nascent understanding of what Christians call original sin. The problem, he sees, is not private property but our own propensity to evil. It is the greed and wickedness in men, rather than the property they own, that is the root cause of the quarrels and dissensions that lead to litigiousness, perjury, and flattery. Even so, Paul did not identify *money* as the root of all evil but the *love of* money (1 Tim 6:10).

Although I do not think the apostles were readers of Aristotle, there is an incident early in Acts that reflects, I believe, an ethos similar to that of Aristotle. The early Christians who "had all things in common" (Acts 2:44) were not coerced into surrendering all their private property but voluntarily sold some of their land to provide for the needs of the saints. Barnabas did so openly and honestly (Acts 4:36-37), but Ananias and Sapphira did so dishonestly, out of a deceitful desire to appear more virtuous than they were (Acts 5:1-11). Peter's (and God's!) condemnation of them has to do with their evil motives rather than an absolute command to redistribute their wealth. The land they sold, Peter explains in Acts 5:4, was theirs to keep and theirs to sell; their sin was not that they refused to give all the money gained from the sale of their private property to the apostles but that they lied about the amount they gained and gave.

BURKE DEFENDS PRIVATE PROPERTY

The profound influence of Aristotle's theories of politics and property on such thinkers as Augustine and Aquinas, Hooker and Thomas Hobbes, Locke and Montesquieu, Burke and Alexis de Tocqueville, Alexander Hamilton and James Madison has proven to be a boon for the Western world, helping to lay the foundations for liberal democracy and free-market capitalism. Unfortunately, in the same way that Aristotle's political thought helped birth justice, stability, and prosperity in Europe and America, Rousseau's rejection of civil society and private property bore destructive fruit in the form of the French Revolution. All seemed well at the start with the relatively bloodless storming of the Bastille in 1789 and the promise to bring liberty, equality, and fraternity to all classes. The promise was short lived, however, with utopian dreams giving way to the execution of Louis XVI and Marie Antoinette and the Reign of Terror (1793–1794), during which aristocracy and clergy were dispossessed of their power, their property, and their lives.

Three years before the Terror, when many Europeans were celebrating the fledgling revolution as a triumph of freedom and justice, Edmund Burke (1729–1797), well-trained in Aristotelian thought, saw with piercing clarity the death and madness that would soon follow. In his *Reflections on the Revolution in France* (1790), Burke, a Whig member of Parliament who supported both Irish and American independence, warned of what the natural upshot would be of the pro-Rousseau/Voltaire, anti-Christian/Aristotelian ethos of the revolutionaries. Although some critics hold that Burke was an Enlightenment deist, I would argue that he was a believing and practicing Christian. In *Reflections*, he affirms "that man is by his constitution a religious animal; that atheism is against, not only our reason, but our instincts; and that it cannot prevail long." He also hails the Christian religion as Britain's "boast and comfort, and one great source of civilization amongst us and amongst many other nations." He further resolves that Britain must "keep an established church, an established monarchy, an established [land-based, hereditary] aristocracy, and an established democracy, each in the degree it exists, and in no greater."[1]

As part of his prophetic critique of the egalitarian excesses of the revolution, Burke defends the central importance of private property along the lines of Aristotle's *Politics*. Here is a complex passage from his reasoned and passionate defense:

> As ability is a vigorous and active principle, and as property is sluggish, inert, and timid, it never can be safe from the invasions of ability, unless it be, out of all proportion, predominant in the representation. It must be represented, too, in great masses of accumulation, or it is not rightly protected. The characteristic essence of property, formed out of the combined principles of its acquisition and conservation, is to be *unequal*. The great masses, therefore, which excite envy and tempt rapacity must be put out of the possibility of danger. Then they form a natural rampart about the lesser properties in all their gradations. The same quantity of property, which is by the natural course of things divided among many, has not the same operation. Its defensive power is weakened as it is diffused. In this diffusion each man's portion is less than what, in the eagerness of his desires, he may flatter himself to obtain by dissipating the accumulations of others. The plunder of the few would indeed give but a share inconceivably small in the distribution to the many. But the many are not capable of making this calculation; and those who lead them to rapine never intend this distribution.[2]

The closing sentence of this paragraph may represent the greatest prophetic utterance in all of Burke's work. Not only in the French Revolution but in the Russian, Chinese, Korean, Vietnamese, Cambodian, Cuban, and Venezuelan Revolutions, the anti–private property communist government never actually

---

[1] Edmund Burke, *Reflections on the Revolution in France*, ed. Thomas H. D. Mahoney (New York: Macmillan, 1986), 103-4.
[2] Burke, *Reflections on the Revolution*, 57-58.

redistributed property to the poor. They simply impoverished everyone, rich and poor alike, to fatten their own coffers. Needless to say, the Marxist-Leninist dictatorship of the proletariat has never "evolved" into a pure communist state where all things are held in common.[3]

Like civilization itself, private property is a tenuous thing. Property is passive and inert; it cannot protect itself from the clever and the strong. It also cannot protect itself from the envy of the masses, a force that has again and again been channeled for evil by demagogues such as Mao Zedong, Pol Pot, and Fidel Castro. The best bulwark, Burke argues, against the dissolution of private property is large holdings of land conserved by hereditary families who are fully invested in their preservation. Burke is not against small landowners, but he insists that property by its nature is unequal and that any attempts to redistribute land on a large scale will more likely lead to chaos and civil war. Such redistribution generally provokes resentment rather than gratitude, as each recipient claims that he has been cheated in the division of property. In any case, the plundering of hereditary land will make no actual difference in the lives of the masses who scramble for mere scraps.

Although I would argue that the American republic that Burke supported found peaceful and effective ways to transition from large feudal landholdings to small home ownership, Burke's predictions have nevertheless proven accurate in terms of the many and continuing revolutions that have followed in the wake of the Bastille and the Terror. Private property needs many safeguards, the most important of which are the qualities that are bred and strengthened by the responsibility that comes with hereditary wealth.

---

[3] Richard Crossman, ed., *The God That Failed* (New York: Columbia University Press, 2001), collects six essays by former communists who recanted their allegiance when they witnessed the upshot of Marxist ideology. *The Black Book of Communism: Crimes, Terror, Repression*, written by Stéphane Courtois and five other authors and translated by Jonathan Murphy and Mark Kramer (Cambridge, MA: Harvard University Press, 1999), documents the outrages committed by Marxist governments across the globe. See also James R. Otteson, *The End of Socialism* (New York: Cambridge University Press, 2014). For a Christian writer who rejected collectivism and defended private property but who was a critic of capitalism, see Hilaire Belloc, *The Servile State* (Milwaukee: Cavalier Books, 2018; originally published in 1912). Belloc and his friend G. K. Chesterton advocated for distributism, their version of the Catholic social teaching of subsidiarity, on which see Thomas C. Behr, *Social Justice and Subsidiarity: Luigi Taparelli and the Origins of Modern Catholic Social Thought* (Washington, DC: Catholic University of America Press, 2019).

PRIVATE PROPERTY AS A SCHOOL OF VIRTUE

"The power of perpetuating our property in our families," argues Burke in a manner that is strongly indebted to Aristotle's *Ethics* and *Politics*,

> is one of the most valuable and interesting circumstances belonging to it, and that which tends the most to the perpetuation of society itself. It makes our weakness subservient to our virtue, it grafts benevolence even upon avarice. The possessors of family wealth, and of the distinction which attends hereditary possession (as most concerned in it) are the natural securities for this transmission. With us the House of Peers is formed upon this principle. It is wholly composed of hereditary property and hereditary distinction, and made, therefore, the third of the legislature and, in the last event, the sole judge of all property in all its subdivisions. The House of Commons, too, though not necessarily, yet in fact, is always so composed, in the far greater part. Let those large proprietors be what they will—and they have their chance of being amongst the best—they are, at the very worst, the ballast in the vessel of the commonwealth. For though hereditary wealth and the rank which goes with it are too much idolized by creeping sycophants and the blind, abject admirers of power, they are too rashly slighted in shallow speculations of the petulant, assuming, short-sighted coxcombs of philosophy. Some decent, regulated preeminence, some preference (not exclusive appropriation) given to birth is neither unnatural, nor unjust, nor impolitic.[4]

Although Burke concedes that hereditary wealth can provoke envy and flattery in lesser men, he champions it as the best nursery for nurturing virtue and benevolence in each generation of landowners. It is those virtues and that benevolence that do the most to preserve society.

Indeed, the British Parliament, England's great bastion of law and liberty, rests itself on such land-based wealth, for the majority of its members are both products and defenders of the properties and distinctions that arise from hereditary possession. Such men, raised to respect land, family, and tradition, are for Burke the ballast that keeps the ship of state steady and on course. While shallow, shortsighted philosophers—Burke clearly has Rousseau and Voltaire in mind—may rage against the aristocracy and its

---

[4] Burke, *Reflections on the Revolution*, 58-59.

hereditary wealth, difference and inequality are not in and of themselves unnatural, unjust, or impolitic. To the contrary, they form the foundation of any true civil society.

LIMITS ON THE RIGHTS OF MAN

The French revolutionaries, Burke writes, speak loudly and long about the rights of man. But what does such a phrase mean, and what are its limits? Burke's answer to this question is at once Judeo-Christian and Aristotelian:

> Men have a right to live by that rule [the law]; they have a right to do justice, as between their fellows, whether their fellows are in public function or in ordinary occupation. They have a right to the fruits of their industry and to the means of making their industry fruitful. They have a right to the acquisitions of their parents, to the nourishment and improvement of their offspring, to instruction in life, and to consolation in death. Whatever each man can separately do, without trespassing upon others, he has a right to do for himself; and he has a right to a fair portion of all which society, with all its combinations of skill and force, can do in his favor. In this partnership all men have equal rights, but not to equal things. He that has but five shillings in the partnership has as good a right to it as he that has five hundred pounds has to his larger proportion. But he has not a right to an equal dividend in the product of the joint stock.[5]

It was likely the terrible institution of slavery in the colonies that led Thomas Jefferson and the signers of the Declaration of Independence to enumerate our inalienable rights as life, liberty, and the pursuit of happiness rather than life, liberty, and property. Although Jefferson's use of the word *happiness* should be taken in the sense that Aristotle uses it in *Ethics*, rather than in the sense of Rousseau's autonomous individual, I think Aristotle himself would have preferred *property* to *happiness*, since the ownership of private property is a necessary precondition to the citizen's pursuit of happiness.

In any case, our Founding Fathers, who sought equality of opportunity and not equality of outcome, would have resonated with Burke's commonsense claim that all men have equal rights but not to equal things. Just as

---

[5] Burke, *Reflections on the Revolution*, 67.

inequality is "neither unnatural, nor unjust, nor impolitic," so forced equality violates human nature, human industry, and human flourishing. It is essential that the citizens of a polis be guaranteed the right to their own industry and to that of their parents and grandparents. They must possess, as well, the right to pass down the fruit of that industry to their children and grandchildren. For Burke and Aristotle alike, the family is the foundation of the state and is the first classroom where we learn about virtue and vice, diligence and sloth, life and death.

USURY AS A MISUSE OF PRIVATE PROPERTY

Were I to end the chapter here, I might seem to be claiming Aristotle as the father of modern, unregulated capitalism. He was not. He believed very strongly in private property and would have been a proponent of free trade, but he also believed that there needed to be limits on the acquisition of wealth. The polis, after all, with its guarantee of private property, does not exist to make its citizens rich but to make them virtuous:

> It is clear then that a state is not a mere society, having a common place, established for the prevention of mutual crime and for the sake of exchange. These are conditions without which a state cannot exist; but all of them together do not constitute a state, which is a community of families and aggregations of families in well-being, for the sake of a perfect and self-sufficing life. . . . The end of the state is the good life, and these are the means towards it. And the state is the union of families and villages in a perfect and self-sufficing life, by which we mean a happy and honorable life. (III.9; 1280b30-1281a2)

For Aristotle, as I said a moment ago, happiness/virtue is the end; private property is merely one of the means for achieving that end. As such, laws that prevent theft and that regulate the exchange of goods are necessary but not sufficient prerequisites for the good life. Private property helps citizens attain the self-sufficiency they need to practice the life of contemplation, but it does not in and of itself guarantee virtue or happiness.

Indeed, there are certain aspects related to trade and the exchange of goods and property that can turn citizens away from the path of virtue. Chief among those is something the Catholic Church once considered a grave sin but that today undergirds our capitalist system: usury. Usury can mean one of two things: the lending of money at excessive rates of interest or the lending of money at any rate of interest. In the Old Testament, God forbids the Jews to practice usury against their own people (Ex 22:25; Lev 25:36-38; Neh 5:6-11), but he does not forbid it with reference to Gentiles (Deut 23:19-20). In the New Testament, Jesus, far from outlawing all usury, rebukes a steward for not having the diligence to put his master's money in the bank so it could at least have accrued interest (Mt 25:27). He does, however, encourage his followers to give without expecting anything in return (Lk 6:34-35) and warns them that they cannot serve both God and money (Mt 6:24).

Despite the lack of a clear restriction against usury in the New Testament, the Catholic Church condemned it during the high Middle Ages. Muslims, as it turns out, also condemned the lending of money at interest, resulting in a Europe and Near East where Jews alone could lawfully practice usury. Although the stereotype of the Jewish banker is no longer true, it was literally true during the high Middle Ages and was, sadly, one of the—if not *the*—chief causes of antisemitism. People who justified their hatred of the Jews on the grounds that they "killed Jesus" were in most cases using that supposedly pious smokescreen to cover their own greed and envy—after all, it seemed like the Jews were getting rich without doing any work. This kind of resentful, envy-inspired antisemitism forms the disturbing background to Shakespeare's *Merchant of Venice*.[6]

But if the New Testament does not forbid usury, why did Catholics and Muslims forbid it? I would argue that the animus against usury goes back as much to the Old Testament as it does to Aristotle's *Politics*. We should not forget that Islam was strongly influenced by Aristotle. As I explained in a note at the end of chapter three, Muslim scholars such as the eleventh-century Avicenna and the twelfth-century Averroes—both of whom Dante designates as virtuous pagans in *Inferno* IV—helped preserve the writings of Aristotle and pass them on to Aquinas and the Catholic Church.

---

[6]For a new study of this sad history, see Rowan Dorin, *No Return: Jews, Christian Usurers, and the Spread of Mass Expulsion in Medieval Europe* (Princeton, NJ: Princeton University Press, 2023).

WHY ARISTOTLE OPPOSED USURY

Why, then, did Aristotle condemn usury? Did he have a good reason, and can we learn from that reason today? We moderns, especially those of us who follow Christ, can learn a great deal from Aristotle's reasoning, even if I do not believe that fair rates of usury are immoral (though the usury that credit-card companies extort from immature teens and college students is nothing less than criminal!).

In *Politics* I.9, Aristotle provides a brief genesis of what we today call capitalism. In the beginning, he explains, the household was self-sufficient, relying on its own property for its sustenance and so having no need to barter goods with neighboring households. As oikos grew into village and village into polis, however, bartering became necessary and eventually expanded to include exchanges of goods from other regions. As the desire for such goods increased, ships were needed to import luxuries from increasingly distant foreign lands. But if sailors were to go on long voyages to acquire foreign goods, then they would need to bring a salable commodity that did not spoil. Enter currency made of nonperishable precious metals that could function as a stable medium of exchange. To protect the trade of foreign goods, armies were formed, and more coins minted to support them.

Alas, once currency was established as the medium of trade, people began to seek it as an end in itself rather than as a means to achieving the goods necessary to live a life of virtue. Thus began what Aristotle calls the art of getting wealth:

> When the use of coin had once been discovered, out of the barter of necessary articles arose the other art of wealth getting, namely, retail trade; which was at first probably a simple matter, but became more complicated as soon as men learned by experience whence and by what exchanges the greatest profit might be made. Originating in the use of coin, the art of getting wealth is generally thought to be chiefly concerned with it, and to be the art which produces riches and wealth; having to consider how they may be accumulated. Indeed, riches is assumed by many to be only a quantity of coin, because the arts of getting wealth and retail trade are concerned with coin. Others maintain that coined money is a mere sham, a thing not natural, but conventional only, because, if the users substitute another commodity for it, it is worthless, and

> because it is not useful as a means to any of the necessities of life, and, indeed, he who is rich in coin may often be in want of necessary food. But how can that be wealth of which a man may have a great abundance and yet perish with hunger, like Midas in the fable, whose insatiable prayer turned everything that was set before him into gold? (I.9; 1257b1-16)

Though Aristotle, unlike Plato and Jesus, rarely illustrates his teachings with vivid and memorable metaphors, he shows himself well capable of doing so in this passage. It is one thing to speak in logical terms of the inability of coins to substitute for the necessities of life; it is another to call up the well-known myth of King Midas and the golden touch. How foolish we are when we pursue Midas's avaricious lust for gold only to learn too late that money cannot satisfy the cravings of our heart, our soul, or even our belly. Be careful what you wish for; you may have the misfortune to get it!

Coin, as coin, does not satisfy. It can only produce an illusion of well-being. When we forget that such commodities are not themselves the good life but only a way of securing the self-sufficiency on which the good life rests, we end up idolizing the means rather than the end. The telos of life is not the accumulation of profit but the cultivation of character. We should not seek to be rich in coin but rich in virtue. When we seek the former, we end up greedy and anxious and lose our sense of limits.

Thus far, Aristotle sounds a bit like Jesus in the Sermon on the Mount, instructing his disciples to seek first the proper goal and telos (see Mt 6:25-34) and not to be blinded by the false promises and endless anxieties of wealth. That is, until Aristotle takes his argument in an unexpected direction:

> There are two sorts of wealth-getting, as I have said; one is a part of household management, the other is retail trade: the former necessary and honorable, while that which consists in exchange is justly censured; for it is unnatural, and a mode by which men gain from one another. The most hated sort, and with the greatest reason, is usury, which makes a gain out of money itself, and not from the natural object of it. For money was intended to be used in exchange, but not to increase at interest. And this term interest, which means the birth of money from money, is applied to the breeding of money because the offspring resembles the parent. Wherefore of all modes of getting wealth this is the most unnatural. (I.10; 1257a38-1258a8)

The Blessings and Dangers of Private Property

For Aristotle, retail trade by coin is unnatural, for it seeks to make gain from coin itself rather than from the good and necessary things that coin is used to purchase. When used as a medium of exchange, money can be a useful tool; when used as a means to make more money, it becomes a mockery of natural procreation. Coin is sterile and inert; it cannot give birth to coin. That is why when traders and bankers try to make wealth off their wealth, they pervert the natural order of things.

WHY DANTE PUT USURERS DEEP IN HELL

This admittedly odd critique of usury was taken up and developed first by Aquinas and then by Dante, who treats usury as a grave sin, far worse than lust, gluttony, hoarding and wasting, wrath and sloth, and heresy. The usurers lie in a subsection of level seven, which punishes various forms of violence. First come the murderers, those who were violent against others; next come the suicides, those who were violent against themselves. Finally are those who are guilty of violence against God (blasphemy), against nature (sodomy), and against art (usury). By art, Dante means the skills that God has given to each of us and that we are responsible to use properly.

Blasphemy, sodomy, and usury are punished in a desert of burning sand, for all three are utterly barren, twisting and perverting all natural forms of procreation. When Dante asks Virgil, in *Inferno* XI, why usury offends God, Virgil replies:

"Philosophy makes plain by many reasons,"
    he answered me, "to those who heed her teachings,
    how all of Nature,—her laws, her fruits, her seasons,—
springs from the Ultimate Intellect and Its art:
    and if you read your *Physics* with due care,
    you will note, not many pages from the start [II.2; 194a21],
that Art strives after her [nature] by imitation,
    as the disciple imitates the master;
    Art, as it were, is the Grandchild of Creation.
By this, recalling the Old Testament
    near the beginning of Genesis, you will see
    that in the will of Providence, man was meant

> to labor and to prosper [Gen 2:15]. But usurers,
> > by seeking their increase in other ways,
> > scorn Nature in herself and her followers."[7]

To Aristotle's argument that usury is unnatural, for it violates the natural laws of procreation, Dante adds an important detail from the creation account of Genesis. Man's call to work the ground was not a result of the fall but a part of God's original plan. The curse was not that Adam would now have to work the ground but that his work would henceforth be harsh and difficult: by the sweat of his brow (Gen 3:17-19).

It is no coincidence that Dante calls the attention of his readers to two passages that come near the beginning of Genesis and *Physics*. He, like Aquinas, counts both as sources of wisdom and authority that, when heeded and properly discerned, clarify the true nature of God, man, and the universe. Usury bypasses the proper use of art, which Dante treats as the child of nature and thus the grandchild of God. As nature reflects and imitates God, so art should reflect and imitate nature. Just as sodomy violates the natural procreative complementarity of the sexes, so usury violates the divine mandate to use our God-given arts to cultivate the natural world and so cause it to blossom. Both leave us stranded in a barren, fruitless world of misdirected sexual desire and dead coin that can neither sustain nor satisfy.

While many Christians on the right condemn sodomy while giving (excessive) usury a pass, many on the left do the exact opposite. Aristotle and Dante can help the church today regain a sense of proportion and propriety, an embrace of our proper design and a healthy desire to cooperate with God, nature, and art to promote life, joy, and human flourishing.

---

[7]Dante, *The Divine Comedy*, trans. John Ciardi (New York: New American Library, 1970), 92-93.

19

THE RULE OF LAW

In chapter sixteen, I explained that, whereas Plato (*Republic* VIII) posits a cycle of constitutions, with each one giving way to a successively worse form, Aristotle (*Ethics* VIII) posits three good forms of government—monarchy, aristocracy, and timocracy—that each degrade into a correspondingly bad form—tyranny, oligarchy, and democracy. In *Politics* III, Aristotle offers a simple test for distinguishing between the three good forms and the three bad ones.

THE ONE, THE FEW, AND THE MANY

> The words constitution and government have the same meaning, and the government, which is the supreme authority in states, must be in the hands of one, or of a few, or of the many. The true forms of government, therefore, are those in which the one, or the few, or the many, govern with a view to the common interest; but governments which rule with a view to the private interest, whether of the one, or of the few, or of the many, are perversions. For the members of a state, if they are truly citizens, ought to participate in its advantages. Of forms of government in which one rules, we call that which regards the common interests, kingship or royalty; that in which more than one, but not many, rule, aristocracy; and it is so called, either because the rulers are the best men, or because they have at heart the best interests of the state and of the citizens. But when the citizens at large administer the state for the common interest, the government is called by the generic name—a constitution. Of the above-mentioned forms, the perversions are as follows: of royalty, tyranny; of aristocracy, oligarchy; of constitutional government, democracy. For tyranny is a kind of monarchy which has in view the interest of the monarch only; oligarchy has in view the interest of the wealthy; democracy, of the needy: none of them the common good of all. (III.7; 1279a25-1279b10)

In *Politics*, Aristotle uses the word *constitution* (often transliterated from the Greek as *polity*) in place of *timocracy*. He also identifies as the chief corrupting factor the attempt to use the power of the polis for the benefit of the one or the few or the many in whom the power is invested rather than for the common good of the polis.

Aristotle is not opposed to sovereignty ("supreme authority") residing in a single monarch, a small group of the best citizens, or the wider citizen body. All three can yield a stable, virtuous polis, but only when sovereignty is exercised on behalf of the polis and not to aggrandize all power in the hands of the one, the few, or the many. So Aristotle explains in chapter seven. At the end of chapter six, he clarifies the distinction by connecting it to the central concern of Plato's *Republic*, justice: "Governments which have a regard to the common interest are constituted in accordance with strict principles of justice, and are therefore true forms; but those which regard only the interest of the rulers are all defective and perverted forms, for they are despotic, whereas a state is a community of freemen" (III.6; 1279a17-21).

How, then, is one to keep the proper balance in a polis between the competing claims of the one, the few, and the many? In particular, how does one balance the desire of the oligarchs for inequality with the desire of the democrats for equality? Aristotle suggests that this balance can be maintained by the law but then temporarily pulls back from that position: "Some one may say that it is bad in any case for a man, subject as he is to all the accidents of human passion, to have the supreme power, rather than the law. But what if the law itself be democratical or oligarchical, how will that help us out of our difficulties? Not at all; the same consequences will follow" (III.10; 1281a34-38). The law can be used to cool the passions of citizens—and to place something above the king—but what if the law is hijacked by the competing agendas of democrats or oligarchs?

THE CHALLENGES OF DEMOCRACY

Aristotle then turns specifically to the possibilities and dangers of a democracy, such as Athens, where sovereignty is in the hands of the many. It is possible, he concedes, to invest power in a group of individuals who are not particularly good on their own but who are good as a unit. Sometimes the whole can be greater than the part, and true efficiency can be achieved by pooling the resources of many. Still, such groupings of people can also result in a disgruntled herd, a resentful mob of disenfranchised citizens.

Solon, who founded the Athenian democracy in about 600 BC, was aware of this danger and took measures to avoid it. Rather than give the people offices of power, he allowed them to elect and hold accountable those who would rule over them. Yes, Aristotle concedes again, the body of citizens may lack the technical skills to judge politicians, but sometimes we need amateurs rather than specialists. Indeed, "if the people are not utterly degraded, although individually they may be worse judges than those who have special knowledge—as a body they are as good or better" (III.11; 1282a16-17). I have no doubt that if Aristotle were alive today, he would criticize our democracy for relying too much on experts and specialists who are cut off both from the people and from common sense.

Having made these qualifications and caveats—all of which are intended to demonstrate how a constitutional government (or polity) can prevent itself from degrading into a disordered democracy that enforces radical equality—Aristotle then returns to the central role that the law must play in a just, well-run polis:

> Laws, when good, should be supreme; and . . . the magistrate or magistrates should regulate those matters only on which the laws are unable to speak with precision owing to the difficulty of any general principle embracing all particulars. But what are good laws has not yet been clearly explained; the old difficulty remains. The goodness or badness, justice or injustice, of laws varies of necessity with the constitutions of states. This, however, is clear, that the laws must be adapted to the constitutions. But if so, true forms of government will of necessity have just laws, and perverted forms of government will have unjust laws. (III.11; 1282b1-14)

The law *should* be the final sovereign, but the political body of magistrates must be prepared to judge when the law is not clear about a particular matter and so needs to be extended and interpreted. Law as law, then, is good, but in an actual polis, the law will only be as good as the constitution it serves.

When the government degrades, the law will end up favoring unjustly the one, the few, the many.

LEX REX OR REX LEX?

Is the best polis, then, one in which the law is king (*lex rex* in Latin) or the king is the law (*rex lex*)? For Aristotle, the ideal is to have a just king act as a lawgiver, but then have those laws be interpreted and enforced by a body of citizens rather than one man:

> The best man, then, must legislate, and laws must be passed, but these laws will have no authority when they miss the mark, though in all other cases retaining their authority. But when the law cannot determine a point at all, or not well, should the one best man or should all decide? According to our present practice assemblies meet, sit in judgment, deliberate, and decide, and their judgments all relate to individual cases. Now any member of the assembly, taken separately, is certainly inferior to the wise man. But the state is made up of many individuals. And as a feast to which all the guests contribute is better than a banquet furnished by a single man, so a multitude is a better judge of many things than any individual. Again, the many are more incorruptible than the few; they are like the greater quantity of water which is less easily corrupted than a little. The individual is liable to be overcome by anger or by some other passion, and then his judgment is necessarily perverted; but it is hardly to be supposed that a great number of persons would all get into a passion and go wrong at the same moment. (III.15; 1286a22-36)

In this passage from *Politics*, we get nothing less than a philosophical-political argument for, and defense of, deliberative democracy. Even if the polis is ruled by a king, the laws are better sifted and applied by a representative body of citizens whose deliberative process can filter out unruly passions and political bribes. Such a body, especially when it is composed of virtuous citizens, is less likely to be corrupted than a single man.

In the past, Aristotle concedes, it was easier for a single ruler to seize control because a good body of virtuous citizens did not yet exist. "But when many persons equal in merit arose, no longer enduring the pre-eminence of one, they desired to have a commonwealth, and set up a constitution" (III.15; 1286b11-13). It is true that such a group of framers and deliberators can become corrupt and slip into an oligarchy or democracy, but Aristotle clearly sees the greatest hope for order and virtue in a state run by a legal code that is open to debate and discussion by a body of the best citizens.

In fact, despite his affinity for virtuous kings, Aristotle does in the end come down strongly on a *lex rex* position that holds up the law as the best stay against corruption: "Therefore he who bids the law rule may be deemed to bid God and Reason alone rule, but he who bids man rule adds an element of the beast; for desire is a wild beast, and passion perverts the minds of rulers, even when they are the best of men. The law is reason unaffected by desire" (III.16; 1287a28-32). The law is not a man that it should give way to disordered desire or allow lust and greed to pervert the course of justice. The law is both divine and rational in its ability to rise above strife and passion.

LAW AS NEUTRAL MEDIATOR

Having established the need for the law to be supreme over the rulers of the polis, Aristotle immediately rebuts a potential argument against his position:

> We are told that a patient should call in a physician; he will not get better if he is doctored out of a book. But the parallel of the arts is clearly not in point; for the physician does nothing contrary to rule from motives of friendship; he only cures a patient and takes a fee; whereas magistrates do many things from spite and partiality. And, indeed, if a man suspected the physician of being in league with his enemies to destroy him for a bribe, he would rather have recourse to the book. But certainly physicians, when they are sick, call in other physicians, and training-masters, when they are in training, other training-masters, as if they could not judge truly about their own case and might be influenced by their feelings. Hence it is evident that in seeking for justice men seek for the mean or neutral, for the law is the mean. (III.16; 1287a32-1287b5)

Would not a patient, the argument goes, prefer to consult a flesh-and-blood doctor rather than an impersonal book of medical procedures? Yes, Aristotle admits, that is true, but then the patient who goes to see a doctor expects that the doctor will be guided by the medical book. And he can trust that that will be the case, for the doctor is not a politician, that he should alter his application of the rules because the patient is a friend or a foe or because he hopes to get a larger fee by doing so. To the contrary, if the doctor fears that his feelings might prevent him from properly applying the techniques laid out in the medical book, he will call in other doctors to help keep him on track.

Now, if the patient has reason to believe that the doctor is in league with his enemies and might have accepted a bribe from them in exchange for poisoning the patient, he would be more apt to go straight to the medical book and leave the doctor out of the equation. Just so, we should be suspicious of political rulers—whether they be one or few or many—who use the law to aggrandize their own power rather than that of the polis and its citizens. For this reason, it is a good thing to look to the law as a neutral mediator—a golden mean—that can adjudicate justice without giving way to an excess or defect of passion. Law, like true virtue, represents the mean between the extremes.

Aristotle's argument for the law has not aged and is as applicable today as it was twenty-four hundred years ago. But he does not stop there. He adds one further sentence that has proven to be a bedrock of legal justice from the Roman republic, to the British parliamentary monarchy, to the American democracy, to such international codes as the Geneva Convention and the United Nations charter: "Again, customary laws have more weight, and relate to more important matters, than written laws, and a man may be a safer ruler than the written law, but not safer than the customary law" (III.16; 1287b5-7). Despite his justification of some forms of slavery and his disparagement of barbarians, Aristotle recognized the existence and sovereignty of unwritten customary laws.

These customary laws are similar to what Christian philosophers and theologians from Augustine to Aquinas have identified with the natural law, unwritten laws that are inscribed in our conscience and so known to all. When the Declaration of Independence appeals to the inalienable rights that all citizens have to life, liberty, and the pursuit of happiness, it appeals to just such customary/natural laws written in the conscience rather than on stone or paper. The Magna Carta of 1215 enumerated rights for the barons, but those rights were understood to rest on the (unwritten) traditional rights of Englishmen, which rights the American colonists also appealed to in their petition for freedom.

ARISTOTLE'S INFLUENCE ON AMERICA'S FOUNDING FATHERS

Although Luther, Calvin, and the early Reformers tended to be suspicious of Aristotle due to his connection to Aquinas and the Scholastics, his musings on law and polity were taken up by a number of sixteenth-century Protestants and came to exercise a shaping force on English and American legal and political thought. Aristotle and his views get favorable treatment, for example, in Richard Hooker's *Laws of Ecclesiastical Polity* (1593–1597) and Samuel Rutherford's *Lex Rex* (1644).

James Harrington's *The Commonwealth of Oceana* (1656) even builds a bridge between the Jewish commonwealth of the Old Testament and Aristotle's legal theories:

> But that we may observe a little further how the heathen politicians have written, not only out of Nature, but as it were out of Scripture: as in the commonwealth of Israel, God is said to have been king, so the commonwealth where the law is king [*lex rex*], is said by Aristotle to be "the kingdom of God." And where by the lusts or passions of men a power is set above that of the law deriving from reason, which is the dictate of God, God in that sense is rejected or deposed that He should not reign over them, as He was in Israel.[1]

The link Harrington forges here between the divine and rational law of the Bible and the equally divine and rational law celebrated in *Politics* III.16 exerted a strong influence on our Founding Fathers, who understood that there was a connection between following (or rejecting) God and following (or rejecting) both customary/natural law and the written laws based on it. Indeed, like Aristotle, the founders came to believe that deliberation of the law—as enshrined first in the Articles of Confederation (1781) and then in the Constitution (1789)—was the best way to cool the lusts and passions of the people.

Although Plato wrote a book called *Laws*, for which Aristotle likely played the role of research assistant, it is Aristotle and not Plato who treated the law as a neutral, dispassionate, rational source of sovereignty and argued that justice is best preserved when a democratic body of representatives deliberates those laws. This Aristotelian understanding of justice is expressed

---

[1]James Harrington, *The Commonwealth of Oceana* (London: Routledge and Sons, 1887), 36.

clearly and powerfully in three of the *Federalist Papers* (1788), all of which were written by James Madison:

> The delegation of the government . . . to a small number of citizens elected by the rest . . . [will] refine and enlarge the public views by passing them through the medium of a chosen body of citizens, whose wisdom may best discern the true interest of their country and whose patriotism and love of justice will be least likely to sacrifice it to temporary or partial considerations.[2]
>
> In all cases a certain number at least seems to be necessary to secure the benefits of free consultation and discussion, and to guard against too easy a combination for improper purposes; as, on the other hand, the number ought at most to be kept within a certain limit, in order to avoid the confusion and intemperance of a multitude. In all very numerous assemblies, of whatever character composed, passion never fails to wrest the scepter from reason. Had every Athenian citizen been a Socrates, every Athenian assembly would still have been a mob.[3]
>
> I shall not scruple to add that [the Senate] may be sometimes necessary as a defense to the people against their own temporary errors and delusions. As the cool and deliberate sense of the community ought, in all governments, and actually will, in all free governments, ultimately prevail over the views of its rulers; so there are particular moments in public affairs when the people, stimulated by some irregular passion, or some illicit advantage, or misled by the artful misrepresentations of interested men, may call for measures which they themselves will afterwards be the most ready to lament and condemn.[4]

The authors of the *Federalist Papers* shared Aristotle's faith in reason and logic as well as his distrust of human lust and passion. Like Aristotle but unlike Plato, they understood that vicious and unjust human behaviors were more often committed out of willfulness than ignorance. Aristotle understood this, even though he lacked the special revelation of Genesis 1–3, which assured Hamilton, Madison, and Jay that man was both good, because he was made in God's image, and evil, because he was fallen.[5]

---

[2]Alexander Hamilton, James Madison, and John Jay, *The Federalist Papers* (New York: New American Library, 1961), no. 10 (p. 82).
[3]Hamilton, Madison, and Jay, *Federalist Papers*, no. 55 (p. 342).
[4]Hamilton, Madison, and Jay, *Federalist Papers*, no. 63 (p. 384).
[5]Although debate continues to rage as to the exact faith of the authors of the *Federalist Papers*, all three clearly wrote out of a Judeo-Christian understanding of the nature of man.

ARISTOTLE AND *SOLA SCRIPTURA*

It is because of our dual nature that governments are necessary and work best when they are mediated by neutral, dispassionate laws that are deliberated on by the right kind and number of citizens. "If men were angels," Madison argues, "no government would be necessary. If angels were to govern men, neither external nor internal controls on government would be necessary."[6] Though Catholics share with Protestants the core biblical belief that man was created in God's image but fallen, they tend to invest order and justice in Plato's philosopher-kings (papal infallibility; the magisterium) rather than Aristotle's laws and deliberation. Likewise, whereas Catholics and Protestants alike believe the Bible is the Word of God, the latter—particularly low-church Protestants—look to that Word as the sole and naked authority for all believers (*sola Scriptura*), while the former look to apostolic succession and church hierarchy.

Even the high-church Protestant Anglican Church, which maintains a focus on creeds, ceremony, hierarchy, and apostolic succession, makes clear that the Bible is the final source of all sovereignty in the church. That is why article XX ("Of the Authority of the Church") of *The Thirty-Nine Articles of Religion of the Church of England* (1562 in Latin; 1571 in English), on which the Anglican Church was founded, states plainly:

> The Church hath power to decree Rites or Ceremonies, and authority in Controversies of Faith: and yet it is not lawful for the Church to ordain any thing that is contrary to God's Word written, neither may it so expound one place of Scripture, that it be repugnant to another. Wherefore, although the Church be a witness and a keeper of Holy Writ, yet, as it ought not to decree any thing against the same, so besides the same ought it not to enforce any thing to be believed for necessity of Salvation.[7]

Whether in church or state, the Protestant mind has tended, in good Aristotelian fashion, to favor *lex* over *rex*, legal over personal, objective over subjective, rational over mystical, deliberation over compulsion. I quoted

---

[6] Hamilton, Madison, and Jay, *Federalist Papers*, no. 51 (p. 322).
[7] *The Thirty-Nine Articles of Religion of the Church of England*, in *The Creeds of Christendom*, 6th ed., ed. Philip Schaff, rev. David Schaff (Grand Rapids, MI: Baker, 1996), 3:500.

above this key line from *Politics* III.16: "Therefore he who bids the law rule may be deemed to bid God and Reason alone rule, but he who bids man rule adds an element of the beast." An evangelical such as myself might rewrite this to read, "Therefore he who bids the Bible rule may be deemed to bid God and Reason alone rule, but he who bids tradition and church hierarchy rule adds an element of the beast." That British civil servants still take an oath to the monarch while American political leaders swear to uphold the constitution reveals the deep Catholic roots of England and the even deeper Protestant roots of America.

PART 5

HOW TO MAKE BEAUTIFUL THINGS

20

DEFENDING THE ART OF RHETORIC

ARISTOTLE'S TEACHER WAS NO FAN OF RHETORIC. In fact, he devotes much of his dialogue *Gorgias* to exposing rhetoric as a form of flattery that does nothing to provide or promote knowledge or virtue. It should come as no surprise that Plato would feel thus, especially after Gorgias the Sophist defines rhetoric in a manner befitting a teacher for hire:

> [Rhetoric is] the ability to persuade with words judges in the law courts, senators in the Senate, assemblyman in the Assembly, and men in any other meeting which convenes for the public interest. Since it is perfectly true that by virtue of this power you will have at your beck and call the physician and the trainer, that businessman of yours will turn out to be making money for somebody else! Not for himself will he make it, but for you who have the power to speak and persuade the vast majority.[1]

According to Gorgias, the only function of the art of rhetoric is to persuade; the art itself is indifferent to good or evil, right or wrong, justice or injustice. In short, its goal is not to teach or to improve but to win.

PLATO: RHETORIC IS A NEGATIVE KNACK

Unsatisfied, as he usually is with the definitions of his interlocutors, Socrates pushes Gorgias to narrow down his definition. He responds by saying that rhetoric is the "sort of persuasion . . . used in law courts and other public gatherings . . . and it deals with justice and injustice."[2] But Socrates keeps pressing him. There is surely a difference between persuasion that produces true knowledge and persuasion that produces belief

---

[1] Plato, *Gorgias*, trans. W. C. Helmbold (Indianapolis: Library of Liberal Arts, 1952), 10 (452e).
[2] Plato, *Gorgias*, 12 (454b).

without certainty. Socrates concludes that rhetoric "effects a persuasion which can produce belief about justice and injustice, but cannot give instruction about them."[3]

But Gorgias will not be so easily trapped by Socrates. Rhetoric, he insists, is about persuasion, plain and simple, and persuasion is about winning:

> If a rhetorician and a physician should come to any city you please and have occasion to debate in the assembly or any other public gathering as to which of them ought to be elected public physician, the doctor would be utterly eclipsed, and the capable speaker would, if he chose, be elected. And likewise in a contest with any other craftsman whatsoever, the rhetorician would win his own election against all opposition of any kind; for not a single craftsman is able to speak in a crowd, on any subject in the world, more persuasively than the rhetorician. This is to show you how great and splendid is the power of his art.[4]

What Gorgias here proclaims with pride is the very thing that worries Socrates (Plato): that someone who has true knowledge can be beaten by a rhetorician who lacks it. Rhetoric, like sophistry, neither seeks nor clarifies the truth; it merely spins it in a direction that is advantageous to the rhetorician.

No, Socrates concludes, rhetoric is not "an artistic pursuit at all, but that of a shrewd, courageous spirit which is naturally clever at dealing with men; and I call the chief part of it flattery. It seems to me to have many branches and one of them is cookery, which is thought to be an art, but according to my notion is no art at all, but a knack and a routine."[5] Just as gymnastics and medicine heal the body, while cosmetics and cookery merely flatter it, so legislation and justice heal the soul, while sophistry and rhetoric merely flatter it. Cosmetics and cooking, sophistry and rhetoric are knacks rather than true arts, for they do not proceed by any established method; they may even lead to evil, for they seek pleasure rather than the ultimate good. But that evil is far worse in the second pair, for they damage the soul and not the body.

---

[3]Plato, *Gorgias*, 14 (455a).
[4]Plato, *Gorgias*, 15 (456b-c).
[5]Plato, *Gorgias*, 23-24 (463b).

ARISTOTLE AND SAYERS: RHETORIC IS A POSITIVE ART

There can be little doubt that Aristotle wrote his *Rhetoric*, at least in part, to rescue and rehabilitate the reputation of rhetoric from its negative treatment in *Gorgias*. In three lengthy books, Aristotle defends rhetoric and lays down systematic rules and methods for its practice, thus confuting Plato's argument that rhetoric is not a proper art but only a knack. Until the twentieth century, Christian educators agreed with Aristotle's defense of rhetoric by making the teaching of it a central element of education. Indeed, the foundational medieval trivium of grammar, logic (or dialectic), and rhetoric treated the third as essential to the shaping of wise, virtuous, morally self-regulating citizens.

The decay of trivium-based education in twentieth-century England prompted Christian apologist, novelist, and public intellectual Dorothy Sayers (1893-1957) to read a paper at Oxford titled "The Lost Tools of Learning" (1947). In it, she lays the blame for a troubling social phenomenon on the loss of the classical trivium in education.

> Has it ever struck you as odd, or unfortunate, that today, when the proportion of literacy . . . is higher than it has ever been, people should have become susceptible to the influence of advertisement and mass propaganda to an extent hitherto unheard of and unimagined? Do you put this down to the mere mechanical fact that the press and the radio and so on have made propaganda much easier to distribute over a wide area? Or do you sometimes have an uneasy suspicion that the product of modern educational methods is less good than he or she might be at disentangling fact from opinion and the proven from the plausible?[6]

In the absence of key facts about history, literature, philosophy, and science (grammar), as well as the ability to think critically, parse syllogisms, and expose logical fallacies (logic) and to construct, articulate, and defend coherent arguments and systems of thought (rhetoric), modern citizens are left at the mercy of advertisers and propagandists.

---

[6] Dorothy Sayers, "The Lost Tools of Learning," in *The Great Tradition: Classic Readings on What It Means to Be an Educated Human Being*, ed. Richard M. Gamble (Wilmington, DE: ISI Books, 2007), 603. I discuss Sayers's essay at length in chapter thirteen of *Passing the Torch: An Apology for Classical Christian Education* (Downers Grove, IL: IVP Academic, 2025).

I would go so far as to suggest that the loss of (Aristotelian) logic in modern secular *and* Christian schools has led to a troubling decrease in doctrinal, theological, and philosophical literacy among the last few generations of church-raised children. Even those who believe find it difficult, if not impossible, to express their beliefs in a logically sound, rhetorically effective manner. They may have memorized a few names and events from the Bible, but they lack the ability to put those facts together into a coherent worldview. They can no more identify the presuppositions on which modern (and postmodern) agendas rest than they can present a compelling case for Christianity that appeals to head and heart, logic and emotion, reason and imagination alike.

Rather than review the rhetorical devices and techniques Aristotle patiently unpacks, I will focus on how he answers Plato's critique while conceding much of what Gorgias has to say. As I do, I will keep in mind that Aristotle never wanders far from the practical applications of rhetoric as a weapon against injustice. Plato wrote *Gorgias* after the execution of Socrates, and he slips into his dialogue several warnings from Socrates's interlocutors that he should learn rhetoric himself lest he need to defend himself in court. In response to these warnings, Socrates boldly replies: "Do you really think that this is the object of our lives: to live as long as possible, to lavish all our care upon the cultivation of those arts which may save us from danger—just as you keep urging me to cultivate the rhetoric that may keep me safe in the law courts?"[7]

Plato clearly agreed with Socrates on this point; the preservation of life is not worth even the tiniest compromise, seeming or otherwise, with truth. Aristotle, as he demonstrates in his *Rhetoric*, did not; though he was no relativist, he was realistic enough to recognize that justice often needs a helping hand from rhetoric.

RHETORIC AS AN AID TO TRUTH AND JUSTICE

"Rhetoric is useful," Aristotle explains, "because things that are true and things that are just have a natural tendency to prevail over their opposites,

---

[7] Plato, *Gorgias*, 88 (511b-c).

so that if the decisions of judges are not what they ought to be, the defeat must be due to the speakers themselves, and they must be blamed accordingly" (I.1; 1355a21-24). Aristotle firmly believed that we live in an ordered, purposeful, and ultimately ethical cosmos where there is a natural tendency for truth and justice to prevail. When they do not, the fault does not always lie with the judge (or magistrate) in charge. Often, the real fault lies with the legal or political orator whose weak grasp of rhetoric fails to convince the judge of the right side of the issue at hand. The rhetoric used to nudge the judge to that side may call for artistry and perhaps some flattery, but it is technique deployed for the sake of justice.

"Moreover," Aristotle goes on to add,

> before some audiences not even the possession of the exactest knowledge will make it easy for what we say to produce conviction. For argument based on knowledge implies instruction, and there are people whom one cannot instruct. Here, then, we must use, as our modes of persuasion and argument, notions possessed by everybody, as we observed in the *Topics* when dealing with the way to handle a popular audience. (I.1; 1355a24-28)

It is all well and good to take Plato's ivory-tower approach and trust that knowledge, logic, and reason will win out in the end. In the real world, where Aristotle sought to live and write, most jurors and even some judges are not teachable. Argument alone will not prod them toward the way of truth. They must be properly handled by a rhetorician who understands common sense, common opinions, and common emotions.

Rhetoric is a tool for winning; Aristotle does not deny that obvious fact. But that does not mean that it is, as sophistry so often is, a foe of reason and truth.

> We must be able to employ persuasion, just as strict reasoning can be employed, on opposite sides of a question, not in order that we may in practice employ it in both ways (for we must not make people believe what is wrong), but in order that we may see clearly what the facts are, and that, if another man argues unfairly, we on our part may be able to confute him. No other of the arts draws opposite conclusions: dialectic and rhetoric alone do this. Both these arts draw opposite conclusions impartially. Nevertheless, the underlying

> facts do not lend themselves equally well to the contrary views. No; things that are true and things that are better are, by their nature, practically always easier to prove and easier to believe in. (I.1; 1355a28-39)

Like the dialectical approach taken in Plato's dialogues, rhetoric allows the rhetorician and his audience to see both sides of an issue and to hold them in tension. But that tension is a creative one, leading not to philosophical or ethical relativism but to a deeper understanding of what is right and good and true. The genuine rhetorician does not use his skill to convince people of what is false but to confute lies, clarify facts, and guide emotions into proper channels.

THE PROPER USE OF RHETORIC

Rhetoric, like most things in our world, can be misused, but that does not mean we should therefore abandon a uniquely human art that can shield us from harm.

> It is absurd to hold that a man ought to be ashamed of being unable to defend himself with his limbs, but not of being unable to defend himself with speech and reason, when the use of rational speech is more distinctive of a human being than the use of his limbs. And if it be objected that one who uses such power of speech unjustly might do great harm, that is a charge which may be made in common against all good things except virtue, and above all against the things that are most useful, as strength, health, wealth, generalship. A man can confer the greatest of benefits by a right use of these, and inflict the greatest of injuries by using them wrongly. (I.1; 1355b1-7)

Aside from virtue itself, the good things of this world—strength, health, wealth, fame—are all susceptible to being used in destructive ways. The solution is not to cast them aside. A strong man who did not use his physical strength to defend himself from an enemy would be considered a fool. In the same way, an intellectually skilled man who did not use his rhetorical gifts to defend himself from a false accuser would equally earn himself the title of fool.

Plato the great dialectician should have recognized in rhetoric a sister art. He should have seen that "it is the function of one and the same art [rhetoric] to discern the real and the apparent means of persuasion, just as it is the function of dialectic to discern the real and the apparent syllogism. What makes a man a 'sophist' is not his faculty, but his moral purpose" (I.1; 1355b14-18). There are moral and immoral dialecticians just as there are moral and immoral rhetoricians. We must not confuse the faculty (the art) with the moral or immoral use that is made of it.

As every schoolboy until a century ago used to learn, a good exhibition of Aristotelian rhetoric calls for a balance of ethos, pathos, and logos:

> Of the modes of persuasion furnished by the spoken word there are three kinds. The first kind depends on the personal character of the speaker [ethos]; the second on putting the audience into a certain frame of mind [pathos]; the third on the proof, or apparent proof, provided by the words of the speech itself [logos]. Persuasion is achieved by the speaker's personal character when the speech is so spoken as to make us think him credible. . . . Secondly, persuasion may come through the hearers, when the speech stirs their emotions. . . . Thirdly, persuasion is effected through the speech itself when we have proved a truth or an apparent truth by means of the persuasive arguments suitable to the case in question. (II.2;1356a1-21)

There is nothing inherently evil or even negative in the use of ethos, pathos, or logos. When exercised properly and in keeping with virtue, all three are tools for achieving the triumph of justice over injustice, good over evil, truth over falsehood.

RHETORIC IN THE REAL WORLD

Still, to make a proper and effective use of rhetoric, one must heed factors that may seem relativistic and even sophistical. For example, Aristotle teaches the would-be rhetorician to adapt his argument and style to suit the governmental form—democracy, oligarchy, aristocracy, or monarchy—that is practiced in the polis he is addressing. "The most important and effective qualification for success in persuading audiences and speaking well on public affairs," Aristotle explains, "is to understand all the forms of government and to discriminate their respective customs, institutions, and interests. For all men are persuaded by considerations of their interest, and their interest lies in the maintenance of the established order" (I.8; 1365b22-26).

Whatever form of constitution is practiced in the polis, the average citizen will wish to maintain the status quo rather than risk the chaos that naturally accompanies sudden political and social change. Rhetoric that supports proper law and order will tend to be just, good, and true, often using ethos to convince the audience of the goodwill of the speaker, pathos to control unruly passions among the citizen body, and logos to substantiate the benefits of political and social stability.

Aristotle, however, does not stop here in his flirtation with relativism. He goes on to argue that a good rhetorician will allow the situation to dictate whether he should champion the unwritten law over the written, or vice versa.

> If the written law tells against our case, clearly we must appeal to the universal law, and insist on its greater equity and justice. We must argue that the juror's oath "I will give my verdict according to honest opinion" means that one will not simply follow the letter of the written law. . . . If however the written law supports our case, we must urge that the oath "to give my verdict according to my honest opinion" is not meant to make the judges give a verdict that is contrary to the law, but to save them from the guilt of perjury if they misunderstand what the law really means. (I.15; 1375a26-1375b18)[8]

Although, as we saw in the previous chapter, Aristotle was a defender of the unwritten (customary) law, he was realistic enough to see that there are situations when justice can be achieved only by appealing to the written law over the unwritten. As before, such a use of the art of rhetoric only slips into sophistry when it is guided by immoral motives that seek to disrupt the path of justice rather than to ensure that it remains on course.

Indeed, the same goes for the effective use of the evidence of witnesses in court. "If you have no witnesses on your side, you will argue that the judges must decide from what is probable. . . . If you *have* witnesses, and the other man has not, you will argue that probabilities cannot be put on their trial"

---

[8]Fans of Greek tragedy who are eager to proceed to the next two chapters on Aristotle's *Poetics* will be happy to know that Aristotle illustrates the first half of this passage by referencing Antigone, who, in the play by Sophocles that bears her name, appeals to the unwritten law of piety as something that trumps Creon's manmade law forbidding the proper burial of her brother Polyneices because he attacked Thebes.

(I.15; 1376a18-23). The same *also* goes, rather disturbingly, for promoting or repudiating evidence gained by the torture of witnesses:

> It is not hard to point out the available grounds for magnifying its value, if it happens to tell in our favour, and arguing that it is the only form of evidence that is infallible; or, on the other hand, for refuting it if it tells against us and for our opponent, when we may say what is true of torture of every kind alike, that people under its compulsion tell lies quite as often as they tell the truth. (I.15; 1376b33-1377a4)

CAN CHRISTIANS USE RHETORIC?

Surely such reasoning must be incompatible with a Christian approach to rhetoric—or is it? Jesus himself calls on his followers, whom he sends out as sheep among wolves, to be "wise as serpents, and harmless as doves" (Mt 10:16). He also in one of his parables unexpectedly commends a dishonest steward who, about to be fired by his master, uses guile to ingratiate himself with his master's debtors. Rather than rebuke or imprison the unjust steward, the master applauds him, "because he had done wisely." Jesus then makes the connection himself to his followers: "for the children of this world are in their generation wiser than the children of light" (Lk 16:8).

In his sermons in Acts, Paul increases the power of his message by a careful use of rhetorical strategies that reflect the teachings of Aristotle's *Rhetoric*, perhaps filtered through Cicero. Even more polished is the defense he makes before King Herod Agrippa II (see Acts 26), a speech that so impresses the sophisticated, Roman-educated Agrippa that he declares that Paul has done nothing wrong and could have been set free had he not already appealed his case to Caesar (Acts 26:30-32).

In the second century AD, a trio of Christian apologists—Aristides, Justin Martyr, and Athenagoras—who had previously been educated Gentiles used their rhetorical skills to defend the Christian faith before the emperors Hadrian, Antoninus Pius, and Marcus Aurelius. All three held up Socrates—the master of Aristotle's master—as their role model for both reason and persuasion, logos (word) and praxis (action). They respected the martyrdom of Socrates and were quite willing to give up their own lives for Christ (as Justin later did), but that did not prevent them from making the best use they could of Aristotelian logic and rhetoric to (successfully) win the favor and mercy of the emperor.

Here, for example, is how Athenagoras begins his "A Plea for the Christians" before the enlightened emperor Marcus Aurelius, author of *Meditations*, a classic work of Stoic philosophy that has long been respected by Christian thinkers:

> In your empire, greatest of sovereigns, different nations have different customs and laws; and no one is hindered by law or fear of punishment from following his ancestral usages, however ridiculous these may be. . . . Among every nation and people, men offer whatever sacrifices and celebrate whatever mysteries they please. . . . And to all these both you and the laws give permission so to act, deeming, on the one hand, that to believe in no god at all is impious and wicked, and on the other, that it is necessary for each man to worship the gods he prefers, in order that through fear of the deity, men may be kept from wrong-doing.[9]

Rather than try to convince the emperor of the truth of Christianity, Athenagoras uses the power of his rhetoric to build a bridge between himself and his pagan audience. As Aristotle and his American political heirs appeal to common law, so Athenagoras follows Aristotle's rhetorical lead in adapting his speech to the time, place, and occasion offered him. By doing so, he does not reduce Christianity to one of many religious truths but argues that it deserves a voice and political protection in a pluralistic society.

THE ARISTOTELIAN RHETORIC OF POLYCARP

But perhaps the supreme example of Aristotelian rhetoric to come down to us from the early church was uttered by Polycarp, the aged and reverend bishop of Smyrna who laid down his life for Christ in the middle of the second century.[10] In his unforgettable replies to the governor who tried and condemned him in the arena, Polycarp embodies the ethos, pathos, and logos that marked the height of Aristotelian rhetoric. It did not save him

---

[9]Athenagoras, "A Plea for the Christians," in *Ante-Nicene Fathers*, ed. Philip Schaff (Christian Classics Ethereal Library, 2000), 2:281.

[10]I discuss Polycarp, Aristides, Justin Martyr, and Athenagoras's speeches at length in chapters five and six of *Ancient Voices: An Insider's Look at the Early Church* (Middletown, RI: Stone Tower, 2022).

from the martyr's fire, but it clarified for all time the truth and the justice, the goodness and the beauty of Christ and the Christian faith.

Despite being in his nineties, Polycarp was dragged into a Roman arena and interrogated by the pagan governor. Had he recanted his beliefs, he would have been set free. Instead, he stood tall and fearless, testifying to Christ by his actions, for which there was little precedent in the Greco-Roman world, and by his words, which possess all the wit, poise, and elegance of Aristotle's rules for rhetoric.

Thus, when the governor commands Polycarp to repent and say away with the atheists, Polycarp turns the command back against his accuser (the governor) and accusers (the crowd) with a rhetorical flourish that has powerful emotional appeal. With the grand gesture of a Greco-Roman orator, Polycarp passes his hand over the heads of the pagan crowd and proclaims, "Away with the impious."

Outmaneuvered by Polycarp's reply, the governor tells him point-blank that he must reject Christ if he wishes to be released. In response, Polycarp changes his tone from the defiantly theatrical to the intensely personal and emotional: "Eighty and six years have I served him, and he never did me wrong; and how can I now blaspheme my King that has saved me?" The Greek Demosthenes and the Roman Cicero would have been hard pressed to effect such a sudden modulation in ethos and pathos.

But Polycarp does not stop there. When the governor insists that he swear by the genius of Caesar, Polycarp combines the personal (ethos) and emotional (pathos) force of his rhetoric with a direct appeal to reason (logos): "If you are so vain as to think that I should swear by the genius of Cesar, as you say, pretending not to know who I am, hear my free confession. I am a Christian. But if you wish to learn what the doctrine of Christianity is, grant me a day and listen to me." The common sense of Polycarp's reply is as simple as it is powerful. If a man of Polycarp's age and position in the church were to suddenly recant his faith, he would cease to be the person he is. No, if the governor truly wishes to know why Polycarp will not swear to another deity, he should set a time and date with him so that he can explain at leisure the doctrines of Christianity.

At this point, defeated by Polycarp's rhetoric (which is as truthful as it is persuasive), the governor deflects attention away from himself by giving Polycarp permission to turn and convince the crowd of his innocence. Polycarp, however, refuses the offer: "I have thought proper to give you a reason; for we have been taught to give magistrates and powers appointed by God, the honour that is due to them, as far as it does not injure us; but I do not consider those the proper ones before whom I should deliver my defence." Once again, Polycarp turns the argument back against his judge, all the while using his rhetorical skill to smuggle in a message to the governor: it is not I who am a threat to you, for I serve a God who commands us to respect and honor civic leaders such as you, but this unruly crowd that knows nothing of truth, goodness, or beauty.

Failing to defeat Polycarp in debate, the governor threatens him instead. But with each threat, Polycarp uses his rhetorical powers to turn the punishment in his favor, transforming his weaker position into the stronger one—not for the sake of winning an argument (like the Sophists whose rhetoric Plato so despised) but for the higher purpose of truth (like Aristotle). Thus, when the governor threatens to feed him to the lions, Polycarp responds: "Call them. For we have no reason to repent from the better to the worse, but it is good to change from wickedness to virtue." Or again, when the governor threatens fire, Polycarp calmly replies: "You threaten fire that burns for a moment and is soon extinguished, for you know nothing of the judgment to come, and the fire of eternal punishment reserved for the wicked. But why do you delay? Bring what you wish."

In the end, Polycarp is bound to the stake and set on fire, but not before he utters his last words, a prayer that makes use of every device taught in Aristotle's *Rhetoric*:

> Father of thy well-beloved and blessed Son Jesus Christ, through whom we have received the knowledge of thee. The God of angels and powers, and all creation, and of all the family of the righteous, that live before thee, I bless thee that thou hast thought me worthy of the present day and hour, to have a share in the number of the martyrs and in the cup of Christ, unto the resurrection of eternal life, both of the soul and body, in the incorruptible felicity of the holy Spirit. Among whom may I be received in thy sight, this day, as a rich and ac-

ceptable sacrifice as thou the faithful and true God hast prepared, hast revealed and fulfilled. Wherefore, on this account, and for all things I praise thee, I bless thee, I glorify thee, through the eternal high priest, Jesus Christ, thy well-beloved Son. Through whom glory be to thee with him in the Holy Ghost, both now and for ever. Amen."[11]

Combining the literary devices of pagan rhetoric with the cadences of the Bible, Polycarp fashions a prayer that is as beautiful as it is forceful. Note the power of ethos here in the way Polycarp states the true foundation of his position and makes it clear he would consider it an honor to join the ranks of Christian martyrs. Note also the power of pathos, the way he conjures a vision of his death as a pure sacrifice good and acceptable to God. Note finally the power of logos as he summarizes all of salvation history into his prayer. Surely what we encounter here, as in all of Polycarp's replies, is a baptizing of the best of pagan rhetoric to serve the purposes of God, his followers, and his kingdom.

---

[11] Although a separate account exists of the martyrdom of Polycarp, I quote it here as it appears in book IV, chapter 15 of *The Ecclesiastical History* of Eusebius Pamphilus, trans. Christian Frederick Cruse (Grand Rapids, MI: Baker, 1994), 146-48. Only the portions in quotation marks are directly quoted.

21

REDEEMING THE ART OF IMITATION

WE SAW IN CHAPTER FIVE that Aristotle disagreed with Plato's theory of the Forms, preferring to locate the essence and telos of things down and within rather than above and outside. We saw in chapter eighteen that Aristotle more forcefully rejected Plato's proposed socialistic community of women in favor of the necessity and virtue of private property. Finally, we saw in the previous chapter that Aristotle, in sharp contrast to Plato, found much use and goodness in the art of rhetoric. In this chapter we will see that Aristotle, who parted ways with Plato in the areas of philosophy, politics, and rhetoric, also parted ways with him on the nature, function, and status of the arts.

PLATO THROWS DOWN THE GAUNTLET

Although Plato's numerous and unforgettable myths and allegories confirm him as one of the most creative thinkers of all time, Plato himself harbored a deep suspicion and distrust of the arts. Indeed, in *Republic* X (see 595a-608b), he regretfully but unapologetically kicks the poets out of his perfect state. One of his reasons for doing so, as we will see in the next chapter, stemmed from his belief that poetry appeals to our weaker, baser emotions. But his suspicion of the arts went deeper than that, for it rested on and was informed by his foundational beliefs about the nature of reality.

For Plato, the things of our world, whether physical objects such as trees and dogs or abstract concepts such as justice and beauty, are finally imitations, or shadows, of the real Trees, Dogs, Justice, and Beauty that exist eternally and without change in the World of Being. The role of the philosopher as well as of the geometer is to push past the earthly imitations of our World of Becoming to commune with the heavenly Forms. The role of the scientist is to work as well as he can with the world as we know it. But the role of the artist is neither to reach out to the Forms nor to discern the laws of the things of our world. He seeks instead to imitate the things in our world that are themselves already imitations. As such, poetry, and the arts in general, is twice removed from the Forms, imitations of imitations, shadows of shadows.

So Plato believed, but he was not unwilling to have his mind changed. After enumerating his reasons for kicking out the poets, he concludes by making a magnanimous offer and laying down a vigorous challenge to the defenders of the arts: "Even so, we shall declare that if poetry that is imitative and aims to provide pleasure can show cause why it should find a place in a well-governed city, we should be glad to welcome its return from exile." If either poets or critics, writing in either poetry or prose, "can argue that poetry is not only delightful but also a blessing to the life of men and well-governed cities," Plato will be happy to allow the poets to return to his city.[1]

ARISTOTLE ON MIMESIS

From the Greek Aristotle to the Roman Horace, the medieval Dante to the Renaissance Philip Sidney, the neoclassical Alexander Pope to the Romantic Percy Bysshe Shelley, the Victorian John Henry Newman to the modernist T. S. Eliot, generations of poets and critics have taken up Plato's challenge and mounted apologies for the arts. Aristotle's was the first, and in many ways it gave the impetus for all those that would follow. It is in fact hard to exaggerate the influence of the *Poetics* on Western aesthetics. Aristotle supplied poetry with categories, genres, and criteria that are still with us today. Just as he dissected logic and science, metaphysics and psychology, social science and political science, ethics and rhetoric, showing how each discipline works and what its end should be, so he took apart the elements that made Homer's epics and Sophocles's tragedies great in order to provide a manual for how to create poetry that will last.

Rather than deny Plato's argument that poetry is a mimetic art (*imitation* in Greek is *mimēsis*), Aristotle treats mimesis as the proper aesthetic tool for achieving the proper aesthetic end. Here is Aristotle's simple but influential

---

[1]Plato, *The Republic*, trans. Richard W. Sterling and William C. Scott (New York: Norton, 1985), 298. The quoted passage can be found at 607c-d.

definition of tragedy, which he considered to be the highest poetic genre: "A tragedy, then, is the imitation of an action that is serious and also, as having magnitude, complete in itself; in language with pleasurable accessories, each kind brought in separately in the parts of the work; in a dramatic, not in a narrative form; with incidents arousing pity and fear, wherewith to accomplish its catharsis of such emotions" (VI; 1449b24-28).

In the next chapter I will take up catharsis and its link to pity and fear. Here I will zero in on Aristotle's contention that tragedy is an imitation (mimesis) of an action (praxis). Far from taking us away from the truth and reality of the action, the imitation of it increases its seriousness, its magnitude, and its completeness. A process of perfection and intensification, not one of declension and diminution, mimesis adds dramatic fullness and wholeness to an event that would otherwise be ordinary and mundane. Although here Aristotle defines tragedy as the mimesis of a praxis, a few lines later he makes it clear that what is created by the mimetic process is specifically the plot of the tragedy.

THE PLOT IS THE TELOS OF TRAGEDY

Whereas a tragedy is composed of six distinct elements or parts—Aristotle identifies them as "Fable or Plot [*mythos* in Greek], Characters, Diction, Thought, Spectacle and Melody" (VI; 1450a9)—"it is the action in it, i.e. its Fable or Plot, that is the end and purpose of the tragedy; and the end is everywhere the chief thing" (VI; 1450a22-23). Modern readers are likely to expect Aristotle to elevate character over plot (mythos), to make it the end and soul of the tragedy, but he does the opposite: "Tragedy is essentially an imitation not of persons but of action and life, of happiness and misery. All human happiness or misery takes the form of action; the end for which we live is a certain kind of activity, not a quality. Character gives us qualities, but it is in our actions—what we do—that we are happy or the reverse" (VI; 1450a16-19).

Let us not forget that when Aristotle speaks of action in relation to tragedy, he does not mean a random action or event but the imitation (mimesis) of an action (praxis) that yields a plot (mythos). If I seem to belabor this point, it is only because Aristotle does so himself. The plot is the chief and proper end (telos) of tragedy in the same way that happiness is the telos of man, health is the telos of medicine, the form is the telos of matter, the soul is the telos of the body, and the final cause is the telos of all motion. Just as scientists cannot do their work fully if they do not know the final cause of a thing, so physicians, ethicists, and literary critics cannot ply their trades if they do not know that health, happiness, and the plot are the ends, respectively, of medicine, man, and tragedy.

In *Ethics*, virtue plays the central role, for it is what allows us to achieve the end of happiness; in *Poetics*, mimesis takes center stage, for it is only by way of the mimetic process that a praxis can be transformed into a mythos. In the real world, actions and events happen without purpose, logic, or plan. Not so the plot, which has an integrity, a wholeness that one rarely encounters in day-to-day life. Neither random nor haphazard, the plot of a tragedy forms a whole, and that whole, explains Aristotle in his uncommonly commonsensical way, "is that which has beginning, middle, and end" (VII; 1450b26).

STORY VERSUS PLOT

Some might suppose that all one needs to achieve that wholeness in a tragedy is to center it on a single character: say, Oedipus or Antigone, Electra or Orestes, Achilles or Odysseus. But that is the case neither with tragedy nor with that other great mimetic (imitative) art, epic:

> The Unity of a Plot does not consist, as some suppose, in its having one man as its subject. An infinity of things befall that one man, some of which it is impossible to reduce to unity; and in like manner there are many actions of one man which cannot be made to form one action. One sees, therefore, the mistake of all the poets who have written a *Heracleid*, a *Theseid*, or similar poems; they suppose that, because Heracles was one man, the story also of Heracles must be one story. Homer, however, evidently understood this point quite well, whether by art or instinct, just in the same way as he excels the rest in every other respect. In writing an *Odyssey*, he did not make the poem cover all that ever befell his hero—it befell him, for instance, to get wounded on Parnassus and also to feign madness at the time of the call to arms, but the two incidents had no probable or necessary connexion with one another—instead of doing that, he took an action with a Unity of

the kind we are describing as the subject of the *Odyssey*, as also of the *Iliad*. The truth is that, just as in the other imitative arts one imitation is always of one thing, so in poetry the story, as an imitation of action, must represent one action, a complete whole, with its several incidents so closely connected that the transposal or withdrawal of any one of them will disjoin and dislocate the whole. For that which makes no perceptible difference by its presence or absence is no real part of the whole. (VIII; 1451a16-35)

Homer knew better than to include everything that Achilles or Odysseus ever did in his *Iliad* and *Odyssey*. What gives those epics their unity is not that they are focused on a central character but that the *Iliad* is centered on the rage of Achilles and the *Odyssey* on the homecoming of Odysseus. How did Homer achieve that unity? By way of the mimetic process: that is, by so imitating the lives of Achilles and Odysseus as to leave out all that is extraneous to the plot of the *Iliad* and *Odyssey*.

What Aristotle offers at the end of the quoted passage is nothing less than an organic theory of poetry. Just as every part of a healthy, living person, dog, or orange performs some necessary function within the whole—such that the artificial removal or addition of a part would change the essential nature of the thing—so a well-structured plot will contain no more and no fewer scenes than are needed to achieve the purpose of the whole. In an action or story that has not been transformed by the mimetic process, the episodes follow each other randomly, without any discernible order or purpose. In an organic plot that has been purified by imitation, each scene follows the previous one in accordance with the aesthetic rather than historical laws of probability and necessity.

The poet's function, Aristotle explains, "is to describe, not the thing that has happened, but a kind of thing that might happen, i.e. what is possible as being probable or necessary." It is for that reason that Aristotle can declare boldly, and in defiance of Plato, that "poetry is something more philosophic and of graver import than history, since its statements are of the nature rather of universals, whereas those of history are singulars. By a universal statement I mean one as to what such or such a kind of man will probably or necessarily say or do—which is the aim of poetry, though it affixes proper names to the characters" (IX; 1451a36-1451b10).

The story of Oedipus is about a particular man fated to commit the taboo crimes of patricide and incest. The plot of Sophocles's *Oedipus* is about a universal man whose unswerving devotion to the solving of riddles and the well-being of his city presses him on to reveal the tragic truth about his own life. The story of Oedipus is a tale of existential horror and despair; the plot of *Oedipus* is an affirmation of human dignity and courage. The difference between the story and the plot is imitation: mimesis, by extracting from the story all that is most universal and ennobling in humanity while trimming away all that is base and ignoble, produces a tragedy for all times—one that takes us closer to, not further away from, the truth about God, man, and the universe. The Aristotelian poet, we might say, is like an alchemist who, by extracting the essence of things, transforms base metals into gold.

FASHIONING COMPLEX PLOTS

Of course, *Poetics*, inasmuch as it is a manual for writing good tragedies, does make helpful distinctions between good plots and weak ones. For Aristotle, complex plots whose climaxes are brought about by a reversal (a sudden change of fortune) and/or a recognition (a sudden change from ignorance to knowledge) are superior to simple ones that do not make use of either. As for the reversals and recognitions, they "should each of them arise out of the structure of the Plot itself, so as to be the consequence, necessary or probable, of the antecedents. There is a great difference between a thing happening *propter hoc* [Latin for "because of this"] and *post hoc* ["after this"]" (X; 1452a18-21). Episodic plots proceed *post hoc*, for there is only a loose, chronological link between the scenes; organic plots proceed *propter hoc*, for the connection between one scene and the next is causal and purposive.

Mimetic design brings us closer to the truth; one might say it reveals the eternal and metaphysical realities that lie both beyond and within the physical. As such, true poetry is at its core philosophical. More than that, it is apocalyptic (a Greek word that, like its Latin equivalent, *revelation*, means "uncovering"), for it rips aside the veil of the familiar to reveal deeper patterns and meanings that lurk behind the quotidian events of people's lives and the wider movement of history. Indeed, by uniting the general truths of philosophy with the particular facts of history, the mimetic-born tragic plot embodies, if not incarnates, truths we might not otherwise be able to perceive or access.

FROM THE PAGAN ARISTOTLE TO THE CHRISTIAN SIDNEY

In answer to Plato's disparagement of imitation, Aristotle held up a higher vision of mimesis that transforms poetry from a mother of delusions into a vehicle for reaching truth. By doing so, he also inadvertently provided scores of Christian poets, critics, and poet-critics with a foundation, a system, and a vocabulary for defending poetry against its Christian detractors past and present, who, like Plato, dismiss poetry as frivolous at best and deceitful at worst. One of the greatest of those Christian poet-critics was a soldier, diplomat, author, and courtier to Queen Elizabeth I, Sir Philip Sidney (1554–1586).

In his delightful and witty "An Apology for Poetry," Sidney combines Aristotle's pagan, Greco-Roman defense of poetry with a biblical, Judeo-Christian worldview in a manner reminiscent of Augustine, Aquinas, and Dante. Poetry, Sidney explains, is "an art of imitation, for so Aristotle terms it in his word *mimesis*, that is to say, a representing, counterfeiting, or figuring forth—to speak metaphorically, a speaking picture; with this end, to teach and delight." Sidney grounds his definition of poetry in the Greek Aristotle's *Poetics*, as filtered through the Roman Horace's "The Art of Poetry": which, elaborating on *Poetics*, adds the phrases "speaking picture" and "teach and delight." He then, in the next sentence, illustrates the power and truth of his definition by referencing the Bible: "Of this [poetry] have been three general kinds. The chief, both in antiquity and excellency, were they that did imitate the inconceivable excellencies of God. Such were David in his Psalms; Solomon in his Song of Songs, in his Ecclesiastes and Proverbs; Moses and Deborah in their Hymns; and the writer of Job."[2]

Note that what is being imitated in Sidney's examples from the Bible are "the inconceivable excellencies of God." Here is poetry that does not take us further away from heavenly truths but closer to them. David, Solomon, Moses, and Deborah do not imitate an earthly avatar of the divine but go directly to the divine to compose their poetic paeans. The same is the case,

---

[2] Sir Philip Sidney, "An Apology for Poetry," in *Critical Theory Since Plato*, rev. ed., ed. Hazard Adams (New York: HBJ, 1992), 146.

Sidney argues, for secular poets who "imitate to teach and delight; and to imitate borrow nothing of what is, hath been, or shall be; but range, only reined with learned discretion, into the divine consideration of what may be and should be. These be they that, as the first and most noble sort may justly be termed *vates*."³

THE POET AS PROPHET

Earlier in his essay, Sidney defines *vates* in a way that lifts up even the pagan poet from a mere imitator, in the Platonic sense, to a poet-prophet: "Among the Romans a poet was called *vates*, which is as much as a diviner, foreseer, or prophet."⁴ It is because of the poet's power to see both into and beyond that he can draw out that which should be rather than merely that which is. It is also why, as Aristotle suggests, he can combine and thus surpass the strengths and virtues of history and philosophy:

> Now doth the peerless poet perform both: for whatsoever the philosopher saith should be done, he giveth a perfect picture of it in someone by whom he presupposeth it was done; so as he coupleth the general notion with the particular example. A perfect picture, I say, for he yieldeth to the powers of the mind an image of that whereof the philosopher bestoweth but a wordish description: which doth neither strike, pierce, nor possess the sight of the soul so much as that other doth.⁵

Whether the poet be an ancient Greek such as Homer or Sophocles or an ancient Hebrew such as David or Solomon, his mimetic skill and prophetic status allow him to do something that neither the historian nor the philosopher can: make something real and immediate and vigorous to the soul of the reader or listener. The general notions of philosophy and the particular examples of history alone do not pierce "to the dividing asunder of soul and spirit, and of the joints and marrow," as the inspired Scriptures do (Heb 4:12). To do so, the two must come together incarnationally as one flesh. But they can only do so via the magic of mimesis.

---

³Sidney, "Apology for Poetry," 146.
⁴Sidney, "Apology for Poetry," 144.
⁵Sidney, "Apology for Poetry," 148.

All the arts, Sidney explains, from astronomy to geometry, music to law, rhetoric to logic, physics to metaphysics, are ultimately grounded in and limited by nature. Not so poetry, which begins but does not end in the natural world:

> Only the poet, disdaining to be tied to any such subjection, lifted up with the vigor of his own invention, doth grow, in effect another nature, in making things either better than nature brings forth, or, quite anew, forms such as never were in nature, as the Heroes, Demigods, Cyclopes, Chimeras, Furies, and such like: so as he goeth hand in hand with nature, not enclosed within the narrow warrant of her gifts, but freely ranging within the zodiac of his own wit.[6]

Poetry alone can escape the boundaries of our world to soar upward, recreating and refashioning all it touches. Its movement is not away from reality but toward greater reality. It seeks not shadows but substances that are richer and fuller. Poetry is that which "worketh, not only to make a Cyrus, which had been but a particular excellency, as nature might have done, but to bestow a Cyrus upon the world, to make many Cyruses, if they will learn aright why and how that maker made him."[7]

MADE IN THE IMAGE OF A MAKER

Poetry understands and respects what nature has made while yearning to perfect it, to draw out of it its more essential and eternal nature. Thus far Aristotle might have gone, but Sidney extends the argument to take in the Christian revelation that teaches that we were made not only by but in the image of a divine, creative, personal Maker:

> Neither let it be deemed too saucy a comparison to balance the highest point of man's wit with the efficacy of nature; but rather give right honor to the Heavenly Maker of that maker, who, having made man to His own likeness, set him beyond and over all the works of that second nature: which in nothing he showeth so much as in poetry, when with the force of a divine breath he bringeth things forth far surpassing her doings, with no small argument to the

---

[6]Sidney, "Apology for Poetry," 145.
[7]Sidney, "Apology for Poetry," 145.

incredulous of that first accursed fall of Adam, since our erected wit maketh us know what perfection is, and yet our infected will keeps us from reaching unto it.[8]

Without denying a divine breath to philosophy, Sidney accords the highest honors to the poet, who most closely shares in his Maker's power of making. Indeed, poetry comes closer than philosophy to mitigating the effects of the fall by allowing us to reach for and grope after the perfection we knew in Eden.[9]

Though the infection of original sin prevents us from achieving that perfection, poetry signals ahead to the new nature that awaits us in the kingdom: "And he that sat upon the throne said, Behold, I make all things new" (Rev 21:5). The poet beckons backward to the perfections of Eden even as, by the power of mimesis, he affords us a glimpse of the greater perfections of the new Jerusalem to come: "And the Spirit and the bride say, Come. And let him that heareth say, Come. And let him that is athirst come. And whosoever will, let him take the water of life freely" (Rev 22:17).

---

[8]Sidney, "Apology for Poetry," 145.
[9]"Fantasy remains a human right: we make in our measure and in our derivative mode, because we are made: and not only made, but made in the image and likeness of a Maker." J. R. R. Tolkien, "On Fairy-Stories," in *Leaf and Niggle* (Boston: Houghton Mifflin, 1965), 55.

22

PURGING AND PURIFYING THE EMOTIONS

PLATO'S SUSPICION OF MIMESIS was not the only source of his disparagement of the arts. He worried, as well, that poetry appealed not to the superior, rational part of our soul but to the inferior, appetitive part. When we listen to poetry being recited by rhapsodes or actors, we are too often drawn into excesses of emotion and grief that are detrimental to the health of the individual soul and the body politic. Even when we "see a man impersonate the kind of character that we would despise and reject in ourselves . . . we do not disapprove; instead, we enjoy ourselves and praise the performance" (605e).[1]

SHOULD CHRISTIANS GO TO THE THEATER?

Whereas Plato would have us live our lives in accordance with the dictates of reason, poetry stirs up negative and irrational emotions within us—impiety, despondency, lamentation, idleness, recklessness, licentiousness—that we would do well to repress for our own good and that of our city:

> Sex, anger, and all desires, as well as all the pleasures and pains that make their presence felt in whatever we do—on all these poetry has the same effect. It makes them grow great instead of drying them up. It establishes them as our governors when instead they should be the ones governed if we are to become men who are better and happier instead of worse and more miserable. (606d)[2]

In every age, there have been some, often many, Christian individuals and groups that have shared Plato's belief that the arts inspire sinful behavior, rebelliousness, and madness. The theater, in particular, has been treated as

---
[1]Plato, *The Republic*, trans. Richard W. Sterling and William C. Scott (New York: Norton, 1985), 296.
[2]Plato, *Republic*, 297.

ground zero for every conceivable form of decadence and immorality. Can parents and the wider society risk having their young men and women be exposed to the strong emotions displayed and celebrated in theaters, cinemas, and auditoriums? Can anything good come of such things?

Luckily for lovers of poetry and the arts, Aristotle, who provided a positive and beneficial way to understand the telos and function of mimesis, provided as well a positive and beneficial way to respond to the emotion-inducing aspects of tragedy and epic recitation. That response is captured in a single Greek word that has been hotly debated for over two millennia and that is generally transliterated into English: catharsis.

THE CATHARSIS OF PITY AND FEAR

Let us begin by restating Aristotle's definition of tragedy: "A tragedy, then, is the imitation of an action that is serious and also, as having magnitude, complete in itself; in language with pleasurable accessories, each kind brought in separately in the parts of the work; in a dramatic, not in a narrative form; with incidents arousing pity and fear, wherewith to accomplish its catharsis of such emotions" (VI; 1449b24-28). The plot, as we saw in the previous chapter, is the telos of tragedy, but the achievement of that telos serves to bring about a particular response by means of something Aristotle terms the catharsis of pity and fear.

There are two basic ways to translate *catharsis*: as "purgation" and as "purification." Whichever one we choose, there must necessarily be a link between it and the emotions of pity and fear—neither of which emotion Plato viewed in a positive light. If we choose *purgation*, then the meaning seems to be that the experience of watching a well-constructed tragic plot will result in the purging away of the "weaker" emotions of pity and fear, leaving us stronger and more balanced. If we choose *purification*, then the plot will purify and perfect pity and fear, transforming them, at least temporarily, into stable, healthy emotions. The former suggests a therapeutic process similar to an enema or emetic. The latter suggests a spiritual process similar to the way aggressiveness can be transmuted by prayer and obedience into a tool for serving God with courage and resolve.

Far from a surrender to irrational, "unmanly" emotions, catharsis frees us from such emotions while simultaneously reorienting them to serve the cause of reason, virtue, and constancy. But how is a playwright to produce such a catharsis? After laying down rules for mimetic plot construction, Aristotle proceeds to take up that very question:

> The next points after what we have said above will be these: (1) What is the poet to aim at, and what is he to avoid, in constructing his Plots? and (2) What are the conditions on which the tragic effect depends? We assume that, for the finest form of Tragedy, the Plot must be not simple but complex [that is, include a reversal and/or recognition]; and further, that it must imitate actions arousing pity and fear, since that is the distinctive function of this kind of imitation. (XIII; 1452b28-32)

TRAGIC HEROES AND TRAGIC FLAWS

Aristotle's logic and clarity do not fail him, even when he turns his attention to a seemingly subjective topic such as poetry. If the desired effect of tragedy is catharsis, and if catharsis relies on the proper arousal of pity and fear, then the playwright must be careful to compose his plot in such a way that it will produce in the audience the right kind and degree of pity and fear.

> It follows, therefore, that there are three forms of Plot to be avoided. (1) A good man must not be seen passing from happiness to misery, or (2) a bad man from misery to happiness. The first situation is not fear-inspiring or piteous, but simply odious to us. The second is the most untragic that can be; it has no one of the requisites of Tragedy; it does not appeal either to the human feeling in us, or to our pity, or to our fears. Nor, on the other hand, should (3) an extremely bad man be seen falling from happiness into misery. Such a story may arouse the human feeling in us, but it will not move us to either pity or fear; pity is occasioned by undeserved misfortune, and fear by that of one like ourselves; so that there will be nothing either piteous or fear-inspiring in the situation. (XIII; 1452b32-1453a7)

Our pity, Aristotle explains, is aroused when we see someone suffer a fate that he does not deserve, that seems out of proportion to his deeds and character. Our fear, in contrast, is aroused when we see someone like ourselves suffer, suggesting that the same fate might befall us. Despite his stubbornness and kingly pride, Oedipus does not deserve the terrible fate that befalls him in the play. Indeed, it is because he is not a wicked man that we can identify with him and so fear—not that we will kill our father and marry our mother but that we may someday learn something about ourselves that will destroy us.

Pity and fear are not aroused by a plot in which a good man suffers a reversal from good to bad fortune, for such a situation so irks and offends us that we withhold our emotional engagement. Even worse is a plot that presents a wicked man rising from bad to good fortune; we feel neither pity for the man nor fear for ourselves. A plot about a wicked man falling from good to bad fortune may inspire in us a simple sense of justice, but it will not provoke the necessary pity or fear. "There remains, then," Aristotle concludes, using his signature method of ethical reasoning, "the intermediate kind of personage, a man not pre-eminently virtuous and just, whose misfortune, however, is brought upon him not by vice and depravity but by some error of judgement, of the number of those in the enjoyment of great reputation and prosperity; e.g. Oedipus, Thyestes, and the men of note of similar families" (XIII; 1453a7-11). The word *error* in Greek, *hamartia*, is often translated "tragic flaw." Aristotle, however, makes it clear that the tragic movement of the hero from good to bad fortune is not brought on by a vice or depravity (pride, envy, wrath, avarice, sloth, gluttony, lust) but by some kind of error or misjudgment: literally, a missing of the mark. It is in the mean between the extremes of the perfectly good man, the paragon of virtue, and the wicked, vicious man that Aristotle, not surprisingly, finds the golden mean.

Although Aeschylus, Sophocles, and Euripides all wrote tragedies in which the reversal or recognition brought about a happy ending, Aristotle preferred tragedies that ended sadly, for those elicited from the audience the maximum degree of pity and fear. As we have seen, the proper kind of pity and fear leads to a catharsis that purges and/or purifies emotions that might otherwise weaken and degrade us. Such a defense on the part of Aristotle was vital to answer the objections of Plato, but it continues to be vital for Christians tempted to dismiss tragedy, if not all poetry, as a force that distracts at best and leads astray at worst. There has always been a strain within Christianity that has shared Plato's suspicion of the arts as promoters of lies (bad view of mimesis) and instigators of dangerous emotions (absent the catharsis of pity and fear).

TRAGEDY IN THE BIBLE

In the previous chapter, I quoted Sidney's argument that the Bible itself is filled with poetry. It also, I would add, contains much tragedy. Samson is a hero out of a Greek tragedy, a figure whose misdirected desires lead him to pain, sorrow, and death. Bible readers cannot help but feel pity for the severity of his defeat and disgrace, while feeling fear that they might make similar rash decisions and so find themselves in a spiritual and emotional, if not physical, prison, blinded to God's path for them. The same is true of King Saul, whose errors seem so minor in the face of his mighty downfall. So hopeful a beginning; so terrible an ending. He stands as a cautionary tale for all Christians.

There are also elements of tragedy (and catharsis) in King David, that man after God's own heart whose sin with Bathsheba tears his family apart, as there are in King Hezekiah, whose great faith fails him at the end when he foolishly shows the temple treasures to the Babylonian envoys and is told by God that those very treasures will one day be plundered by Babylon (see 2 Kings 20:12-19). Of course, the central tragedy of the Bible is the crucifixion. Though Good Friday does give way to Easter Sunday and to Christ's defeat of Satan, sin, and death, Christians who attend a passion play in a theater or on the screen will find their emotions of pity and fear powerfully purged and purified.

MILTON DEFENDS TRAGEDY

Chief among those Christian groups whose low view of tragedy was even greater than that of Plato were the English Puritans of the seventeenth century who rebelled against the art-loving Stuarts and who shut down the theaters. One of the most famous of those Puritans, one who agreed to and publicly defended the execution of King Charles I, was John Milton (1608–1674). Yet, despite his strong Puritan views, Milton was a great defender of the arts. The reason for this is that Milton's education was steeped in the Greco-Roman classics, leading him to acknowledge the central thesis of this book: that Christians have learned and can continue to learn profitable things from pagan writers such as Homer, Sophocles, Plato, Aristotle, and Virgil.

Milton knew his Aristotle well and, like him, was an apologist for the arts, poetry, and freedom of expression. Having written *Paradise Lost* and *Paradise Regained* in imitation of the epics of Homer and Virgil, the elder Milton turned to Greek tragedy, especially those of Sophocles, for his last major work of poetry. Whom would he choose as the subject of his biblical tragedy? None other than Samson.

As the author of a book centered on Aristotle's influence on Christianity, I find it most fortunate that Milton appended a short introduction to his play, *Samson Agonistes*, titled "Of that Sort of Dramatic Poem Which Is Called Tragedy." In it, he offers a Christian take on catharsis similar to Sidney's Christian take on mimesis:

> Tragedy, as it was anciently composed, hath been ever held the gravest, moralest, and most profitable of all other poems: therefore said by Aristotle to be of power by raising pity and fear, or terror, to purge the mind of those and such-like passions, that is to temper and reduce them to just measure with a kind of delight, stirred up by reading or seeing those passions well imitated. Nor is nature wanting in her own effects to make good his assertion: for so in physic things of melancholic hue and quality are used against melancholy, sour against sour, salt to remove salt humors. Hence philosophers and other gravest writers, as Cicero, Plutarch, and others, frequently cite out of tragic poets, both to adorn and illustrate their discourse. The Apostle Paul himself thought it not unworthy to insert a verse of Euripides [actually Menander's comedy, *Thais*] into the text of Holy Scripture, I Cor. 15.33, and [German Calvinist] Paraeus commenting on the Revelation, divides the whole book as a tragedy, into acts distinguished each by a chorus of heavenly harpings and song between.[3]

In contrast to many of his fellow Puritans, Milton, guided by Aristotle's *Poetics*, rejected the belief that tragedy degrades the emotions or scruples of those who watch or read it. To the contrary, it is grave, reverent, and profitable for the strengthening of morals.

---

[3]John Milton, *Samson Agonistes*, in *Paradise Regained, Samson Agonistes, and the Complete Shorter Poems*, ed. William Kerrigan, John Rumrich, and Stephen M. Fallon (New York: Modern Library, 2012), 327.

Milton makes careful use of both meanings of catharsis. On the one hand, it purges the mind of pity, fear, and such-like emotions; on the other, it purifies those same emotions by tempering them: that is, bringing them into a proper harmony that allows the viewer/reader to experience a higher delight in what are normally felt to be negative, unwelcome emotions. Note that the catharsis of pity and fear rests on seeing those emotions "well imitated" on the stage or in the book. There can be no true catharsis without effective mimesis.

As for the scientific means by which catharsis brings harmony and delight, Milton compares its purgative/purifying effects to homeopathic medicine. To cure melancholy, one must find herbs that have a similar effect and then apply them in such a way that like cures like: salty against salty, sweet against sweet. This effect, Milton argues, was known equally to higher pagan writers (Cicero and Plutarch), biblical writers (Paul), and Protestant interpreters of the Scriptures (Paraeus).

ARISTOTLE AND MILTON AS AESTHETIC PURISTS

Indeed, Milton catalogs pagan and Christian politicians, philosophers, and theologians who aspired to the title of tragedian:

> Heretofore men in highest dignity have labored not a little to be thought able to compose a tragedy. Of that honor Dionysius the elder was no less ambitious than before of his attaining to the tyranny. Augustus Cesar also had begun his *Ajax*, but unable to please his own judgment with what he had begun, left it unfinished. Seneca the philosopher is by some thought the author of those tragedies (at least the best of them) that go under that name. Gregory Nazianzen, a Father of the Church, thought it not unbeseeming the sanctity of his person to write a tragedy, which he entitled, *Christ Suffering*. This is mentioned to vindicate tragedy from the small esteem, or rather infamy, which in the account of many it undergoes at this day with other common interludes; happening through the poet's error of intermixing comic stuff with tragic sadness and gravity; or introducing trivial and vulgar persons, which by all judicious hath been counted absurd; and brought in without discretion, corruptly to gratify the people. And though ancient tragedy use no prologue, yet using sometimes, in case of self-defense, or explanation, that which Martial calls an epistle; in behalf of this tragedy coming forth after the ancient manner,

much different from what among us passes for best, thus much beforehand may be epistled.[4]

Milton lists these names as a way of defending tragedy from its detractors, from those who consider it vulgar and beneath the attention of literate audiences. The reason for this low opinion, Milton argues, is that too many modern tragedians compromise the proper gravity of tragedy by mixing in comic interludes—as, in fact, Shakespeare himself did.

Milton, in composing his Christian-classical tragedy, will not stoop to the masses; he will not gratify their desire for comedy but remain true to the purity and seriousness of the genre Aristotle praised so highly. In the golden age of Athens, playwrights such as Aeschylus, Sophocles, and Euripides did not have to preface their tragedies with a prologue defending their genre and their aims. Milton breaks that rule in his introduction because he feels that he must explain to his fellow Englishmen the proper way a tragedy should be composed and the proper effect it should have on an audience.

By such means do the pagan Aristotle and Christian Milton defend the integrity and moral seriousness of tragedy. Yet, both include in their apology a caveat for those who cannot separate their (often legitimate) concern about the licentiousness of actors from the purity of the tragic form itself. At the end of his introduction, Milton explains that his "work never was intended" for the stage but is meant to be read in private.[5] As for Aristotle, he explains that the plot of a tragedy "should be so framed that, even without seeing the things take place, he who simply hears the account of them shall be filled with horror and pity at the incidents; which is just the effect that the mere recital of the story in *Oedipus* would have on one. To produce this same effect by means of the Spectacle is less artistic, and requires extraneous aid" (XIV; 1453b4-8).

Aristotle and Milton are aesthetic purists, but in a way that is subtly different from that of Plato. Aristotle, we saw in chapter twelve, does not measure justice against the Platonic Form of Justice but against the actions of a just man. So here, Aristotle and Milton hold up as their measure not the

---

[4]Milton, *Samson Agonistes*, 327-28.
[5]Milton, *Samson Agonistes*, 328.

Form of Tragedy but the taste of a cultured, educated, nonvulgarized audience. Though this may sound elitist to modern ears, it reveals Aristotle and Milton's poetics to be both ideal and practical, appealing to transcendent standards while simultaneously bringing the arts down to earth and making them accessible to those willing to do the hard work of refining their palate to enjoy and be improved by the fine wine of tragedy.

Christians who have been raised to distrust the arts, on either moral or aesthetic grounds, would do well to study not only the Christian Milton but the pagan Aristotle as well. Even if such an education does not free the Christian to take profit and enjoyment from Greek tragedy, it will allow him to understand with greater clarity and to experience with greater intensity the tragedy of Christ betrayed, arrested, beaten, and crucified.

Conclusion
ARISTOTLE THE PROPHET

I HAVE ARGUED MANY TIMES in this book that Aristotle is more practical in his vision and approach than Plato. I would therefore like to conclude by highlighting a political warning in *Politics* that, while it is directed to the fractured democracy of Aristotle's Athens, is strongly relevant to the fractured democracies of the modern West. Though its pragmatically prophetic power was recognized over sixty years ago by C. S. Lewis, we today would do well to attend carefully to Aristotle's warning.

Aristotle devotes many chapters of *Politics* to discussing the forces that preserve, as well as those that deconstruct, the various forms of government. Here he focuses on the good and bad effects of an education that either upholds or violates the spirit of a democratic or oligarchic constitution:

> The best laws, though sanctioned by every citizen of the state, will be of no avail unless the young are trained by habit and education in the spirit of the constitution, if the laws are democratical, democratically or oligarchically, if the laws are oligarchical. For there may be a want of self-discipline in states as well as in individuals. Now, to have been educated in the spirit of the constitution is not to perform the actions in which oligarchs or democrats delight, but those by which the existence of an oligarchy or of a democracy is made possible. Whereas among ourselves the sons of the ruling class in an oligarchy live in luxury, but the sons of the poor are hardened by exercise and toil, and hence they are both more inclined and better able to make a revolution. And in democracies of the more extreme type there has arisen a false idea of freedom which is contradictory to the true interests of the state. For two principles are characteristic of democracy, the government of the majority and freedom. Men think that what is just is equal; and that equality is the

supremacy of the popular will; and that freedom means the doing what a man likes. (V.9; 1310a15-31)

Although democracies and oligarchies will be served by different educational methods and outcomes, they will only be well served if their education respects the laws and the ethos that lie at the core of their democratic or oligarchic constitution.

As readers of the *Ethics* would expect, Aristotle identifies as a good education one that fosters the kinds of habits needed to perpetuate the laws and the constitution of the polis. If those laws and that constitution are oligarchic, the habits instilled will be those necessary for preserving an oligarchy; if they are democratic, they will be those necessary for preserving a democracy. But such will not happen unless the leaders and educators of the polis are vigilant. Without proper supervision and discipline, the children of the oligarchs will slip into living luxurious lives with no care for the suffering or grievances of the poor. As for the unsupervised and undisciplined children of the democrats, they will begin to demand and worship radical autonomy and a leveling form of equity.

Writing in 1959, while England was finally experiencing post–World War II prosperity, Lewis, who was as influenced by the logic, philosophy, and theology of Plato as he was by the ethics, aesthetics, and political science of Aristotle, saw the dangers prophesied by Aristotle manifesting themselves in Europe and America. In "Screwtape Proposes a Toast," he has his senior devil address the Tempter's Training College on how to use the West's almost idolatrous worship of democracy to its own undoing and damnation.

Near the end of his speech, Screwtape celebrates what the democratic ethos, when left unsupervised and undisciplined, leads to:

> For "democracy" or the "democratic spirit" (diabolical sense) leads to a nation without great men, a nation mainly of subliterates, full of the cocksureness which flattery breeds on ignorance, and quick to snarl or whimper at the first sign of criticism. And that is what Hell wishes every democratic people to be.... It is our function to encourage the behaviour, the manners, the whole attitude of mind, which democracies naturally like and enjoy, because these are the very things which, if unchecked, will destroy democracy. You would almost wonder that even humans don't see it themselves. Even if they don't

read Aristotle (that would be undemocratic) you would have thought the French Revolution would have taught them that the behaviour aristocrats naturally like is not the behaviour that preserves aristocracy. They might then have applied the same principle to all forms of government.[1]

The French aristocrats were destroyed by the French revolutionaries, for they chose to overindulge their aristocratic privileges rather than acquire the habits of wisdom, virtue, and noblesse oblige that are needed to sustain an aristocracy. From this alone, the citizens of Lewis's day should have realized what Aristotle taught in *Politics*: that the behavior democrats like is not the same behavior that will allow their system to endure. But then, many today would consider reading the "elitist" Aristotle an undemocratic thing to do. How dare you lift yourself above the crowd? Do you think you are smarter than I am?

Civilization, especially democratic civilization, is a tenuous thing that must be as carefully weeded, watered, and pruned as a garden. If we take the blessings bestowed on us by our democracy and use them to pull everyone else down to our level or to demand no accountability for our actions, then we shall be washed away like the foolish builder who built his house on the sand (see Mt 7:24-27); or, to switch parables, like the evil servant who, thinking his master will be away for a long time, begins to beat his fellow servants and indulge his every appetite. When the master returns suddenly and unexpectedly, he will seize that evil man and tear him to pieces (see Mt 24:45-51).

Though he lived and died long before Jesus taught his parables, Aristotle knew full well that choices have consequences and that the habits we cultivate determine the types of people we become and the kinds of societies in which we live. He understood the microcosm of human behavior as well as he did the macrocosm of the starry heavens; and he understood, too, the reason, logic, and virtue that bind them together.

He still has much to teach us today: if only we will have ears to hear!

---

[1] C. S. Lewis, *The Screwtape Letters*, rev. ed. (New York: Collier Books, 1982), 169-70.

GLOSSARY

accident: *see* substance and accident

actuality and potentiality: whereas an object's physical matter possesses the potential to be organized, that potentiality can only be rendered real and concrete (actualized) by its form. God, as the ultimate form behind all things, exists in a state of pure actuality.

allegory: a kind of figurative, metaphorical language in which a writer finds a hidden, spiritual meaning in a story that may or may not be historically true.

atomism: the belief that all there is in the world are atoms (indivisible bits of matter) and the void; as the atoms move ceaselessly through the void, they occasionally swerve, causing collisions with other atoms that form into the various compounds we see. This naturalistic, proto-Darwinian theory was held by pre-Socratic philosophers Leucippus and Democritus and rejected by Aristotle. The theory is best expressed in Lucretius's epic poem *On the Nature of Things*.

catharsis: a well-constructed plot will so move its audience to pity and fear as to produce a catharsis of those emotions. *Catharsis* can be translated as "purgation" or "purification." According to the purgation theory of catharsis (described in Milton's preface to *Samson Agonistes*), tragedy works like an enema or an emetic, cleansing us of our emotions of pity and fear and leaving us more fit and able to face the rigors of life. According to the purification theory of catharsis, tragedy does not so much purge our emotions as purify them. Whereas the former theory is therapeutic in nature, the latter is more spiritual, suggesting that tragedy, like suffering, can strengthen our faith and resolve by testing and trying them like gold in the fire.

Causeless Cause: *see* Unmoved Mover

correspondence theory of truth: there is a real, one-to-one correspondence between the things we see around us and the things we say about those things.

deduction: a method of logical thinking that proceeds downward from self-evident premises and assumptions to a specific conclusion. Deductive reasoning is generally expressed in the form of a syllogism.

deism: the belief that God is like a divine watchmaker who creates the watch, winds it up, and then lets it run on its own. Another name for the God of deism is the God of the philosophers, a removed and impersonal God who makes no moral demands on us.

efficient cause: *see* four causes

ether: *see* four elements

ethos: *see* rhetoric

final cause: *see* four causes

form and matter: whereas the matter of an inanimate or animate object is its external, physical shape (its body), its form is its internal, invisible essence (its soul).

formal cause: *see* four causes

four causes: Aristotle identifies four causes for any given object: the material cause is the physical matter out of which the object was made (the marble out of which Michelangelo's David was built); the formal cause is the form or archetype or blueprint on which the object was modeled (the bipedal shape of a man); the efficient cause is the direct and primary cause of the object coming into being (the sculptor Michelangelo); the final cause is the purposeful end (or telos) for which the object was made (to glorify God and man).

four elements: beginning with the pre-Socratic philosophers and stretching into the Renaissance, European thinkers believed that our physical world was composed of four material elements (earth, air, fire, and water) that served as the building blocks of all other things. As the four elements collided and combined with each other, they transformed into all the other compounds that exist in our endlessly changing world beneath the moon. While earth and water tend to fall to the center, air and fire tend to move away from it. While earth is cold and dry, and water is wet and dry, air is hot and wet, and fire is hot and dry. The movement downward from fire to earth is called condensation; the movement upward, rarefaction. Most thinkers also believed in a fifth element (ether) that existed in the unchanging heavens above the moon.

God of the philosophers: *see* deism

golden mean: virtue represents the mean between the extremes. For example, the virtue of courage lies midway between cowardice (its lack) and foolish bravado (its excess).

Great Chain of Being: an ordered, hierarchical vision of the universe that can be traced back to Aristotle in which every creature, organic and inorganic, physical and spiritual, occupies a rung on a cosmic ladder that stretches from inanimate rocks to God.

hylomorphic: composed of two Greek words that mean "matter" and "form." Aristotle used the word to highlight the intimate union between our body (matter; potentiality) and our soul (form; actuality), an intimacy that disallows reincarnation. Aquinas and Dante Christianized Aristotelian hylomorphism to include the biblical teaching of the resurrection of the body.

imitation: *see* mimesis

induction: a method of logical thinking that proceeds upward from facts, figures, and observations toward a general inference.

infinite regress: if we do not posit an ultimate starting point to motion that does not itself move (that is, the Unmoved Mover), a paradox occurs whereby the origin of motion is endlessly deferred: that is to say, we regress backward infinitely without ever reaching a starting point.

influence: the belief that as the seven planets and the constellations rotated in the heavens, they shed down a celestial influence that drew certain metals out of the earth and personality types out of men. Though the concept of influence lies behind astrology—which teaches that the planets and stars that shone on a person at the moment of his birth (his horoscope) determine his destiny—not all medievals accepted influence as deterministic. Yes, the planets shed down their influence, but it is up to us to receive that influence in a proper way. Thus, the influence of Mars, depending on how it is received, can make a man a brave soldier or a merciless killer.

law of noncontradiction: something cannot be itself and its opposite at the same time and in the same way.

logos: *see* rhetoric

material cause: *see* four causes

matter: *see* form and matter

***mimēsis*:** Greek for "imitation." Whereas Plato saw mimesis in the arts as a process that removes us further from the truth, Aristotle saw it as a process that draws us closer to the truth. The story of Oedipus, which is long and disjointed, becomes, when it is run through the purifying mimetic process of the great playwright Sophocles, the tight, unified plot of the tragedy *Oedipus the King*. The great mimetic poet Homer transformed the episodic lives of Achilles and Odysseus into the cohesive, organic plots of the epics *Iliad* and *Odyssey*. In a story, events follow each other chronologically; in a plot, they follow causally, in accordance with necessity and probability.

monism: the belief that all is one and that what we experience with our senses as motion and change is an illusion.

oikos: a household that functions as an economic unit. Oikos is the root of our word *economics*, which means, literally, the "laws of the household." For Aristotle, the oikos is the model for the polis (the state or city-state) about which he writes in his *Politics*. The Greek polis lies at the root of such words as *politics, political*, and *politician*. The Roman equivalent of polis is *civitas*, the root of such words as *city, civility, civilian, civilization*, and *citizen*.

ontological argument: an argument for the existence of God put forward by Anselm that relies on Aristotle's arguments that form/actuality must precede matter/potentiality. Anselm defines God as "a being than which nothing greater can be conceived" and then argues that there must be an origin to our conception of God that is greater than our conception. Since a God who exists is necessarily greater and more perfect than one who does not, if God does not exist, then our conception of him is greater than God, which Anselm rejects as absurd.

pathos: *see* rhetoric

plot: *see mimēsis*

polis: *see* oikos

potentiality: *see* actuality and potentiality

practical thinking: *see* three kinds of thinking

primum mobile: the highest sphere that spins out of love for God and in turn sets all the other spheres in motion. The phrase means "first mover" in Latin.

productive thinking: *see* three kinds of thinking

reductio ad absurdum: an argument that exposes foundational weaknesses in a claim by showing what happens if that claim is taken to its "logical" conclusion.

rhetoric: the art of persuasion, toward which Plato harbored a negative view but Aristotle a positive one. Aristotle treated rhetoric as an art that could be misused but that, when properly used, strengthened truth and justice. He taught that a good rhetorical speech would balance a threefold appeal to ethos (emphasizing the personal character of the speaker), pathos (appealing to the emotions of the crowd), and logos (building a logical case based on proof and reason).

seven planets: moving outward from the central earth the seven ancient and medieval planets spun eternally in perfect, concentric circles: Moon, Mercury, Venus, Sun, Mars, Jupiter, Saturn. The earth was not considered a planet, for *planet* in Greek means "wanderer," and the earth neither moved nor spun.

seven virtues: *see* virtue

soul: the actualizing form that animates and exists prior to all living things. The soul is the cause and telos of the body, and not vice versa. Aristotle believed that all plants and animals had souls: the vegetable soul provides life, nutrition, and reproduction; the sensitive animal soul provides all of these but adds motion, desire, perception, and thought; the rational human soul provides all of the above but with the vital addition of reason and understanding. Soul and body exist together in a hylomorphic union.

story: *see mimēsis*

substance and accident: while the essence of something is its substance (that which makes a dog a dog, a tree a tree, and a man a man), those things we use to modify those substances (*brown* dog, *tall* tree, *musical* man) are known as accidents. Accidents describe a quality of a substance without being essential to the nature of that substance: a white dog is still a dog.

syllogism: a three-step proof that begins with a major premise, which is assumed rather than proven; a minor premise, which is an observable fact; and a conclusion, which results from the two premises. Here is an example: major premise (all men are mortal); minor premise (Socrates is a man); therefore, conclusion (Socrates is mortal).

telos: purposeful end. All things in the universal have a built-in telos that directs them toward their proper end. According to Aristotle, the proper telos (chief end) of man and virtue is happiness.

theoretical thinking: *see* three kinds of thinking

three kinds of thinking: Aristotle distinguishes between theoretical thinking (which teaches us how to reason logically and how to observe and understand the motions of the heavens and the earth), practical thinking (which teaches us how to behave virtuously and to get along civilly), and productive thinking (which teaches us how to make things of beauty). Theoretical, practical, and productive thinking can be linked, respectively, to the true, the good, and the beautiful.

tragedy: *see* catharsis and *mimēsis*

transubstantiation: a uniquely Catholic understanding of the Lord's Supper that relies on Aristotelian categories. During the Mass, the bread and wine retain their physical accidents while being transformed, in their substance, to the body and blood of Christ.

Unmoved Mover: one of Aristotle's designations for God; though God sets all things in the universe in motion, he himself neither moves nor changes. A second and related designation for God is Causeless Cause, which posits that while God is the cause of all things, he himself was not caused by anything outside himself. As Unmoved Mover and Causeless Cause, God exists in a state of pure actuality.

usury: the lending of money at excessive rates of interest, or, alternatively, the lending of money at any rate of interest. In the Old Testament, God forbids the Jews to practice usury, but the New Testament does not repeat this command. Aristotle argued against usury, influencing medieval Catholics, by way of Aquinas and Dante, to do the same. Islam still forbids usury.

virtue: a kind of moral/ethical excellence that is built up by habit rather than emotion and that finds its telos in the formation of a state of character that, having been properly trained and habituated, naturally chooses virtue over vice and feels proper pleasure at the choice. Medieval theologians distinguished between the four classical (or cardinal) virtues of courage, self-control, wisdom, and justice, of which Plato and Aristotle knew, and the theological (or Christian) virtues of faith, hope, and love, which awaited the special revelation of Christ and the New Testament. Collectively, they are known as the seven virtues.

BIBLIOGRAPHICAL ESSAY

GENERAL

In this book, I have used the translations of Aristotle's works anthologized in *The Basic Works of Aristotle*, edited by Richard McKeon (New York: Random House, 1941). This inexpensive and very handy fifteen-hundred-page book is not complete, but it has all you need contained in a well-made, well-printed volume. For a shorter, six-hundred-page anthology of Aristotle's essential works, see *An Aristotle Reader*, edited by J. L. Ackrill (Princeton, NJ: Princeton University Press, 1987). If you would like to own the complete Aristotle, I suggest the excellent two-volume *Complete Works of Aristotle*, revised Oxford translation, edited by Jonathan Barnes (Princeton, NJ: Princeton University Press, 1984). The complete works of Aristotle can also be purchased for a nominal fee on Kindle. In the sections below, I will suggest a few editions of individual works I have found useful.

For the general reader who wants an accessible overview of all Aristotle's work, I would suggest the following five books, all of which I consulted in preparing this book.

1. Mortimer Adler's *Aristotle for Everybody: Difficult Thought Made Easy* (New York: Touchstone, 1978) is the best place to start. Rather than quote passages from Aristotle, it engages the reader directly in the kind of thinking one encounters in Aristotle. It is low on jargon and high on clarity. For those who want to go deeper, Adler includes an epilogue in which he directs readers to the exact books and chapters in Aristotle that cover the material he highlights in his chapters.

2. A. E. Taylor's *Aristotle*, revised edition (Mineola, NY: Dover, 1955) is the next stop. It manages to synthesize in a mere one hundred pages the full breadth, and much of the depth, of Aristotle's thought. It also

argues, much to my delight, that Aristotle is not so different from Plato as is often believed.

3. J. L. Ackrill's *Aristotle the Philosopher* (Oxford: Clarendon, 1981) takes 150 pages to cover Aristotle's main contributions to philosophy, but he does it well. I find him a bit thicker than Taylor, but he is accessible to the careful reader, and his book is well-organized and takes the time to dialogue directly with Aristotle.

4. Sir David Ross's *Aristotle* (London: Methuen, 1964) comes in at three hundred pages. Along with Ackrill, Ross is an accomplished translator of Aristotle, and that insight finds its way into his challenging analysis of Aristotle's work and thought. He is quite thorough in his overview and is particularly good on *Ethics* and *Politics*.

5. Jonathan Lear's *Aristotle: The Desire to Understand* (Cambridge: Cambridge University Press, 1988) focuses its overview of Aristotle around the theme he identifies in his subtitle. It bogs down at parts, but its central theme opens up different areas of Aristotelian thought.

To these five, I would add the delightful fifty-page chapter on Aristotle in Will Durant's *The Story of Philosophy* (New York: Washington Square, 1961). Another delightful but surprisingly incisive overview of Aristotle is to be found in Max Lerner's introduction to Aristotle's *Politics*, translated by Benjamin Jowett (New York: Modern Library, 1943). Although Werner Jaeger's *Aristotle: Fundamentals of the History of His Development* (Oxford: Oxford University Press, 1950, 1962) is hard to find, it is a seminal work by a great classicist.

I have not included in this bibliography such non-Aristotelian works as Alasdair McIntyre's *After Virtue* that I discuss in the body of the book and cite in the footnotes.

PART ONE

Robin Waterfield's translation of Aristotle's *Physics* (Oxford: Oxford University Press, 2008) is very good; it includes thorough notes by David Bostock that help parse some of the more obscure language and arguments. *Aristotle's Revenge: The Metaphysical Foundations of Physical and Biological Science*, by the passionate and accessible Catholic philosopher Edward Feser

(Neunkirchen-Seelscheid, Germany: Editiones Scholasticae, 2019) is a great read that shows the continued relevance of Aristotle in the sciences. Throughout my *Atheism on Trial: Refuting the Modern Arguments Against God* (Eugene, OR: Harvest, 2018) I refer to Aristotle's writings on logic, science, and metaphysics to answer the atheists and secular humanists of his day (and ours). An interesting recent perspective on the impact of Aristotle on medieval science is given in Richard E. Rubenstein's *Aristotle's Children: How Christians, Muslims, and Jews Rediscovered Ancient Wisdom and Illuminated the Dark* Ages (Boston: Houghton Mifflin, 2003).

PART TWO

The Penguin Classics edition of *Metaphysics*, translated by Hugh Lawson-Tancred (New York: Penguin, 1999), is very good. Though Aristotle's direct influence on Christianity does not begin in earnest until the dawn of the Middle Ages, a recent book has done the hard work of tracing the slow growth of Aristotelian thought in the Christian world from the second to the sixth century: Mark Edwards's *Aristotle and Early Christian Thought* (London: Routledge, 2019). *The Routledge Philosophy Guidebook to Aristotle and the Metaphysics*, by Vasilis Politis (London: Routledge, 2004), is a concise and helpful guide. Edward Feser's *Scholastic Metaphysics: A Contemporary Introduction* (Neunkirchen-Seelscheid, Germany: Editiones Scholasticae, 2014) does an excellent job defining and describing scholastic terminology. *Aristotle in Aquinas's Theology*, reprint edition, edited by Gilles Emery and Matthew Levering (Oxford: Oxford University Press, 2018), clarifies links between Aristotle and Aquinas in the spirit of this book.

PART THREE

The standard and best translation of *The Nicomachean Ethics* remains that of David Ross. The 2009 edition from Oxford has been revised with an introduction and notes by Lesley Brown and is well worth a careful read. *The Cambridge Companion to Aristotle's Nicomachean Ethics*, edited by Ronald Polansky (Cambridge: Cambridge University Press, 2014) is a helpful resource. For a breezy and practical gloss on *Ethics*, see Andrew Younan's *Advice from Aristotle: Life Lessons from the Nicomachean Ethics* (Eugene, OR:

Cascade, 2022); Younan is a priest in the Chaldean Catholic Church. A second breezy take on *Ethics* can be found in Conor Gallagher's *If Aristotle's Kid Had an iPod: Ancient Wisdom for Modern Parents* (Charlotte, NC: Saint Benedict, 2014). One more practical look at *Ethics* that also brings in Aquinas is Charles Nemeth's *Finding Happiness in a Complex World: Rules from Aristotle and Aquinas* (Nashua, NH: Sophia Institute, 2022). I devote a chapter to friendship in my *On the Shoulders of Hobbits: The Road to Virtue with Tolkien and Lewis* (Chicago: Moody, 2012). For Aristotle's thoughts on educating in virtue, see Gary Hartenburg's *Aristotle: Education for Virtue and Leisure* (Camp Hill, PA: Classical Academic Press, 2022).

PART FOUR

I am very partial to *The Politics of Aristotle*, edited and translated by Ernest Barker (Oxford: Oxford University Press, 1958). The notes are extensive, and Barker uses frequent brackets to insert phrases that help clarify what Aristotle is saying. The best modern translation and commentary is *Aristotle's Politics*, second edition, translated and with an introduction, notes, and glossary by Carnes Lord (Chicago: University of Chicago Press, 2013). A handy edition that includes Aristotle's catalogue of the Athenian Constitution is *Aristotle: The Politics and the Constitution of Athens*, edited by Stephen Everson (Cambridge: Cambridge University Press, 1996). *Aristotle: Democracy and Political Science*, by Delba Winthrop (Chicago: University of Chicago Press, 2018), offers both a fine reading of *Politics* and an incisive look at the dangers of excessive democracy. Another study that takes up freedom, equality, and virtue in democracy is Jill Frank's *A Democracy of Distinction: Aristotle and the Work of Politics* (Chicago: University of Chicago Press, 2005).

PART FIVE

I would highly suggest *Aristotle's Art of Rhetoric*, translated and with an interpretative essay by Robert C. Bartlett (Chicago: University of Chicago Press, 2019). There are many great editions and translations of *Poetics*. I am partial to the translation by S. H. Butcher, which is available in numerous inexpensive editions, though it is worth picking up the *Norton Critical Edition of Poetics*, edited by Michelle Zerba and David Gorman, who revised the translation of James Hutton (New York: Norton, 2018). It includes helpful excerpts from Plato and Aristotle that give context for *Poetics*, excerpts from later literary theorists (such as Sidney) who were influenced by it, and a series of contemporary interpretive essays. My two favorite analyses of *Poetics* are S. H. Butcher's *Aristotle's Theory of Poetry and Fine Arts*, fourth edition (Mineola, NY: Dover, 1951) and Gerald F. Else's *Plato and Aristotle on Poetry* (Chapel Hill: University of North Carolina Press, 2011).

Critical Theory Since Plato, revised edition, edited by Hazard Adams (New York: HBJ, 1992), is my go-to resource for critical essays in the tradition of *Poetics*. M. H. Abrams's *The Mirror and the Lamp: Romantic Theory and the Critical Tradition* (Oxford: Oxford University Press, 1971) is an excellent guide to the mimetic theories of Aristotle. I devote two lectures to *Poetics* as well as lectures to Horace, Sidney, Shelley, and others influenced by *Poetics* in *From Plato to Postmodernism: Understanding the Essence of Literature and the Role of the Author*, a twenty-four-lecture series from the Teaching Company, 1999. I devote a section to Greek tragedy in my *From Achilles to Christ: Why Christians Should Read the Pagan Classics* (Downers Grove, IL: IVP Academic, 2007).

Aristotle in a New Perspective: Introduction to the Theory of the Four Discourses, by Brazilian author Olavo de Carvalho (Boston: Ashman, 2022), offers a fascinating new look at Aristotle that draws connections among his poetics, rhetoric, analytics, and dialectic.

SCRIPTURE INDEX

OLD TESTAMENT

Genesis
1–3, *206*
1:27, *55*
2:7, *108*
2:15, *198*
2:24, *42*
3, *139*
3:17-19, *198*
13:1–14:20, *170*
28:1-5, *170*
29, *152*
46:1-7, *170*

Exodus
22:25, *194*

Leviticus
25:36-38, *194*

Deuteronomy
23:19-20, *194*

Joshua
2:18, *125*

1 Samuel
16:7, *117*

2 Kings
20:12-19, *238*

Nehemiah
5:6-11, *194*

Job
1:1-5, *170*
19:26, *42*

Psalms
2:12, *74*

Proverbs
1:10-16, *143*
2:12-15, *143*
4:14-17, *143*
23:9, *143*

Isaiah
6, *99*

NEW TESTAMENT

Matthew
1:5, *125*
5–7, *119*
5:44, *141*
6:24, *194*
6:25-34, *196*
7:24-27, *245*
10:16, *219*
23, *119*
24:45-51, *245*
25:27, *194*

Mark
10:7-9, *42*
12:25, *54*
12:41-44, *126*

Luke
1:37, *9*
6:34-35, *194*
10, *153*
10:18, *98*
10:38-42, *153*
16:8, *219*
18:11-12, *134*
18:13, *157*
18:14, *134*
22:31-34, *127*

John
15:1-8, *173*

Acts
2:44, *187*
4:36-37, *187*
5:1-11, *188*
5:4, *188*
20:35, *127*
26, *219*
26:30-32, *219*

Romans
5:8, *143*
7:19, *112*
12:20, *141*

1 Corinthians
4:15-16, *114*
11:1, *114*
11:3, *170*
12:12-31, *173*
13:12, *182*
13:13, *183*
15:44, *106*

2 Corinthians
9:7, *127*

Galatians
6:7, *118*

Ephesians
5:21–6:9, *170*

Philippians
3:17, *114*
4:9, *114*

Colossians
3:18–4:1, *170*

2 Thessalonians
3:7-9, *114*

1 Timothy
6:10, *187*

Hebrews
4:7, *31*
4:12, *231*
11:31, *125*
13:8, *32*

James
1:17, *33*
1:22, *118*
2:19, *118*

1 Peter
3:7, *170*
3:10, *112*

Revelation
4, *99*
21:5, *233*
22:17, *233*

ALSO BY THE AUTHOR

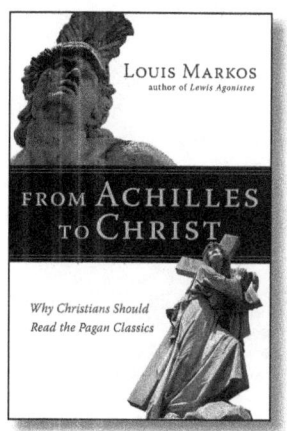

From Achilles to Christ
978-0-8308-2593-6

From Plato to Christ
978-0-8308-5304-5

Passing the Torch
978-1-5140-1130-0